First World War
and Army of Occupation
War Diary
France, Belgium and Germany

9 DIVISION
Divisional Troops
B Squadron Glasgow Yeomanry,
Divisional Cyclist Company
and 50 Brigade Royal Field Artillery
8 May 1915 - 17 September 1919

WO95/1751

The Naval & Military Press Ltd
www.nmarchive.com
Published in association with The National Archives

Published by

The Naval & Military Press Ltd

Unit 10 Ridgewood Industrial Park,

Uckfield, East Sussex,

TN22 5QE England

Tel: +44 (0) 1825 749494

www.naval-military-press.com

www.nmarchive.com

This diary has been reprinted in facsimile from the original. Any imperfections are inevitably reproduced and the quality may fall short of modern type and cartographic standards.

© **Crown Copyright**
Images reproduced by permission of The National Archives, London, England, 2015.

Contents

Document type	Place/Title	Date From	Date To
Heading	1751/1		
Heading	9th Division "B" Sqdn Glasgow Yeo. May 1915-Mar 1916. To 5 Corps.		
Heading	War Diary 9th Division. "B" Squadron Glasgow Yeomanry 11th May To 30th Septr. 1915.		
Heading	9th Division "B" Squadron Q.O. Glasgow Yeomanry 11 May to 30 Sep 1915 Vol. I		
War Diary		11/05/1915	30/09/1915
Heading	War Diary 9th Division "B" Squadron Glasgow Yeomanry October-November 1915.		
Heading	9th Division "B" Sqn Glasgow Yeomanry Oct-Nov Vol.2		
War Diary		01/10/1915	30/11/1915
Heading	War Diary 9th Division. "B" Squadron Glasgow Yeomanry. December 1915.		
Heading	9th Div "B" Sq Ye 3		
War Diary		01/12/1915	31/12/1915
Heading	9th Div "B" Sq Glasgow (Lanarkshire) Yeo Vol. 4.		
War Diary		01/01/1916	31/01/1916
Heading	9 "B" Sq: G"law Yeo: Vol. 5		
War Diary		01/02/1916	29/02/1916
Heading	B Sq G'law Yeo Vol. 6.		
War Diary		01/03/1916	31/03/1916
Heading	1751/2		
Heading	9th Division 9th Cyclist Coy. May 1915-May 1916.		
Heading	War Diary 9th Division 9th Cyclist Company May 1915.		
Miscellaneous	Confidential. Officer, i/c Records, Hounslow.	15/11/1915	15/11/1915
Miscellaneous	Officer, i/c Records, Hounslow.	14/11/1915	14/11/1915
Heading	9th Division. 9th Cyclist Coy. 1st Part Vol. I May15.		
Heading	9th Divisional Cyclist Company War Diary 11th May to 31st May 1915.		
War Diary		11/05/1915	11/05/1915
War Diary	Havre.	12/05/1915	16/05/1915
War Diary	Hondeghem.	17/05/1915	17/05/1915
War Diary	Moate-Boom.	18/05/1915	31/05/1915
Heading	War Diary 9th Division 9th Cyclist Company June 1915.		
Heading	9th Division. 9th Div Cycl Coy. Vol. I June 15.		
War Diary		01/06/1915	28/06/1915
Heading	War Diary 9th Division 9th Cyclist Company July 1915.		
Heading	9th Division 9th Cyclist Vol. 2 July 15.		
Heading	Confidential. War Diary of 9th Div Cycle Coy. From July 1st 1915-July 31st (inclusive) (Volume. III).		
War Diary	Locon.	01/07/1915	31/07/1915
War Diary	Locon.	18/07/1915	18/07/1915
Heading	War Diary 9th Division 9th Cyclist Company. August 1915.		
Heading	9th Div. Cyclist Vol.3 August 15.		
War Diary	War Diary August 1915 9th Division Cyclist Company.		

War Diary	Locon.	02/08/1915	17/08/1915
War Diary	Gonnehem.	17/08/1915	31/08/1915
Heading	War Diary 9th Division. 9th Cyclist Company September 1915.		
Heading	9th Div Cycls Coy. Vol. 4.		
Heading	War Diary of 9th Division Cyclist Company From 1st September 1915. to 30th September 1915 (inclusive) Volume. 4		
War Diary	Cens la Vallee	01/09/1915	02/09/1915
War Diary	Bethune.	03/09/1915	30/09/1915
Heading	Amendment of War Diary of 9th Division Cyclist Company 27th September 1915. Volume 4.		
War Diary	Bethune.	27/09/1915	27/09/1915
Heading	War Diary 9th. Division 9th. Cyclist Company October 1915.		
Heading	9th Division 9th Div. Cycl: Coy Vol 5 Oct 15.		
Heading	9th Divisional Cyclist. Company War Diary October, 1915.		
War Diary	Bethune.	01/10/1915	03/10/1915
War Diary	Wippenhoek	04/10/1915	31/10/1915
Heading	War Diary 9th. Division 9th. Cyclist Company November 1915.		
Heading	9th Division 9th Cyclist Coy Vol. 6 Nov.15.		
Heading	War Diary of 9th Division Cyclist Company From 1st November 1915 To 30th November 1915 (inclusive) Volume No. 6.		
War Diary	Wippenhook.	01/11/1915	30/11/1915
Heading	War Diary 9th. Division 9th. Cyclist Company December 1915.		
Heading	9th Div. 9th Cyclist Coy Vol; 7.		
Heading	War Diary of 9th Division Cyclist Company From, 1st December 1915 to 31st December 1915 (inclusive) Volume. 7.		
War Diary	Wippenhook.	01/12/1915	16/12/1915
War Diary	Merris.	16/12/1915	31/12/1915
Heading	9th Div Cyclist Vol. 8 Jan.		
Heading	War Diary of 9th Division Cyclist Company From 1st January to 31st January 1916 Volume 8.		
War Diary	Merris.	01/01/1916	24/01/1916
War Diary	Trois Arbes	24/01/1916	31/01/1916
Heading	War Diary of 9th Division Cyclist Company Volume.9 From 1st February 1916 to 29th February 1916		
War Diary	Trois Arbres Steenwerck.	01/02/1916	29/02/1916
War Diary		01/02/1916	29/02/1916
War Diary	Trois Arbres Steenweerck.	03/02/1916	29/02/1916
War Diary		01/02/1916	29/02/1916
Miscellaneous	Divisional Mounted Troops Order by Major Macfarlane, O/C Divn. Mounted Troops. Appendix 1.	09/02/1916	09/02/1916
Heading	War Diary of 9th Division Cyclist Company Volume.10 From 1st March 1916. to 31st March 1916.		
War Diary	Trois Arbres Steenwerck.	01/03/1916	30/03/1916
Heading	War Diary of 9th Division Cyclist Company From 1st April, 1916 to 30th April 1916. Volume.11.		
War Diary	Trois Arbres Steenwerk.	01/04/1916	10/04/1916
War Diary	Ebblinghem	11/04/1916	12/04/1916
War Diary	Harlettes.	12/04/1916	27/04/1916

Type	Description	Start	End
War Diary	Ebblinghem.	27/04/1916	27/04/1916
War Diary	Trois Arbres Steenwerk.	30/04/1916	30/04/1916
Miscellaneous	Date of Courses. Appendix A.		
Miscellaneous	Sketch of proposed Syllabus of Training for Divisional Squadrons and Cyclists-Second Army. Appendix B.		
Heading	War Diary of 9th Division Cyclist Company From 1st May, 1916. To 31st May, 1916. Volume.12.		
War Diary	Trois Arbres Steenwerck.	01/05/1916	23/05/1916
War Diary	Les. Trois Arbress Steenwerck.	26/05/1916	26/05/1916
War Diary	Les. Trois Arbress Steenwerck.	19/05/1916	19/05/1916
Heading	1751/3.		
Heading	9th Division 50th Bde R.F.A. May 1915-1919 Sep.		
Heading	Headquarters 50th Brigade R.F.A. (9th Division) May-September 1915.		
Heading	Confidential War Diary of The 50th Brigade Royal Field Artillery. From May 9th 1915 To Sept 30th 1915. Volume.I		
War Diary	Bordon Camp.	08/05/1915	09/05/1915
War Diary	Southampton.	10/05/1915	10/05/1915
War Diary	Havre.	11/05/1915	11/05/1915
War Diary	Helfaut	12/05/1915	16/05/1915
War Diary	Steenwerck	17/05/1915	17/05/1915
War Diary	Ploegsteert.	18/05/1915	12/06/1915
War Diary	Le Pt. Mortier.	13/06/1915	18/06/1915
War Diary	Bourecq.	21/06/1915	30/06/1915
War Diary	Rue D/Vaches.	30/06/1915	01/07/1915
War Diary	Gorre.	02/07/1915	01/08/1915
War Diary	Loisne.	02/08/1915	14/08/1915
War Diary	Lecleme.	15/08/1915	30/08/1915
Heading	War Diary Headquarters, 50th Brigade R.F.A. (9th Division) September 1915.		
War Diary	Cuinchy.	01/09/1915	30/09/1915
Heading	Headquarters 50th Brigade R.F.A. (9th Division) October 1915.		
Heading	Confidential War Diary of The 50th Brigade Royal Field Artillery 9th (scottish) Div October 1915.		
War Diary	Cuinchy.	01/10/1915	02/10/1915
War Diary	(Near) Poperinghe.	03/10/1915	16/10/1915
War Diary	South Of Ypres-Zillebeke Railway.	17/10/1915	31/10/1915
Heading	Headquarters 50th Brigade R.F.A. 9th Division November 1915.		
Heading	9th Division 50th Bde. R.F.A. Vol.2 Nov 15.		
War Diary	South Of Ypres-Zillebeke Railway.	01/11/1915	30/11/1915
War Diary			
Heading	Headquarters. 50th Brigade R.F.A. 9th Division December 1915.		
Heading	9th Division 50th Bde. R.F.A. Vol. 3.		
War Diary	Near Ypres.	01/12/1915	01/12/1915
War Diary	South Of Ypres-Zillebeke Railway.	02/12/1915	02/12/1915
War Diary	Bde Hdqrs at Kruistraat In Aschery-pasition.	03/12/1915	23/12/1915
War Diary	Bollezeele.	24/12/1915	29/12/1915
Heading	9th Division Artillery. 50th Bde Royal Field Artillery. January 1916.		
Heading	Confidential War Diary 50th. Brigade R.F.A. For January 1916.		
War Diary	Bollezeele.	01/01/1916	09/01/1916

War Diary	Caestre.	10/01/1916	27/01/1916
War Diary	M. Ploegsteert.	28/01/1916	31/01/1916
Miscellaneous	Addenda to War Diary of October 1915		
Heading	9th Division. Artillery. 50th Bde. Royal Field Artillery February 1916.		
Heading	Confidential War Diary of 50th Brigade Royal Field Artillery 9th (Scottish) Division For February 1916.		
War Diary	Near Ploegsteert.	01/02/1916	28/02/1916
Miscellaneous	Ammunition field during Feb.		
Heading	9th Division Artillery. 50th Bde Royal Field Artillery. March 1916.		
Heading	Confidential War Diary 50th Brigade R.F.A. 9th (Scottish) Division March 1916.		
War Diary	Near Ploegsteert.	01/03/1916	31/03/1916
Heading	9th Division Artillery. 50th Bde Royal Field Artillery. April 1916.		
Heading	Confidential War Diary 50th Brigade R.F.A. 9th (Scottish) Division April 1916.		
War Diary	Near Ploegsteert. Bde. H.Q B11 d3.7.	01/04/1916	30/04/1916
Miscellaneous	Appendix I. Showing Pritions And Zones Of Fire Of Centre Group Batteries		
Heading	9th Division Artillery. 50th Bde Royal Field Artillery May 1916.		
Heading	Confidential War Diary 50th Brigade R.F.A. 9th (Scottish) Division May 1916. Vol.8		
War Diary	Near Ploegsteert Bde. H.q B 1123. 7.	01/05/1916	31/05/1916
Heading	9th Division Artillery, 50th Bde Royal Field Artillery, June 1916		
War Diary	Therouanne.	01/06/1916	30/06/1916
Heading	9th Div. XIII. Corps. Division Transferred To IV. Corps, First Army, 25.7.16. War Diary Headquarters, 50th Brigade, R.F.A. July 1916.		
Miscellaneous	Brigade Major 9th Divl Artillery	03/08/1916	03/08/1916
Heading	Confidential War Diary 50th Brigade R.F.A. 9th (Scottish) Division July 1916. Vol. 10		
War Diary	Mai Montauban Ref Smap Montauban1/2,000.	01/07/1916	31/07/1916
Miscellaneous	Casualties During The Operation On The Somme.		
Heading	9th Division Artillery, 50th Bde Royal Field Artillery August 1916.		
Miscellaneous	9th Div Artillery ER 139.	01/09/1916	01/09/1916
Heading	Confidential War Diary of The 50th Brigade. R.F.A. 9th (Scottish) Division August-1916. Vol.11.		
War Diary		01/08/1916	31/08/1916
Miscellaneous	Ammunition Expended (From 15th).		
Heading	9th Division Artillery, 50th Bde Royal Field Artillery, September 1916.		
Heading	Confidential War Diary of The 50th Brigade R.F.A. 9th (Scottish) Division September 1916.		
War Diary	Near Carency Map Reference X To Sheet 36 B.S.E.S To Sheet 36 C.S.W.	01/09/1916	30/09/1916
Heading	9th Division. Artillery. 50th Bde Royal Field Artillery. October 1916.		
Miscellaneous	H.Q. R.A. 9th. Division. Ex 151.	01/11/1916	01/11/1916
Heading	Confidential War Diary of The 50th Brigade R.F.A. 9th (Scottish) Division October 1916. Vol 13.		

War Diary	Near Carency (vimy Ridge) Maps X To 36 B.S.E. S 36 C.S.W. (1/20,000).	01/10/1916	12/10/1916
War Diary	Ref. 1/20,000 57c SW.	13/10/1916	13/10/1916
War Diary	Near High Wood Of Bazenting Grand Map 57c S.W. 1/20,000.	14/10/1916	31/10/1916
Miscellaneous	Ammunition Expended during October.		
Heading	9th Divisional Artillery. 50th Bde. R.F.A. November, 1916.		
Heading	Confidential War Diary 50th Brigade R.F.A. 9th (Scottish) Division November 1916.		
War Diary	Near High Wood.		
War Diary	H.Q. S10 C 4.7. Reference To 57c S.W. 1/20,000.	03/11/1916	29/11/1916
Miscellaneous	Casualties Officers. Wounded Lt L.W. Jacobson 5/11/16.	05/11/1916	05/11/1916
Heading	9th Divisional Artillery 50th Bde. R.F.A. December, 1916.		
Heading	War Diary 50th Brigade R.F.A. 9th (Scottish) Division. June 1916.		
Miscellaneous	H.Q. 9th D.A. EK 158.	01/01/1917	01/01/1917
Heading	Confidential War Diary 50th. Brigade R.F.A. 9th (Scottish) Division. December 1916.		
War Diary	Bouret Sur Canche Near Frevent.	01/12/1916	26/12/1916
War Diary	Arras Sheet 51 B N.W. 3 1/10,000.	27/12/1916	31/12/1916
Heading	Confidential. War Diary. 50th Brigade R.F.A. 9th (Scottish) Division. January. 1917.		
War Diary	Arras Sheet 51B N.W. 3 1/10,000.	04/01/1917	31/01/1917
Miscellaneous	Brigade Major, R.A. 9th. Division.	01/03/1917	01/03/1917
Heading	Confidential War Diary. 50th Brigade R.F.A. 9th (Scottish) Division. February 1917.		
War Diary	Arras Sheet 51B N.W. 3 1/10,000.	14/02/1917	20/02/1917
Heading	Confidential War Diary. 50th. Brigade R.F.A. 9th (Scottish) Division March 1917.		
War Diary	Map Reference To Arras 51B N.W. 3 1/10,000.	08/03/1917	31/03/1917
Miscellaneous	Making A Total For The Brigade of		
Heading	Confidential War Diary 50th: Brigade R.F.A. 9th: (Scottish) Division April 1917.		
War Diary	Arras.	02/04/1917	02/04/1917
War Diary	Fampoux.	03/04/1917	03/04/1917
War Diary	Sheet 51B. N.W. 1/20,000.	04/04/1917	30/04/1917
War Diary	Confidential War Diary. 50th Brigade. R.F.A. 9th (Scottish) Division. May, 1917.		
War Diary	Arras.	01/05/1917	01/05/1917
War Diary	Fanpoux Sheet 51B. N.W. 1/20,000.	02/05/1917	31/05/1917
Miscellaneous	Total Casualties For The Month Of May:-		
Heading	Confidential War Diary For June, 1917. 50th Brigade. R.F.A. 9th (Scottish) Division.		
War Diary	Sheets 51B.N.W. & 51B.S.W.	01/06/1917	05/06/1917
War Diary	Sheets 51B.N.W. & 51B.S.W.	01/06/1917	30/06/1917
Miscellaneous	Honours & Awards. For Services Since September 1916.		
Miscellaneous	Total Casualties For The Month Of June.		
Miscellaneous	50th. Bde. No. E.X. 216. Left Group Order For Minor Operation.	12/06/1917	12/06/1917
Miscellaneous	16 Pounder Barrage Table Y.		
Miscellaneous	4.5 Howitzer Barrage Table C.		
Miscellaneous	E.K. 216/2.		

Miscellaneous	E.K. 216/4/	24/06/1917	24/06/1917
Miscellaneous	10th Brigade No. B. 398. O.C.50th Bde R.F.A.	22/06/1917	22/06/1917
Miscellaneous	4th Division "G"	12/06/1917	12/06/1917
Miscellaneous	Report On Raid By Royal Irish Fusiliers-24th June 17.	24/06/1917	24/06/1917
Diagram etc	Right Battn Front I.14.		
Map			
Heading	Confidential War Diary July.1917. 50th. Brigade R.F.A.9h. (Scottish) Division. Vol. 22.		
War Diary	Ref Sheet 51B.S.W.	01/07/1917	31/07/1917
Miscellaneous	Casualties During July.		
Heading	Confidential War Diary. August 1917. 50th. Brigade R.F.A. 9th (Scottish) Division. Vol.23		
War Diary	Sheet 57C NE. 57C SE.	01/08/1917	31/08/1917
Heading	Confidential War Diary. September 1917. 50th. Brigade R.F.A. 9th. (Scottish) Division. Vol.24.		
War Diary	Ref. Sheet 28. N.W. 28. N.W.	01/09/1917	30/09/1917
Heading	Confidential War Diary. October 1917. 50th Brigade R.F.A. 9th. (Scottish) Division.		
War Diary		01/10/1917	31/10/1917
Miscellaneous	Casualties for October.		
Heading	Confidential War Diary. November 1917. 50th Brigade R.F.A. 9th. (Scottish) Division. Vol 26.		
War Diary		01/11/1917	30/11/1917
Miscellaneous	Casualties During Nov.		
War Diary		01/12/1917	31/12/1917
Miscellaneous	Casualties for the Month of December.		
War Diary	Sheet 57c.	01/01/1918	31/01/1918
Miscellaneous	Casualties During January.	01/02/1918	01/02/1918
War Diary		01/02/1918	28/02/1918
Heading	9th Div. War Diary. Headquarters. 50th Brigade, R.F.A. March 1918.		
War Diary		01/03/1918	31/03/1918
Heading	9th Divisional Artillery. 50th Brigade R.F.A. April 1918.		
Miscellaneous	Headquarters, 9th Div.	30/04/1918	30/04/1918
War Diary		01/04/1918	29/07/1918
Miscellaneous	During Meteren Operation.	01/08/1918	31/10/1918
Miscellaneous	Honours Awards		
War Diary		01/11/1918	30/11/1918
Miscellaneous	Honours & Awards (November).		
War Diary		01/12/1918	31/12/1918
Miscellaneous	Honours Awards		
War Diary		01/01/1919	31/01/1919
War Diary	Honoues Awards January 1919.	09/01/1919	09/01/1919
War Diary	Solingen.	01/02/1919	30/04/1919
War Diary	Solingen.	15/04/1919	26/04/1919
War Diary	Solingen.	24/03/1919	30/06/1919
War Diary	Solingen	28/06/1919	13/07/1919
War Diary	Niederem Bt.	14/07/1919	17/09/1919

(75)

9TH DIVISION

'B' SQDN GLASGOW YEO.
MAY 1915 - MAR 1916

TO 5 CORPS

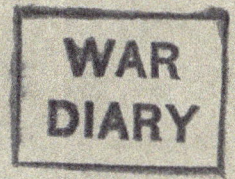

9TH DIVISION.

"B" SQUADRON GLASGOW YEOMANRY.

11TH MAY TO 30TH SEPTR. 1915.

9th K'zaim

121/7598
9th Dn

"B" Squadron O.C. Charge

Subedar Jemadar

Sikh, Dogra & Mus.

Vol. I

in both fighters

WAR DIARY

of B. Squadron, Yeoman Lovatts   Army Form C. 2118.

INTELLIGENCE SUMMARY.

May 1915

(Erase heading not required.)

Instructions regarding War Diaries and Intelligence Summaries are contained in F. S. Regs., Part II. and the Staff Manual respectively. Title pages will be prepared in manuscript.

Hour, Date, Place	Summary of Events and Information	Remarks and references to Appendices
11th May 1915	Left Bulford at 5 P.M. Bd horses at Nuvalle and Leicester & arrived at Southampton	From 11th May to 20th May
12. May.	at 1 P.M. rest day & put horses & men straight on Board Boat and sailed at 5 P.M.	
13	Were at Havre at daylight & got into Harbour about 8 A.M. were disembarked at once & went to Rest Camp No 3, got there at 2 PM & left at 10 PM. & entrained.	
14	Left Havre at 4 AM. were in train all day & arrived at St Omer at midnight & detrained at once	
15	2nd horse to Bomech here horses were picketted & men in hamlets. Left St Omer at 4 PM & arrived Labuca in afternoon	
16	Left St Omer at 1 P.M. rode to Offaire & arrived at Willinghem at 4 P.M. the bay of all night fall	
17	Left at 6 AM & rode by Gautier, Halterre, Baillent & arrived at Le Venier at 2 PM was a very hot day & either ridden or forage carried	
18	Exercised horses.	
19	that exercise to Esterium & frame left at 1 PM & arrived Steenvoorde at 4.30 P.M.	
20	Exercised horses in frame & had drund Exercise dismtd in frame	

WAR DIARY of 1st B Ignatn Royal Warwick

Army Form C. 2118.

INTELLIGENCE SUMMARY.

May 1915

(Erase heading not required.)

Instructions regarding War Diaries and Intelligence Summaries are contained in F.S. Regs., Part II and the Staff Manual respectively. Title pages will be prepared in manuscript.

Hour, Date, Place	Summary of Events and Information	Remarks and references to Appendices
21st May	Started to do a scheme but it came on very wet & we stopped. Had rifle ammunition & dest inspection afternoon.	From 21st May to 31st May
22"	Exercised horses — forenoon, sword drill & afternoon.	
23	Rest easy day Sunday	
24	Left at 9 AM & did a Philly scheme with 6 ydales got back 5 PM	
25	Left at little inspection & forenoon Arms etc — afternoon	
26	Did our Philly scheme - forenoon to a 3 mile hand gallop	
27	Left 8.30 AM & did our Philly scheme & got back 3 PM	
28	Exercised horses	
29	Exercised horses	
30	Sunday. Church Parade at 5.30 PM.	
31	Exercised horses — forenoon, left at 5.30 P.M. & marched to Regatmt & went into trenches along with Royal Warwicks. Marched about 8 miles. Left enough men to look after horses till we came away.	

WAR DIARY or INTELLIGENCE SUMMARY

Army Form C. 2118.

(Erase heading not required.)

J. B. Lynton Shaggan Yeomanry June 1915

Hour, Date, Place	Summary of Events and Information	Remarks and references to Appendices
1st June	Devr: Rendrs at Phosphat, very hot day at Chor —	
2	Left Rendrs at 1 AM. Arrived Phol & h Wells got there	
	3 AM. Did no examples	
3	Did — how trial taken	
4	Did — Chor — frmen — argul exercise — flanus	
5	Set everything ready to move. Left at 7 PM & mode of Salame	
	got there at 5 AM	
6	Marsile. Rateg to Barna got there —	
7	Had easy all day	
8	Exercised horses & frmen	
9	Did a patrol scheme — frmen	
	Left at 6 AM. d.t. by patrol scheme all by feels	
	& got back at 1 PM.	
10	Exercised in frmen, dismounted parade & flamen	
11	Did patrol scheme — frmen, rifle inspection & drinl drill	
	— flamen	
12	Exercised horses & frmen	
13	Church parade — frmen	
14	Exercised horses & frmen & dismounted schene —	
	flamen	

WAR DIARY of R. Sparshor, Glasgow Yeomanry Army Form C. 2118.
INTELLIGENCE SUMMARY. June 19/15

(Erase heading not required.)

Instructions regarding War Diaries and Intelligence Summaries are contained in F. S. Regs., Part II and the Staff Manual respectively. Title pages will be prepared in manuscript.

Hour, Date, Place	Summary of Events and Information	Remarks and references to Appendices
16th June	Breakfast 4 A.M. Started all day to be ready to entrain.	
17	Ditto.	
18	Ditto. moved to 3 horse lines	
19	Did orderly ordered till N.C.Os ~ pierriere	
20	Church Parade ~ pierriere. Billey parade in pierriere	
21	Did orders ~ pierriere. Orders to move St Venant + 3 hours notice (cancelled)	
22	Off at 8:30 A.M. Rode to near St Venant + spent day ~ the Forest will the whole Squadron, returned at 4.30 P.M.	
23	Did ~ Robilly scheme	
24	Ditto.	
25	Exercised horses ~ pierriere + rode to to Lully. Very wet.	
	2:30 P.M. + rode to le Lully. Very wet.	
26	Exercised horses ~ pierriere, got orders at 9 P.M. to move on Sunday.	
27	Church Parade ~ pierriere. got order not to move till 28th	
28	Exercised ~ morning. Left ~ evening + rode through Ellers back to the Billets at Pierriere	
29	Exercised horses ~ pierriere. Rifle Inspection in afternoon	
30	Left at 1:30 P.M. + rode through Robeay to Quentin arrived there at 5 P.M. + got into Billets.	

WAR DIARY of J.B. Lyndon, Glasgow Yeomanry

Army Form C. 2118.

INTELLIGENCE SUMMARY

July 1915.

(Erase heading not required.)

From 1st July to 15th July

Hour, Date, Place	Summary of Events and Information	Remarks and references to Appendices
1st July	Examined knees — [illegible] & trenches N.E. of [illegible] cove & no attack to no.	
2nd	One of enemy [illegible] from the westward to run up cliff at 1.30 & made to see down side of cliff & also 4 Mar.	
3rd	Examined knees by boats — [illegible]	
4th	Bund knees — [illegible] all [illegible]	
5th	Examined knees — [illegible] Rifle [illegible] & small [illegible]	
6th	Examined [illegible] enemy's trenches — no	
8th	[illegible] examined knees	
9th		
10th		
11th	One 9 day [illegible] [illegible] was [illegible] [illegible] & [illegible] & out of [illegible] & night [illegible]	Officers lately returned here [illegible] & [illegible]
12th	One 9 d 538 F. [illegible] Officers (2) [illegible] [illegible] not [illegible]	
13th	Ditto	
14th	Ditto	
15th	Examined knees — [illegible] the any — [illegible]	

WAR DIARY of B Squadron Shagun Lancers

Army Form C. 2118.

INTELLIGENCE SUMMARY. July 1915

(Erase heading not required.)

Instructions regarding War Diaries and Intelligence Summaries are contained in F. S. Regs., Part II. and the Staff Manual respectively. Title pages will be prepared in manuscript.

Hour, Date, Place	Summary of Events and Information	Remarks and references to Appendices
16 July	Squadron digging at Redoubt at Featherbed.	for 16 July to 31 July
17 "	Ditto	
18 "	Ditto	
19 "	"	
20 "	"	
21 "	"	
22 "	"	
23 "	"	
24 "	"	
25 "	"	
26 "	"	
27 "	Party 12 men to the dugouts for remounts, remainder engaged.	
28 "	Squadron of digging at Featherbed.	
29 "	Squadron of digging at Featherbed.	
30 "		
31 "		

WAR DIARY of B. Squadron, Glasgow Yeomanry

Army Form C. 2118.

INTELLIGENCE SUMMARY.

(Erase heading not required.)

August 1915. from 1st August to 13th August

Instructions regarding War Diaries and Intelligence Summaries are contained in F.S. Regs., Part II. and the Staff Manual respectively. Title pages will be prepared in manuscript.

Hour, Date, Place	Summary of Events and Information	Remarks and references to Appendices
1st August	Church Parade. All by chiefs & prison. Everything quiet.	
2"	Squadron of digging at Redoubt & Featherbed.	
3"	Ditto	
4"	"	
5"	"	
6"	"	
7"	Church Parade — prison & everything quiet.	
8"	Squadron of digging Redoubt at Featherbed.	
9"	Squadron started for harbour at 5 P.M. of 9th	
10"	Featherbed	
11"	Menu — Trenches all day, all very quiet.	
12"	1 Trenches all day, very quiet. Relief [?] Trenches at 8 P.M. got billetted at [?]	
13"	1 Trenches, left them at 8 P.M. got billetted at [?] morning then [?] day at [?] we ne [?] arrived at Ballilla at 3.30 A.M.	

WAR DIARY of B Squadron, Shagya Yeomanry

INTELLIGENCE SUMMARY.   August 1915

Army Form C. 2118.

Hour, Date, Place	Summary of Events and Information	Remarks and references to Appendices
14th August	Squadron had easy day after being in trenches.	
15 "	Squadron were up working at R.E. Store.	
16 "	A Gunner & 25 men to Rue Cailloux at Hazebrouck to held R.O. Drill & Loud men to our Division may to take over trenches they got back to Billets at 1 AM.	
17 "	Left at 1 PM. & went 5 klms to Terre de Vallee got there 2.30 & went into Billets which authorized Horses on had left & ponies next day	
18 "	Exercised horses - freen & cleaned up & after	
19 "	Were inspected by Lord Kitchener at Busnes the whole Brigade were drawn up till - field	
20 "	Squadron did troop drill - ponies & men jumping	
21 "	Exercised horses - freen	
22 "	Church Parade - horses exercised	
23 "	Squadron did troop drill & troop exercise	
24 "	Party of 50 men left at 6 AM to billets for remount to the division & ratter the men at Busnes to different units	

WAR DIARY of B. Squadron Glasgow Yeomanry Army Form C. 2118.

or

INTELLIGENCE SUMMARY. August 1915

(Erase heading not required.)

Instructions regarding War Diaries and Intelligence Summaries are contained in F. S. Regs., Part II. and the Staff Manual respectively. Title pages will be prepared in manuscript.

Hour, Date, Place	Summary of Events and Information	Remarks and references to Appendices
25 August	Horses inspected — fairly easy of them.	For 25 & 26 & 31st August
26"	Squadron did yet filled & took Exercises	
27"	Shelled the Lt. Squadron across country now the ditches.	
28"	Exercised horses.	
29"	Church Parade in forenoon	
30"	Squadron was all Lt. side not across country over ditches	
31"	Squadron we all out across country over the ditches. There was a great improvement in the horses jumping the ditches.	

WAR DIARY of B Squadron Sharpshooters, Army Form C. 2118.
or
INTELLIGENCE SUMMARY. September 1915

(Erase heading not required.)

Hour, Date, Place	Summary of Events and Information	Remarks and references to Appendices
1st September	Horses at exercise — groom	
2"	Horses at exercise & groom, 2nd & 3rd groups & everybody who could — Gloves — pipeclaying to army	
3"	Left at 1 P.M. & rode through Bethune & were billeted just on outskirts of town on the Beuvry side	
4"	Horses at exercise — groom — no change. Whole Sqdn all 4 at 7 head 9 diggy trench & telephone wires	
5"		
6"		
7"		
8"		
9"		
10"		
11"		
12"		
13"	Squadron were inspected by General Gough.	
14"	Left Bus 16 Lancers case & took over Convent (while them which consisted of Armoury, bicycles & M. Water trailer bars.	

Army Form C. 2118.

WAR DIARY of B. Squadron Shagra Hussars

or

INTELLIGENCE SUMMARY.

(Erase heading not required.)

Instructions regarding War Diaries and Intelligence Summaries are contained in F.S. Regs., Part II. and the Staff Manual respectively. Title pages will be prepared in manuscript.

September 1915.   From 15 September to 24 September

Hour, Date, Place	Summary of Events and Information	Remarks and references to Appendices
15 September	Squadron was at day Petihlly below under Capt. Hoare. Instructions from Brig. Gen. O'Dowda came informing that new Comdt of Wells & Lines ordered 16 Sept Hoare returned to Regiment.	
16 September	Squadron at day below under Brig Brig Bullivant and at Egbab & Kedes Zar	
17		
18		
19		
20	Horses exercised – (men & sit gully thing sunk 3 pts. Horses exercised (men & sit gully)	
21st	Quiet day. On of my Attendants. Squadron was at day Below with Cyclists under Major Reynolds.	
22nd	2nd day of bombardment. Horses at exercise.	
23rd	3rd day of bombardment. Horses at exercise.	
24	Fourth & last day of bombardment. Horses at exercise (men + getting everything ready – spare pr & hot evening meal)	

WAR DIARY of 2nd Squadron Glasgow Yeomanry

Army Form C. 2118.

INTELLIGENCE SUMMARY. September 1915

(Erase heading not required.)

Instructions regarding War Diaries and Intelligence Summaries are contained in F.S. Regs., Part II. and the Staff Manual respectively. Title pages will be prepared in manuscript.

Hour, Date, Place	Summary of Events and Information	Remarks and references to Appendices
25th September	Reveille 3:30 A.M. & man & horse at horse at 4.30. Waited & orders till 7:30 A.M. Set orders to move off to saddle to Bonnes. Then at Vermelles when we stood mounted awaiting till 3 PM. Then got orders to return to saddle to Bonnes. Got there & watered out our Report to us told Horses were left as it. Another Patrol to went off & Elmes was told at Sailly had Stome Patrol'd at same for in trenches wounded & sent front a foot dies them we told 5 the try for 1½ hrs under heavy fire & Sailly bought in 4 & had the information asked. Off spirs bit up under Mr. Ellis (cpl Burl & 6 bm more under Sgt tree but attend the channel informer the Mr. Hay was sent out in another direction & returned to BHQrs at 6 PM. It was a very wet & stormy evening.	From 25th September to 30th September
26th September	Squadron stood to all day & in riding order.	
27th September	Got order at 7.15 A.M. to mount and move off at 8 AM & ride right up to Vermelles & stood there about 2 hours. Then got orders to leave horses & go to trenches. Left as we as pair lines where it opens, to cut the further back as they were a way & as we gave orders to move in tell of the trenches under 2d Brigade orders line. 6 yds were under my Sergt till fire all day - we returned at 8 PM. Left horses at 8 PM. [Capt Officer] to Major Hunter left for Hunes & wherever had the horses had to tie off ca Bonnes we wanted food & were ungalloped as they stand all night. Did not unsaddle.	
28th September	Returned to Billets at Bethune 10:30 a.m. & had easy all day.	
29.	Heavy rain incessantly however that orders to go to our Billets - Bethune at there were immediately cancelled & other orders to join 5 troops on Afternoon, orders & had would arrive later.	
30th September	Stood to all day. Went orders to move carried.	

WAR DIARY

9th Division.

"B" Squadron Glasgow Yeomanry.

October — November 1915.

9th K warrun

"B" Sqn. Glasgow Yeo'
Ot- Nov-nl
Vol. 2

31/7708

Army Form C. 2118.

B. Squadron
Sherwood Rangers

WAR DIARY
of
INTELLIGENCE SUMMARY.
(Erase heading not required.)

October 1915. From 1st to 12th

Instructions regarding War Diaries and Intelligence Summaries are contained in F. S. Regs., Part II. and the Staff Manual respectively. Title pages will be prepared in manuscript.

Hour, Date, Place	Summary of Events and Information	Remarks and references to Appendices
1st October	Received orders to move tomorrow, got everything packed ready.	
2nd "	Moved off at 3 A.M. & moved to Mevagissey. Slow & dusty all day, very dull rainy windy even.	
3rd October	Moved off at 9 A.M. & rode through Bodlow, Gorsecliffe to Wyndford, slow & then billetted, first in border of Belgium & found Belgians en Billet — night settled down.	
4th October	Busy all day billets settled down.	
5th October	Commenced building stables (to house, pitting long Hp Pts	
6th "	Examined horses — early morning & walked & walking over stables all day.	
7th "	Squadron Drill soon ready — morning & afternoon entered.	
8th "	Squadron Drill came early & in the mud & letter, wire & busy stable building — German.	
9th "	Gun section at drill, Rifle & (minor at) stables — German.	
10th "	Set orders that S.O.S. all defence of trenches.	
11th "	Several started at 2 A.M. & thought it was very bally, washed, & we at still wanted, horses rode ill stably. Orders to stables — German.	
12th "	Had Route of times before trying billet for early, got 8 cent horse started watching stables — German.	

WAR DIARY
or
INTELLIGENCE SUMMARY.

Army Form C. 2118.

B. Squadron
Slough Training
October 1915
From 13th to 27

(Erase heading not required.)

Hour, Date, Place	Summary of Events and Information	Remarks and references to Appendices
13 October	Squadron Drill - [illegible] at stable billets - [illegible]	
14 October	1st relief O.R - D.R would inspect horses (not hay) in all troops & stables - [illegible]	
15 "	D.R inspected horses & was very pleased & said the 8 which Major Hall had out at stables - [illegible] Exercised early & everyone at stables - [illegible] Exercised - [illegible] at stable billets - [illegible]	
16 "		
17 "		
18 "		
19 "		
20 "		
21 "		
22 "		
23 "	Watered & stables - [illegible]	
24 "	Exercised horses early & had an church parade, other worked - stables - [illegible] Church service at 11 A.M. & it was a very wet [illegible]	
25 "	Horses & everyone [illegible] Major Ryott left us to rejoin his regiment. Everyone very sorry	
26 "	Exercised horses - fairer - watered & stables - [illegible] It was very cold & wet all day	
27 "	Squadron received news from 3.30 till 10.30 AM	

B. Squadron
Sharpur Stannery Army Form C. 2118
October 1915.
from 28th to 31st

WAR DIARY
or
INTELLIGENCE SUMMARY
(Erase heading not required.)

Instructions regarding War Diaries and Intelligence Summaries are contained in F. S. Regs., Part II. and the Staff Manual respectively. Title Pages will be prepared in manuscript.

Place	Date	Hour	Summary of Events and Information	Remarks and references to Appendices
	28 October		At Graham + 20 men were arranged and Sherrson which were despatched to the King's Shore one of well parties [illegible] and that.	
	29 October		Exercised horses and early morning + worked in stables afterwards.	
	30 October		Exercised horses + early morning worked in stables afterwards.	
	31 October		Church Parade at 11 A.M. A very wet day.	

Army Form C. 2118.

WAR DIARY
B. Squadron
Glasgow Yeomanry
INTELLIGENCE SUMMARY

(Erase heading not required.)

November 1915 from 28.6.30

Instructions regarding War Diaries and Intelligence Summaries are contained in F.S. Regs., Part II. and the Staff Manual respectively. Title pages will be prepared in manuscript.

Hour, Date, Place	Summary of Events and Information	Remarks and references to Appendices
1st November	Horses exercised early v ridden rest of day.	
2nd November	" "	
3rd "	" "	
4th "	Horses exercised – grooms v ran v either afternoon. Lt. Tullis v St. John ran at smoking concert in hosp. v 3 Division others.	
5th "	Horses exercised – grooms v ran v either afternoon.	
6th "	Horses "	
7th "	Horses exercised early rang Church Parade – Marcelia Run at 11 a.m.	
8th "	Horses exercised – grooms, run at Stables v platoon	
9th "		
10th "		
11th "		
12th "		
13th "		
14th "	Horses exercised – grooms. Lt. Tullis went to France & return for a week to Capt. Bucky.	

WAR DIARY or INTELLIGENCE SUMMARY

Army Form C. 2118

B. Squadron
Glasgow Yeomanry
November 1916. From 28'6'30'

(Erase heading not required.)

Instructions regarding War Diaries and Intelligence Summaries are contained in F.S. Regs., Part II. and the Staff Manual respectively. Title Pages will be prepared in manuscript.

Place	Date	Hour	Summary of Events and Information	Remarks and references to Appendices
	15 November		Horses exercised & groomed – men in stables.	
	16		Parade detail to take a rest leaving – Sunday	
	17		Horses exercised & groomed & men tidying stables afterwards.	
	18		"	
	19		"	
	20		Horses exercised early & ten days leave – stables afterwards.	
	21		Horses exercised early. Church Parade at 11 a.m.	
	22		All gone on out to Steenvoorde to land convoy with lads for stables	
	23		Horses exercised – groomed. Lt. Gillies, Gillen & Pitman out and strong parade of men detailed to find them out.	
	24		Lt. Gillies left party of 12 on road about strong finale.	
	25		Horses exercised: groomed in stables after.	
	26		"	
	27		"	

WAR DIARY or INTELLIGENCE SUMMARY

Army Form C. 2118

13 Squadron, Glasgow Germany

November 28, 29, 30.

Place	Date	Hour	Summary of Events and Information	Remarks and references to Appendices
	28 November		Aeros exercised early. Church service & Parade went up to 28 Brigade. 2/Lt L. of duties as Observers. Lt. Ephraim & Sergt Reid out up to Brandt school to take a radio course & bombing.	
	29 November		Aeros exercised early & in at stables afterwards. Nine reinforcements arrived.	
	30"		Nothing behind for no draught but good very heavy.	

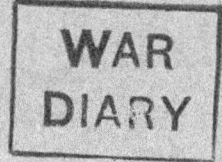

9TH DIVISION.

"B" SQUADRON GLASGOW YEOMANRY.

DECEMBER 1915.

"B. M: G'pur Flo:
Vol: 3

15/7935

WAR DIARY

Army Form C. 2118

B. Squadron
Sherpur Germany ? No 4 gola
December, 1915.

INTELLIGENCE SUMMARY
(Erase heading not required.)

Instructions regarding War Diaries and Intelligence Summaries are contained in F. S. Regs., Part II. and the Staff Manual respectively. Title Pages will be prepared in manuscript.

Place	Date	Hour	Summary of Events and Information	Remarks and references to Appendices
	1st December		Horses exercised early. One Troop & man old Patrol Stables under Lt. Jackson & Lt. Gillie had a fairly stiff Stuff training.	JJP
	2nd December		Horses exercised early. Lt. Gillie had Troop at Burby's funeral. Everyone at Stables - gymnar. Lt. Jackson had our troop doing Patrol Schemes.	JJP
	3rd December		Horses exercised early in & Stables gymnar.	JJP
	4th December		Horses exercised early in & Stables gymnar. Lt. Spiers & Sgt. Reid returned from Brigade Schools.	JJP
	5th December		Horses exercised early. On General Service. Officers Lt. String arrived from England to join us.	JJP
	6th December		Lt. Gillie and 10 men went to get Remounts at Cesstre. Ten different Units. Lt. Spiers had eight men at Burby. Remainder of men were busy at Stables.	JJP
	7th December		Lt. Gillie took remounts to different Units. Had to get yesterday. Lt. Spiers had same eight men at Burby as yesterday. Remainder of horses exercised under S.S.M. Larter.	JJP
	8th December		Lt. Jackson and 15 men to Cesstre to take over 24 Remounts, 8 for Germany & remainder to different Units, only got one to Units today. Lt. Spiers had 8 men at Burby.	JJP
	9th December		Lt. String exercised horses from 9am till 11am. Lt. Spiers had 8 men Burby in gymnar. Lt. Gallie rode off on radio leave.	JJP

Army Form C. 2118

WAR DIARY B. Squadron
or
INTELLIGENCE SUMMARY Elsegen, Germany
(Erase heading not required.)   from 10 Dec to 16 December
1915

Place	Date	Hour	Summary of Events and Information	Remarks and references to Appendices
	10th December		Exercised horses from 6.45 till 8 A.M. Eight men at Bombing Instruction under Lt. Spiers at 9.30. Remainder working in stables. Everyone saddling - afternoon.	JJP
	11th December		Paraded at 9.30 A.M. everyone earth, three + signal duty + Broken Rides. I took them to stables at Piperinghe + they all had falls. Everyone on saddling - afternoon.	JJP
	12th December 13th December		Exercised horses + grooms + men at saddling afternoons. Lt. Spiers + 14 men to Baesthe for Remounts + delivered them – afternoon. Remainder exercised – morning + had a marching order parade in afternoon, to get things ready for moving to 16th.	JJP
	14 December		Exercised horses + grooms + men were busy getting things packed up for moving on 16th	JJP
	15 December		Three men took three horses to Petr Vet Section which were cast by Vet M. Crashed Cobb etc. Had marching order parade – afternoon the eighth men enjoyed a place at 5 Corps were returned to us.	JJP
	16 December		Reveille 4.30 A.M. Paraded at 8 A.M. + left - no Ritheb to no Ritheb to Zontaline Sundams at front they had all their horses standing inside, however we managed to get all horses under cover at different farms, v everything was well settled down in evening.	JJP

Army Form C. 2118

WAR DIARY
or
INTELLIGENCE SUMMARY

B. Squadron
Elgin Yeomanry
Dec 14th to 27 December 1915

(Erase heading not required.)

Instructions regarding War Diaries and Intelligence Summaries are contained in F. S. Regs., Part II. and the Staff Manual respectively. Title Pages will be prepared in manuscript.

Place	Date	Hour	Summary of Events and Information	Remarks and references to Appendices
	14 December		Horses exercised before breakfast & in afternoon all busy all day – stables & cleaning of billets etc.	JJP
	18 December		Ditto	JJP
	19 December		Ditto. A lot of places have been made at which repairs require been laid.	JJP
	20 December		Ditto	JJP
	21 December		Horses exercised early, men at stables etc in forenoon and the O.C. Inspected all billets & stables in afternoon. The General & Col. Nobody were round – afternoon. Col. visited O.C. Sergeant of all non + Officers were quite infallible. At eight man who were left at H.Q. as Orderly for keyed by, came back at 9 P.M.	JJP
22 December			Horses exercised early, men at stables in forenoon & men were paid in afternoon. Men at stables all forenoon. Stable Parade & Inspection & instruction in use of entire details	JJP
23 December			Horses exercised early, men at stables – afternoon	JJP
24 December			Horses exercised in forenoon, men at stables – afternoon	JJP
25 December			Horses exercised in forenoon. Squadron paraded – forenoon & was marched to Bailleul to Baths. The following promotions were made – Ordins Sergt. Matheson to be Sergt. 2/6pt. McNeill to be Sergt. L/Sgt. Thompson to be Sergt. Also 2/Sgt. Welsh to be Sergt. to be L/Sgt. Ptes. Purdie, Meighen, Morton & Green. Church Parade at 10 A.M. Being had easy all day.	JJP
26 December			Horses exercised in forenoon, St. Mary + the reinforcements which came and did probably done with St. Julian in forenoon. Men at stables in afternoon	JJP
27 December				JJP

WAR DIARY
INTELLIGENCE SUMMARY

Army Form C. 2118

of J.B. Squadron. Glasgow Yeomanry
From 28 December to 31st December 1915.

(Erase heading not required.)

Instructions regarding War Diaries and Intelligence Summaries are contained in F.S. Regs., Part II. and the Staff Manual respectively. Title Pages will be prepared in manuscript.

Place	Date	Hour	Summary of Events and Information	Remarks and references to Appendices
	28th December		Nos 3 & 4 troop exercised horses - (forenoon & at stables rest of day). No 2 troop rest & Route march - forenoon & at stables - afternoon.	JP
	29th December		Every fine in order Lt Gillie started work as Guide to Know the roads to G.H.Q. & 2nd Line & other pords. Remainder of Squadron exercised horses - forenoon & at stables - afternoon	JP
	30th December		The Guides out none of all day. Remainder of Squadron paraded at 7 A.M. in the St Afrique road to Hazebrouck for 49 Remounts & worked the men to different units in the Division.	JP
	31st December		The Guides were out all day. Remainder of Squadron cleaning saddlery etc in forenoon & - afternoon - dismounted parade doing foot drill etc.	JP

Ulick Mackintosh
Major
J.B. Squadron
Queens Own Royal Glasgow Yeomanry.

Glasgow
"B"-Sq: (Lanarkshire) Yeo.
Vol: 4

96 Div.

Army Form C. 2118

WAR DIARY
or
INTELLIGENCE SUMMARY
(Erase heading not required.)

B. Squadron
Glasgow Yeomanry
From 1st to 23rd January 1918.

Place	Date	Hour	Summary of Events and Information	Remarks and references to Appendices
	1st January 1918		Horses exercised early under Lt. Gallie, men were at horses & stables all forenoon. No parade in afternoon.	JJP
	2nd January		Horses exercised early. Church Parade at 11 A.M. men were at stables etc. in afternoon.	JJP
	3rd January		Had a Squadron Parade at 9 A.M. & did Troop Patrols etc. All forenoon. In afternoon & duties of Observers by Sgt. Cromwell. Lt. Paterson, Sergt. Drill & Pte. Wilson attended Brigade School for one weeks instruction.	JJP
	4th January		No 1 & No 2 Troop exercised horses & then cleaned saddlery. No 3 Troop were out doing Patrol Instruction.	JJP
	5th January		Horses exercised. In afternoon a fatigue party were making a grenade pit.	JJP
			Horses exercising - morning & afternoon, cleaning saddlery. The following men went to C.R.A. 21st Division as Head light spotters. Sgt. Peattie, Pte. Dalton, Pte. McAllister, Pte. Yemmel.	
	6th Jany.		Horses exercised - forenoon & in afternoon - saddles etc. & men at Grenade pit in afternoon.	JJP
	7th Jany		Horses exercised - forenoon. The Yeomanry & Cyclist football team played the Argyll & Sutherland Hrs. in afternoon & were beaten by them.	JJP
	8th Jany		Horses exercised in forenoon under Lt. McKie. Had inspection of clothing - forenoon. Football team played 26th Bde. Machine Gun Section - afternoon & won by 6 G.O.	JJP

Army Form C. 2118.

WAR DIARY
or
INTELLIGENCE SUMMARY.

B Squadron Glasgow Yeomanry

(Erase heading not required.)

From 9th Jany to 16th Jany

Hour, Date, Place	Summary of Events and Information	Remarks and references to Appendices
9th Jany	Church Parade at 11.30. Lt. Pearson brought Draft of the 1/1st Lanark Yeomanry Scouts at Parade billeted & all passed as "class" men at various Huts/billets	JJP
10th Jany	Horses exercised in Forenoon had a dismounted parade in afternoon. Lt. Johnson, Sgt. Thompson & Cpl Moore attended at Grenade School for no echo course.	JJP
11th Jany	Exercised horses in forenoon, inspection of Carts & Vehicles & box rations in forenoon. Had dismounted parade in afternoon.	JJP
12th Jany	Exercised horses – forenoon. No use getting saddlery ready for journey into Parade next day.	JJP
13th Jany	Had a mounted order parade – forenoon.	JJP
14th Jany	Horses exercised in forenoon, & had inspection of horses & forenoon. Rifle inspection parade	CWP
15th Jany	Kit parade in forenoon. New saddlery came & turning horses in afternoon.	JJP
16th Jany	Church Parade at 11 AM. Lt. Johnson, Sgt. Thompson & Cpl. Moore finished their Grenade Course & all passed as 1st Class Instructors.	JJP

Army Form C. 2118.

WAR DIARY
or
INTELLIGENCE SUMMARY.

B. Squadron
Glasgow Yeomanry
From 17 Jany 1916 to 24 Jany 1916

(Erase heading not required.)

Instructions regarding War Diaries and Intelligence Summaries are contained in F. S. Regs., Part II. and the Staff Manual respectively. Title pages will be prepared in manuscript.

Hour, Date, Place	Summary of Events and Information	Remarks and references to Appendices
17th Jany. 1916	Roused & ready orders at 2 A.M. & rose therefrom by the troop Commander. While we rode round	JP
18th Jany 19 Jany	Horses exercised – Grooms & vet at saddles etc through. Horses reviewed – Francis Instructor in use of Sabre. Helmets & inspection of details & rifles & others.	JP JP
	Gas filling in will go on tomorrow all day. Gallic 2/6 pm. Inspection Pte Roger. The cellar of the Medical Stores examined – Grooms & men cleaning & afternoon	JP
20th Jany 21st Jany 22nd Jany 23rd Jany	Had a round order Roads Grooms. Had a march order Parade & Grooms & easy afternoon Church Parade at 11 A.M. & easy Gallic all things ready to move tomorrow afternoon	JP JP JP JP
24th Jany.	Left Billets at 8 A.M. & rode to Steenwerck Station to our billets & took over from B Squadron Lothians & Border Horse 25 Tilleries, wet lovely day but threatened rain & snow	JP

Army Form C. 2118

WAR DIARY
or
INTELLIGENCE SUMMARY
(Erase heading not required.)

B. Squadron
Sloan Yeomanry
From 25. Jany. to 31st Jany. 1916

Instructions regarding War Diaries and Intelligence Summaries are contained in F. S. Regs., Part II. and the Staff Manual respectively. Title Pages will be prepared in manuscript.

Place	Date	Hour	Summary of Events and Information	Remarks and references to Appendices
	25 Jany		Horses exercised in forenoon & men all busy at stables & making roads of &	JJP
	26 Jany		" "	JJP
	27 Jany		" "	JJP
	28 Jany		" "	JJP
	29 Jany		" "	JJP
	30 Jany		Horses exercised in forenoon & men busy fixing stables & making roads in Stamou. Four red & 1 N.C.O. detailed to go to Signal Coy. as despatch Riders daily. Church Parade at 11 A.M.	JJP
	31 Jany		Horses exercised in forenoon, men making roads also in afternoon & putting of canvas round stables	JJP

Walter Macfarlane
Major
O.C. &c. Mounted Troops

9

"B" Sq: E' Liv Yeo:
vol: 5

WAR DIARY or INTELLIGENCE SUMMARY

Army Form C. 2118

E. Squadron
Bhopal Lancers
From 1st July 1918 to 12 July 1918

Vol

Place	Date	Hour	Summary of Events and Information	Remarks and references to Appendices
	1st July		Horses exercised in morning & men busy making roads etc. afterwards. Two men were sent to CAESTRE to draw remounts for detachment to replace horses which were killed at Nieppe & to drill all available transport were fitting and for heavy stables. Stifling hot to tracks for two three days inoculation.	JJP
	2nd July		Horses exercised in morning & men busy making roads & horse stables afternoon.	JJP
	3rd July		Horses exercised in morning & men at roads & stables all day	JJP
	4th July		Horses exercised in morning & men in saddlery – afternoon	JJP
	5th July		Horses exercised in morning & men in saddlery – afternoon	JJP
	6th July		Church Parade at 11 A.M. & men were fed – afternoon	JJP
	7th July		Horses were exercised early & men at stables – afternoon	JJP
	8th July		Horses were exercised early & men at stables – morning & saddlery – afternoon	JJP
	9th July		Horses were inoculated for Glanders. Men at saddlery etc.	JJP
	10th July		Horses were exercised morning. Eleven men sent to Tenedos & took over stated 102 mill 50 hr for bipeds, as twenty & bipeds are now to take part of line. Lt. Jackson in command of the Body	JJP
	11th July		Horses exercised morning & men at stables etc. afternoon but men at twelve it was out as had what to know to look after.	JJP
	12th July		Horses exercised early & men at stables afternoon all day.	JJP

Army Form C. 2118

WAR DIARY
or
INTELLIGENCE SUMMARY

(Erase heading not required.)

B. Squadron
Glasgow Yeomanry
From 12 July 1916 to 21 July 1916

Instructions regarding War Diaries and Intelligence Summaries are contained in F.S. Regs., Part II. and the Staff Manual respectively. Title Pages will be prepared in manuscript.

Place	Date	Hour	Summary of Events and Information	Remarks and references to Appendices
	13th July		Horses exercised early & were at stables etc. afternoon.	JJP
	14 July		Horses exercised early, no details for trenches were required – full kit in afternoon.	JJP
	15 July		Horses exercised early, horses were at stables & were at stables & work all day	JJP
	16 July		Horses exercised early. 11 men went to trenches – afternoon & relieved the 11th Squadron. We had two of our dogs. Lt. Judson relieved will relieved party & remained & general party handed over to D. Hill Cyclist Coy. Lt. King from Squadron went to will Party on duty for week.	JJP
	17 July		Horses exercised early, here the relieved for trenches from no night were taken to Baths at Nieppe – afternoon	JJP
	18th July		Horses exercised & greased & ran at stables afternoon	JJP
	19 July		Horses served early & ran at stables all (men) & at stables afternoon. Full of War catastrophe – afternoon	JJP
	20 July		Church Parade 11 A.M. & ran hand – easy & afternoon	JJP
	21st July		Horses exercised early & stables all (men) disposed of Lost, Helmets etc. – afternoon	JJP

Army Form C. 2118

WAR DIARY
or
INTELLIGENCE SUMMARY
(Erase heading not required.)

B. Squadron, Glasgow Yeomanry
From 21st Feby 1916 to 29 Feby 1916

Place	Date	Hour	Summary of Events and Information	Remarks and references to Appendices
	22 Feby		Horses exercised early. At 11 a.m. Sqn. to trenches to relieve Rifle of Horse Rifle Officers. 1st Tp. was told we formed of Third Body for 2nd Bde.	JSP
	23 Feby		Horses exercised early. Sqn. returned from Trenches. Parade after night exercises to Bells of Nickle – afternoon.	JSP
	24 Feby		Horses exercised & harness, harness cleaning & watering – afternoon	JSP
	25 Feby		Horses exercised & harness per Sqn. sent fwd – afternoon	JSP
	26 Feby		Horses exercised – harness the whole troop's own – Troops went to Bands	JSP
	27 Feby		Horses & Lt. Alban – afternoon	JSP
			Divine Services of French troops held at Stables etc afternoon. Final Parade of 11 A.M. we had easy afternoon.	JSP
	28 Feby		Horses exercised –	JSP
			Horses exercised – morning. 11 a.m. went to trenches – afternoon & relieved Rifle Rifle. Lt. Thirs returned & Lt. Lennon. Lieut. Tychwitz took over command of Sqn. went to trenches – duty.	JSP
	29 Feby		Horses exercised early & men at Stables & rounds afterwards.	JSP

Walter Macfarlane
Major

B Sg. G! em leo.
folio B

Army Form C. 2118

WAR DIARY
B. Ignatius
Sharpa Summary

INTELLIGENCE SUMMARY
From 1st March 1916 to 9th March 1916

(Erase heading not required.)

Instructions regarding War Diaries and Intelligence Summaries are contained in F. S. Regs., Part II. and the Staff Manual respectively. Title Pages will be prepared in manuscript.

Place	Date	Hour	Summary of Events and Information	Remarks and references to Appendices
	1st March		Horses exercised early, hosed and douched daily, watered as shown & within tidy institution - Wiring	JPP
	2 March		Horses exercised early, hen do stores & Glenin	JPP
	3 March		Horses exercised & groomed. Kit Parade & Shoes as usual & Hardsoal	JPP
			2.6 mls to Orderlies	JPP
	4 March		Horses exercised & in a saddling flomarde	JPP
	5 March		Horses Kit Parade & as had easy day thus	JPP
	6 March		The 12 hr she had been attached to Coln & duty with other 25 hr as Triffin Road Colinde. Horses exercised early & in a saddling flomarde	JPP
	7 March		Horses exercised early & in a saddling flomarde	JPP
	8 March		Horses exercised early, hosed: Horses now relieved by H.L.I. & the 10 Jeomy did the Route. The 10 Jeomy all when at of the Route.	JPP
	9 March		Horses exercised early, hen the one at of Route and to Billets - Glenin	JPP

Army Form C. 2118

WAR DIARY
or
INTELLIGENCE SUMMARY
(Erase heading not required.)

B. Sanderson
Glasgow Yeomanry
From 10 March 1916 to 21 March 1916

Instructions regarding War Diaries and Intelligence Summaries are contained in F. S. Regs., Part II. and the Staff Manual respectively. Title Pages will be prepared in manuscript.

Place	Date	Hour	Summary of Events and Information	Remarks and references to Appendices
	10 March		Horses exercised early & men on horses & saddling afterwards, gully horses fit & saddlery which had been neglected all were being set to rights.	JP
	11 March		Billets	JP
	12 March		Church Parade & men at saddles - afternoon	JP
	13 March		Horses exercised early & men at horses - Saddlery afternoon gully horses all closed up for kits etc. Stop. hanging - begins next month.	JP
	14 March		Ditto.	JP
	15 March		Ditto	JP
	16 March		Billets. H. C. O's. Had lecture - Picket duties - afternoon	JP
	17 March		Ditto.	JP
	18 March		Ditto. Had Kit inspection & afternoon	JP
	19 March		Men at saddles & horses all day.	JP
	20 March		Men at saddles & horses all day; gully horses clipped & trimmed	JP
	21 March		Church Parade & men at saddles afternoon	JP

Army Form C. 2118

WAR DIARY
or
INTELLIGENCE SUMMARY

(Erase heading not required.)

B. Squadron - Imperial Shaysn Yeomanry from 22 March 1916 to 31st March 1916

Instructions regarding War Diaries and Intelligence Summaries are contained in F. S. Regs., Part II. and the Staff Manual respectively. Title Pages will be prepared in manuscript.

Place	Date	Hour	Summary of Events and Information	Remarks and references to Appendices
	22nd March		Horses exercised × men at Mess & artillery flirmards. No ho one & recruit drafts had men the instruction & flimon	JP
	23rd March		Horses exercised + men at drill & truming & mess flirmards	JP
	24th March		ditto	JP
	25th March		ditto	JP
	26th March		ditto	JP
	27th March		Horses exercised & flimon & had ea tillery instruction & flimon	JP
	28th March		Horses exercised & flimon & men & my lines had veen walks & Observers	JP
	29th March		& full teams in were transferred to & squads Battalions	JP
	30th March		Horses exercised — Common & men & atillery do — flimon	JP
	31st March		"	JP

Walter Macfarlane Major

1751/2

9TH DIVISION

9TH CYCLIST COY.
MAY 1915 – MAY 1916

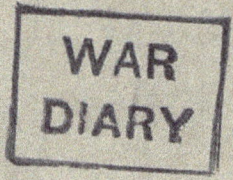

9th Division

9th Cyclist Company.

May 1915.

CONFIDENTIAL.

Officer,
	i/c Records,
		Hounslow.

Herewith War Diary for the months of May and June which, being the duplicate copies of same, we are forwarding to you for safe custody. Please acknowledge receipt.

15/11/15.

...........*Mackintosh Walker, Lt.*........Comdg.
9th. Divisional Cyclist Company.

Officer,
      i/c Records,
           Hounslow.

Reference your letter No. E/20139. I beg to forward the following information.

1. January 7th. 1915.

2. Two platoons were formed from each of the three Infantry Bdes. of the 9th. (Scottish) Division.

3. The Coy. was collected in Aldershot and taken to Eastbury Manor Compton, Surrey on the 7th. January 1915. On the 21st. March 1915, the Coy. moved to OXNEY FARM, BORDON under canvas. On the 11th. of May the Coy. entrained at BORDON station at 11 a.m. for FRANCE

4. As per. War Diary enclosed which is sent to you for safe custody

5. 2/Lt. I.D. Munro. killed September, 11th. 1915.
   2/Lt. S.E. Tidy. wounded September, 27th. 1915.
   Capt. C.C.K. Campbell. Missing. September. 27th. 1915.
   The following were recommended for their gallant action on September, 26th. 1915.
   Capt. C.C.K. Campbell. Pte. 3149. Liddell. J.

6. Drafts Despatched.
6. 2/Lt. E.J. Ritchie was transferred to the 173rd. Coy. R.E. a tunnelling Coy. on the 24th. of September, 1915.

   Drafts Received.-
   Officers.
   2/Lt. G. Blunden. June 18/15.
   2/Lt. S.E. Tidy. Sept. 27/15.
   2/Lt. H.R. Alexander. Oct. 17/15.
   2/Lt. H.N. Crowe.   Oct. 17/15
   2/Lt. S.M. Gilbert.   Oct. 17/15.

   Other Ranks received at various times.
   66.

7. Nil.

14/11/15.

                                C. Mackintosh Walker, Lt. Comdg
                                9th. Divisional Cyclist Company.

121/7598

9th Division

9th Cyclist Coy.
1st Part-Vol I

May 15.

7th Divisional Cyclist Company.

War Diary

11th May to 31st May 1915.

Army Form C. 2118.

WAR DIARY
or
INTELLIGENCE SUMMARY.

(Erase heading not required.)

7th Divisional Cyclist Co

Place	Date	Hour	Summary of Events and Information	Remarks and references to Appendices
	May. 11th 1915		Capt. L. L. K. Campbell. Comdg. Capt. J. S. Gordon. Sec-in-com. 2/Lt. R. A. Mackintosh-Walker. 2/Lt. C. D. t. Jerviswa. 2/Lt. J. P. Munro. 2/Lt. L. L. Wemyss. 2/Lt. D. McGowan-Hill. 2/Lt. E. J. Ritchie. Other Ranks. 192.	
		11 a.m.	The Company left BORDON Rly. Station at 11 a.m. and went by rail to SOUTHAMPTON, arriving at 1. p.m. Cycles and horses were embarked on s.s. "INVENTOR" (Harrison line) and the men (less a party under 2/Lt. E. J. Ritchie on the INVENTOR) embarked on s.s. "PANCRAS" (Booth Line)	
		5 p.m.	s.s. "PANCRAS" sailed at 5 p.m.	

Army Form C. 2118.

WAR DIARY
or
INTELLIGENCE SUMMARY.
(Erase heading not required.)

Instructions regarding War Diaries and Intelligence Summaries are contained in F. S. Regs., Part II. and the Staff Manual respectively. Title pages will be prepared in manuscript.

Place	Date	Hour	Summary of Events and Information	Remarks and references to Appendices
Havre	12th May	7 a.m.	S.S. "PANCRAS" arrived in the HAVRE docks about 7 a.m. after a good passage, and men disembarked at 8 a.m.; moving round to another part of the Docks, the cycles, horses, and wagons were unloaded and the day then proceeded to a Rest-Camp for the day. At about 5 p.m. the Ho. Moved off to the Railway Station and entrained. Train left HAVRE about 1-30 a.m.	
	13th "	1-30 a.m.	At 8-30. detrainment started, after which the Ho. S¹ OMER was reached about 6 a.m. Moved off to billets in village of S¹ MARTIN just outside S¹ OMER.	
	14th "		Day, remained at S¹ MARTIN, but went for a short route-march on the 15th.	
	15th "			
	16th "		Day, together with "B" Squadron, Queens Own Glasgow Yeomanry left S¹ OMER at 9-30 a.m. The 10th Battery Motor Machine-Gun Service followed on after us. We reached HONDEGHEM at 3 p.m. and billeted there.	

WAR DIARY or INTELLIGENCE SUMMARY

Army Form C. 2118.

Place	Date	Hour	Summary of Events and Information	Remarks and references to Appendices
HONDEGHEM	17th May	6 A.M.	The Bay. moved off at 6 a.m. for billets at NOOTE BOOM going via METEREN - BAILLEUL and arriving at 11 A.M.	
NOOTE-BOOM	18th "		The Bay. rested.	
"	19th "	2-30 P.M.	At 2-30 P.M. we moved off for billet 1 mile S.E. of STEENWERCK and arrived at 5-30 p.m. 2/Lts. J.D. Munro & E.J. Ritchie proceeded to ARMENTIERES for a Four of instruction in the trenches with the 3rd Batt. J.R.B. returning on 22nd May. Bay. carries on with training by ourselves and doing schemes with the Glasgow Yeomanry and Motor Machine Gun Battery. On Tuesday 25th Captain J.E. Gordon went to hospital with German Measles. Extract of LONDON GAZETTE of 12th May. 2/Lt. E.A. MacIntosh-Walker to be Lieut. dated 12th Feb. Ref. sheet No. 28 1/40,000.	
"	20-30th			
"	31st "	6-30 P.M.	At 6-30 P.M. the Bay. left for the trenches. The cycles were left with the Bay. in Reserve of the 6th Warwicks (T.F.) at T.18.d.4.5.	
		9 P.M.	At about 9 p.m. we moved off for the trenches held by the 8th Warwicks (T.F.) two platoons in the trenches facing MESSINES with their right on the U.8.a.1.5. and then left on the MESSINES - WOUVERGHEM road at U.1.b.1.3. The remaining platoon (No. 2) was at right angles to the rest along the	

Army Form C. 2118.

WAR DIARY
or
INTELLIGENCE SUMMARY.
(Erase heading not required.)

Instructions regarding War Diaries and Intelligence Summaries are contained in F. S. Regs., Part II. and the Staff Manual respectively. Title pages will be prepared in manuscript.

Place	Date	Hour	Summary of Events and Information	Remarks and references to Appendices
	31st May		the MESSINES-WOUVEGHEM Road. The Bn. arrived in the trenches about 10. h.m.	

WAR DIARY

9th DIVISION.

9th CYCLIST COMPANY.

JUNE 1915.

12/7518

9th Hussars

9th div: Gel: Lrs
Vol I
June 15.

Army Form C. 2118.

WAR DIARY
or
INTELLIGENCE SUMMARY.
(Erase heading not required.)

Instructions regarding War Diaries and Intelligence Summaries are contained in F. S. Regs., Part II. and the Staff Manual respectively. Title pages will be prepared in manuscript.

Place	Date	Hour	Summary of Events and Information	Remarks and references to Appendices
	1st June		The night passed quietly. All the officers and men and a number of N.C.O.'s and men went out to listening post No. 4 (Platoon Sergt.) went out as far as the German mine. At this part the German trench is 500 yards away. On the left of the road the distance decreases to 200 yds. After a stand down in the morning 2/3 of the men were able to turn in and sleep in the dug-outs. Between one and two o'clock the trenches were shelled by a "77 m/m or 65 m/m gun with H.E. very little damage was done to the parapet which was hit in several places. Otherwise all was quiet until the day. Left the trenches at about midnight. At 10 h.m. the 6th Warwicks were relieved by their 4th Battalion.	
	June 2nd 3rd & 4th June		Billets were reached about 3 A.M. There were no casualties in the day. Carried on training.	
	June 5th	6-45 P.M.	At 6-45 P.M. Bay moved off for near LILLERS. We arrived in our billets at about 9 P.M. Bills were situated 1 mile N.W. of BUSNES and about 2½ miles by road from LILLERS.	
	June 6th June 7th		Sunday. Carried on Training. Brigade Village fighting at AUCHY-AU-BOIS (a deserted village)	

1577 Wt.W10791/1773 500,000 1/15 D.D.&L. A.D.S.S./Forms/C. 2118.

WAR DIARY
or
INTELLIGENCE SUMMARY.

Army Form C. 2118.

Place	Date	Hour	Summary of Events and Information	Remarks and references to Appendices
	June 14th		Blaringhem. 4 A.M. Coy. ready to move off at 6 A.M. but no orders came during the day. Since 6th June division is in Reserve under G.H.Q. and on about 13th is put under the orders of G.O.C. 1st Army. During the night 12/13th a heavy bombardment has been going on N. of BETHUNE.	
	June 15th		Coy. under orders to move at 1 hour's notice.	
	June 16th		Coy. move under 2 hours notice to move.	
	June 17th		Same time limit.	
	June 18th		Time extended to 3 hours.	
	June 19th		Still under 3 hours notice but Coy. able to go out to FORET DE NIEPPE to inspect line of defences running through forest.	
	June 20th		Sunday. Church Parade.	
	June 21st		Coy. went for route-march via ROBECQUE – MERVILLE – St VENNANT. 2/Lt. A. BLUNDEN joins Coy. for duty from HOUNSLOW.	
	22–23rd		Training as usual.	
	24th		Coy. moves off to billets at St SAUVEUR outside CHOQES arriving at 3.P.M.	
	25–26th		Coy. kept ready to move.	
	27th		Sunday. After a Service the Coy. moves off to billets 1 mile N. of LOCON. at R.31 central (Ref: 1/40,000 sheet 36a)	

Army Form C. 2118.

WAR DIARY
or
INTELLIGENCE SUMMARY.

(Erase heading not required.)

Place	Date	Hour	Summary of Events and Information	Remarks and references to Appendices
	June 18-31st		Carry on with training	

WAR DIARY

9th DIVISION

9th CYCLIST COMPANY.

JULY 1915.

9th K Warren

9th Cyclops
Vol 2

121/7761

July 15

CONFIDENTIAL.

War Diary
of
9th Div: Cycle Coy.

From July 1st 1915 — July 31st (inclusive)

(Volume III)

WAR DIARY
or
INTELLIGENCE SUMMARY.
(Erase heading not required.)

Army Form C. 2118

Place	Date	Hour	Summary of Events and Information	Remarks and references to Appendices
LOCON	JULY 1		Ref. (I Bne) BETHUNE 1/40,000	
	2		Coy parade on training. 2 N.C.Os + 12 men sent on Road Patrols to ROBECQ cross Roads (R.27.K.1)	
	3		and LES CHOQUAUX Tracks (W.17.K.17) Party on unloading	
	4		8 N.C.O.s + 48 men at LOCON Billy guards and Road controls — 1 N.C.O. + 6 men on each as follows :— Bridge guards at LILLE CASAN X28.R.I.I (ii) LOCON PONT TOURNANT X8.C.42 (iii) X.13.d.5.9. (iv) Ecluse d'ESSARS X.19.a.3.1. (v) W24.c.9.1 + (vi) AVELETTE W.17.b.2.1. which also provided a road control at W.17.b.0.0. Road controls at (vii) ESSARS X25.R.2.1. + (viii) GORRE F3.b.5.2. Three eight posts and the three sent out on the 2nd inst. are inspected daily by the trotaly officer who also to go round on a motor bike + notify of casualties, weather + him on the march, as a good weather the district round to hot and but 27 miles and the summing too early 35 seem often seen. 1 Sgt. sent to D.H.Q. on list Went party worth of + a men under two officers sent out to rebuild redoubt at S.13.d.4.8. Working from 1 P.M. + 6 P.M.	
	11			

Army Form C. 2118.

WAR DIARY
or
INTELLIGENCE SUMMARY.
(Erase heading not required.)

Instructions regarding War Diaries and Intelligence Summaries are contained in F. S. Regs., Part II. and the Staff Manual respectively. Title pages will be prepared in manuscript.

Place	Date	Hour	Summary of Events and Information	Remarks and references to Appendices
LOCON	July 12	8 AM to 1 PM	Work party of [?] men about 4 N.C.O.s & [?] from detachment from the company & was inspected by LORD KITCHENER & PRINCE of WALES & accompanying Staff.	
	14	11 PM	Advance party of [?] & Lieutenants & Work [?] party of [?] & men [?] who left [?] at 3.19 & arrived at S. Pol at 3 [?] [?] on [?] [?] the [?] [?] reports and [?] R.E. [?] [?] and [?] acts of R.E. at ENNETOT.	
	25		[?] the month [?] [?] had to find [?] at [?] YM R. & 1st Eng HQ & all these being obtained at night. & also [?] at Cy HQ and a fatigue of [?] men per day for 2 H.R. The work parties were [?] [?] [?] [?] [?] when work was completed. There men from Les Chaqueux [?] at [?] whole [?]	

Army Form C. 2118.

WAR DIARY
or
INTELLIGENCE SUMMARY.   3

(Erase heading not required.)

Instructions regarding War Diaries and Intelligence Summaries are contained in F. S. Regs., Part II. and the Staff Manual respectively. Title pages will be prepared in manuscript.

Place	Date	Hour	Summary of Events and Information	Remarks and references to Appendices
LOCON	JULY 31 18		of the AVELETTE POST return to the Coy. 1 Sgt & 14 O.R. sent on to LE TOURET to run a light railway from X.18.a.3.4. to S.20.a.9.5.	Attached to A Coy 9. 8 the Cyclist Coy

1577 Wt.W10791/1773 500,000 1/15 D. D. & L.   A.D.S.S./Forms/C. 2118.

WAR DIARY

9th DIVISION

9th CYCLIST COMPANY.

AUGUST 1915.

9th Int: Cyclists
Vol: 3

121/7693

August/15

War Diary.

August 1915

9ᵈ Division Cyclist Company.

WAR DIARY or INTELLIGENCE SUMMARY

Army Form C. 2118.

Place	Date	Hour	Summary of Events and Information	Remarks and references to Appendices
LOCON	AUGUST 2		(Ref BETHUNE [COMBINED SHEET])	
			Three men return from bridge guards on LAWE CANAL.	
			Since JULY 29 an officer from the company has had to report to D.H.Q at 9 A.M. to act as Liaison Officer between the Division and the two Infantry Brigades in the trenches. This is carried out by us on alternate days, the Yeomanry providing the officer for the other days. The duties of the Liaison Officer were considerably facilitated by his being able to go round on a motor bicycle.	
	6		2/Lt F. Blunden detached from Company to take charge of the two light railways to the trenches, one being the railway eft referred to on JULY 18, and the other from S.7.d.3.3 to S.15C.8.2.	
	10	6.P.M	2/Lt. Munro — McCowan - Hill with 51 O.R. leave the Company for the trenches of the 28TH I.B.	
	12	11. P.M	The two officers and 51 O.R. return from the trenches. No casualties.	
	14		L/Cpt. C.C.K. Campbell admitted to hospital with poisoned leg.	
	15		2/Lt I.P. Munro admitted to hospital with jaundice.	
	16	7. A.M	2/Lt Ferreira, and 60 O.R. sent out to take charge of redoubts and front stores behind 2nd line trenches for handing them over to 7 4.P.M (relieving 5th) K.R.	

WAR DIARY or INTELLIGENCE SUMMARY

Army Form C. 2118.

Place	Date	Hour	Summary of Events and Information	Remarks and references to Appendices
LOCON	AUGUST 16	(con.)	2/Lt BLUNDEN and all O.R. on Railway & guards return to the company	
		4 P.M.	Company moves into close billets at R.31.a.9.2. to rest room for 28th I.B.	
	17	1 A.M.	2/Lt FERREIRA and all men taken went with him, except (P)-6332 Pte STEWART, wounded, return to Coy	
		2 P.M.	Company moves off for billets CENSE LA VALLÉE (VIOLDALE) and bivouac	
GONNEHEM	19		Company inspected with the Division by LORD KITCHENER at P.31.d.6.8.	
	26		2/Lt MUNRO Re returned from Hospital. 2/Lt MUNRO detached from Company and proceed to Rouches Roted by 1st Div which are to be taken over by the IV. as Divisional Scout Officer.	
	29	6 A.M.	One Officer and 30 O.R. sent to FOSSE No 3 or BETHUNE to dig in telephone wires. Party returned at 3:30. Distance covered to and from to and 29 miles.	
	30	6 A.M.	Some digging party sent out	

Army Form C. 2118.

WAR DIARY
or
INTELLIGENCE SUMMARY. 3

Place	Date	Hour	Summary of Events and Information	Remarks and references to Appendices
GONNEHEM	August 31		Except for the digging parties on 29th & 30th since moving to GONNEHEM the Company has been engaged in having during the period of rest. On 30th a second Lt/Qt was sent to D.H.Q. as a clerk	

WAR DIARY

9TH DIVISION.

9TH CYCLIST COMPANY.

SEPTEMBER 1915.

9th Stirl: Cycls. Coy.
Vol: 4

121/738.

Fight in
28 Sept 1915

War Diary
of
9th Division Cyclist Company

From 1st September 1915. To 30th September 1915. (Inclusive.)

Volume 4

(Wheeler) tot Bolen Capt
Commanding 9th Division Cyclist Company.

Army Form C. 2118.

WAR DIARY
or
INTELLIGENCE SUMMARY.
(Erase heading not required.)

Place	Date	Hour	Summary of Events and Information	Remarks and references to Appendices
CUINCHY	Sept 1-2nd		Overhauling carts.	
VALLÉE BETHUNE	3rd	9 A.M.	The mens billet in E.23.B (BETHUNE to left) previously at 10.5 A.M. During the afternoon by about 6 constructing splinter proof shelter. Stretch of shelters completed. All available men employed in wire for 7th Infy Bde at the foot of FOSSE 7 N of BETHUNE.	
	4th		Digging in wire continued in the direction of CHAPELLE	
	5th		finch for cover to cover in to 25 Infy Bde H.Qrs.	
	6th		Trench completed.	
	7th		Digging in wires to the North of VERMELLES for 26 Infy Bde.	
	8th		Part of the trench to the North of Infy Bde was filled in.	
	9th			
	10th		Remainder of trench filled in.	
	11th			
			2/Lt J.B. MUNRO killed by a sniper in Coy's communication trench. The Major General Commanding the Division on a letter to the O.C. Coy, expressed his deepest regret at 2/Lt J.B. Munros death, and testified to the good work done by this Officer as Recce Lieut Officer. A Party sent out digging in wires in SCOTTISH communication to H. Qrs of 26 Infy Bde at RAILWAY WELL.	

Army Form C. 2118.

WAR DIARY
or
INTELLIGENCE SUMMARY.
(Erase heading not required.)

Place	Date	Hour	Summary of Events and Information	Remarks and references to Appendices
BETHUNE	Sept 14th to 15-23		Draft of 1 Sgt and 11 men arrive from HOUNSLOW. He toy together with A one Squadron of GLASGOW YEOMANRY and 10th M.M.G.S. carry out a scheme of training to the N.W. of BETHUNE, Under Capt (Comp Major) PRITCHELL of the IV HUSSARS Commanding Divisl Mounted Troops from the 14th inst. On the 15th final training was rehearsed by Capt HORNE (16th January) who assisted Major PRITCHELL until 19th inst. The object of the training was to make all ranks thoroughly acquainted with their duties in the event of the division attached and the infantry having captured HAINES. The Divl Mounted Troops theory to take up the pursuit. As there was no known line of defence behind the German 2nd line, it which ran in front of LA BASSEE, through HAINES along the ridge to the W of HULLOCH. The Divl Mounted Troops were not expected to get ahead of the infantry until they had reached DOUVRIN as they would have to move up via VERMELLES — AUCHY LES-LABASSEE — HAINES to DOUVRIN. From the latter point the squadron was to advance on BILLY BERCLAU across country, and enter this village from the fields to the South. The Cyclist Coy & machine gun section were to move up and occupy BILLY BERCLAU, and the squadron was to move on to and occupy BEDOLU and the same way and to the	O.P. etc. M. & S.

Army Form C. 2118.

WAR DIARY
or
INTELLIGENCE SUMMARY.
(Erase heading not required.)

Instructions regarding War Diaries and Intelligence Summaries are contained in F.S. Regs., Part II. and the Staff Manual respectively. Title pages will be prepared in manuscript.

Place	Date	Hour	Summary of Events and Information	Remarks and references to Appendices
BETHUNE	24/9		followed up by the Cyclists and Machine Guns. From this point the force was to divide, one party to seize and occupy the bridge at B19b2.1 (BETHUNE continued) across the canal, and the other to the foot bridge at C13a and the bridge at C13c9.7. These points were to be our objective for the first day of the attack. We were to hold them against any troops trying to come from LILLE, as this was known to be one direction. It was hoped that the demonstration made in front of ARMENTIERES the day before would draw the enemy's reserves across the infantry which came up day by day were to relieve the 2nd Mounted Troops. 2/Lt F.J. RITCHIE & Transferred to 173rd Tunnelling Cos, R.E.	P.D.44
	25/9	2.30 A.M.	Roused at 2.30 A.M. The by. marched 2nd Mounted Troops ready (Ref E18d.4.0) to move. went their front by the Squadron of Glasgow Yeomanry. We expected to move	W.D.S.S. W.D.S.S.
		7 A.M.	forward at 6.30 a.m. and join up with the M.M.G.S. on the way. At 7 am a message arrived saying that the guns who were working satisfactorily, and that the 26th Bdes on the right of the Division had taken HOHENZOLLERN redoubt, but we should not	
		8 A.M.	be wanted for another hour. At 8 A.M a message came from Major TRAGNELL at D.H.Q. ordering us forward to SAILLY LABOURSE to where with the Glasgow Yeomanry at 9.15am	
		9.15 A.M.	having on immediately to VERMELLES. On arrival we joined up with the M.M.G.S. Soon after we	

Army Form C. 2118.

WAR DIARY
or
INTELLIGENCE SUMMARY.
(Erase heading not required.)

Instructions regarding War Diaries and Intelligence Summaries are contained in F. S. Regs., Part II. and the Staff Manual respectively. Title pages will be prepared in manuscript.

Place	Date	Hour	Summary of Events and Information	Remarks and references to Appendices
BETHUNE	25th	2:30 PM	reached VERMELLES being five or six hundred prisoners went past. At 2.30 P.M. we received orders to move back to SAILLY-LABOURSE. Whilst we were met by Lt C.A. MACKINTOSH-WALKER who had been anxiety at D.H.Q. to bring word all the time he received an order for us to proceed to HAISNES but it was cancelled immediately.	
	26th	6·30 PM	We arrived at SAILLY-LABOURSE till 8·30 P.M. when we received orders to go out & support	
		1:15 AM	that the 25th Bde. We reached the firing line at 1·15 A.M. We remained in the front line	
		2:30 AM	till 2·30 P.M. when we now return to say the 2nd Bde. who had suffered heavy casualties	
			back to BETHUNE. At 6 P.M. on this date a wounded man crawled up to the Fmd. Amb. by L/2 Platoon. It was reported Capt Campbell O.C. C2 who with the Platoon	
			fought out in the fight to find carried him in successfully although they suffered	
		10 PM	on without any success. We reached BETHUNE at 10 P.M. where we bivouacked on the	
			billets	
	27th	7:30 AM	Orders were received for Coy to report to G.O.C. 26th Inf. Bde. at their H.Qrs. at	
			RAILWAY WELL	
		8:30 AM	2 Lt. S.E. TIDY joined the Coy from HOUNSLOW.	
		9 AM	Coy moved off.	

Page 5

WAR DIARY
or
INTELLIGENCE SUMMARY.
(Erase heading not required.)

Army Form

Instructions regarding War Diaries and Intelligence Summaries are contained in F. S. Regs., Part II. and the Staff Manual respectively. Title pages will be prepared in manuscript.

Place	Date	Hour	Summary of Events and Information	Remarks and references to Appendices
BETHUNE	Sept 27th	11 A.M.	Arrived at VERMELLES, and left the Cyclecader a guard and marched to 21st Inf Bde. M.V.Y.	
		Noon.	After having reported to G.O.C. 21st Inf Bde. And were moved into RAILWAY RESERVE trenches	
		1.30 P.M.	Coy ordered 21st Inf Bde Support trenches in front of HOHENZOLLERN REDOUBT.	
		3.5	C Coy ordered to move up with 8th B.W. was ordered to move up soon to relieve first of the old fire French then on to the few fire trench and finally bayonet the troops in HOHENZOLLERN REDOUBT. This move was carried out with very few casualties. Nos 5 & 6 PLATOONS however did not have the orders passed on to them in time before the charge was ordered and were consequently left behind under Lt. C.A. MACKINTOSH - WALKER.	
			No 1 Platoon under 2nd Lt WEMYSS after reaching the old fire trench got orders to move up to the right but as no word to halt was received along the trench commander went back a short distance and came upon 10th Bn H.L.I. and was ordered by the Major commanding to hold the trench as all the men he could get.	
		5 P.M.	Reinforced to British into the Old fire French but this retirement was followed by	

1577 Wt.W10791/1773 500,000 1/15 D.D.&L. A.D.S.S./Forms/C. 2118.

Army Form C. 2118.

WAR DIARY
or
INTELLIGENCE SUMMARY.
(Erase heading not required.)

Place	Date	Hour	Summary of Events and Information	Remarks and references to Appendices
BETHUNE	2/1		by having the 25o communication trench to the new fire trench, and the men advanced again.	P.M.K.
		7 P.M.	The 25 #1 Pl Bah started to relieve from line trench, and men were ordered to withdraw to the old fire trench and reorganise. About 30 N.C.O's & men of №5 Platoon came back with a number of officers and men of the 25 Pl 41 Pl the men this unit were reorganizing. Eventually all the men aged 26 & bn / Pde were withdrawn to the Old canal fort trench, as O.C. №1 Pl Coln went out and reported to 21st Inf Pde advanced H.Q.rs. and was ordered to bring back at least 2 Platoons.	
			WELL.	
		10 P.M.	2nd Lt BLUNDEN joined this party as it was withdrawing.	
			NARATIVE OF №'s 2 & 4 PLATOONS. afterwards	
			On getting out of 1st 2nd Lt S.E. TIDY was blown up by a shell and was then away suffering from nervous shock. The remainder got out to the trench on the South side of the HOHENZOLLERN redoubt and became mixed with the Infantry. It was now that W/S C.C.K. Campbell was last seen and 2nd Lt C. BLUNDEN.	

Army Form C. 2118.

WAR DIARY
or
INTELLIGENCE SUMMARY.
(Erase heading not required.)

Place	Date	Hour	Summary of Events and Information	Remarks and references to Appendices
BETHUNE	Sept 27th	5 P.M.	was left with a few men under his command. Suddenly some men were seen coming back from the front line, and the men in the support trench, thinking they were withdrawing began to retreat. However the line was rallied & again advanced again. Whitson very much up. 2/Lt BLUNDEN & myself made an attempt at reviving again. Whitson very much up. The support line then went forward & in rear to the 2/Black Watch.	M.H.
		6.30 P.M.	men with him. The support line then went forward through strong machine gun fire. The 9 & Dins refusing to the suffer shit. 2/Lt BLUNDEN with C.O.R returned to support line and then reported to 2nd Camerons to	
		10 P.M.	Bn. H.Q. when he met 2/Lt W.EMYSS.	
		11 P.M.	2/Lts WEMYSS & BLUNDEN were ordered by Major BLACKWELL to return to Billets.	
			NARRATIVE OF Nos 5 & 1 PLATOONS	
		3 P.M.	Nos 5 & 6 PLATOONS remained in the support trench and were nearly all hit	
			Reaving 28 casualties out of 50 O casualties	
		6 P.M.	Lt C.A. MACKINTOSCH-WALKER received orders to retire. Nos 5 & 1 Platoons to	
		8.30 P.M.	Railway reserve trench. where they joined up with the Glasgow Yeomanry. Lt C.A. MACKINTOSCH-WALKER received orders to return to Billets.	
		10.30 P.M.	Arrived in Billets at 10.30 P.M.	

Army Form C. 2118.

Page 8.

Instructions regarding War Diaries and Intelligence Summaries are contained in F. S. Regs., Part II. and the Staff Manual respectively. Title pages will be prepared in manuscript.

WAR DIARY
or
INTELLIGENCE SUMMARY.
(Erase heading not required.)

Place	Date	Hour	Summary of Events and Information	Remarks and references to Appendices
BETHUNE	27th	5 A.M.	Capt Sander & 2 Lt WEMYSS returned to billets. Total casualties during 25th & 26th 1 man Killed. WOUNDED — 2/Lt S.E. TIDY. O.R. MISSING. Capt C.C.K. Campbell.	M.H.
	29th -30th		Coy was reorganising and overhauling kit.	R.H.S.

1577 Wt.W10791/1773 500,000 1/15 D. D. & L. A.D.S.S./Forms/C. 2118.

Amendment of War Diary

of

9th Division Cyclist Company.

27th September 1915.

Volume 4.

C.A. Bachilor Walker Capt.
Commanding 9th Division Cyclist Company

Army Form C. 2118.

WAR DIARY
or
INTELLIGENCE SUMMARY.
(Erase heading not required.)

Place	Date	Hour	Summary of Events and Information	Remarks and references to Appendices
BETHUNE	2/4		KILLED ———— 1 O.R. WOUNDED ———— 2¹ᵗ S.E. Tidy. ———— O.R. 35. MISSING ———— Capt. C.K. Campbell.	App. M.S.S.

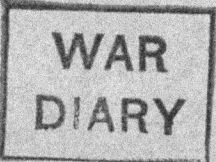

9 th. DIVISION

9 th. CYCLIST COMPANY

OCTOBER 1915

121/7518

9th Division

9th Divl: Cycl: Coy
Vol 5
Oct 15.

7th Divisional Cyclist Company.

War Diary, October, 1915.

Army Form C. 2118.

WAR DIARY
or
INTELLIGENCE SUMMARY.
(Erase heading not required.)

Place	Date	Hour	Summary of Events and Information	Remarks and references to Appendices
BETHUNE	Oct. 1	2.30 P.M.	2/Lts Ferreira & Blundon with 4 O.R moved off to take charge of the unoccupied camps of IX"Div. in IV Corps area. The remainder of the Coy stop in billets and are informed to move.	
	2	9 A.M.	The Company leaves billets, after rendezvousing on the BETHUNE - LOCON Road proceeds via ESTAIRE - VIEUX BERQUIN to MERRIS with the Sect Mobile Column. Progress as far as ESTAIRE was very slow owing to the Company having to overtake a column of 4 batteries of the IX"Div. Artillery and pass one brigade of the infantry and one of artillery of the MEERUT Div. moving S.	
		noon	When halted outside NEUF BERQUIN instructions were received from MAJOR PRAGNELL to send 1 Sgt & 39 O.R. to ABEELE at once. Sgt Park was despatched with 34 O.R. to report to Camp Commandant and 5 O.R. to Signals, both of IV Corps.	
		1.30 P.M	Coy arrived in MERRIS and went into billets.	
	3	10 A.M.	Coy moved off via METEREN to BOESCHEPE arriving at 11.30 A.M.	
		2.30 P.M.	Moved into billets on FRANCO-BELGIAN frontier in the POPERINGHE- BOESCHEPE Road	

WAR DIARY or INTELLIGENCE SUMMARY

Army Form C. 2118.

Place	Date	Hour	Summary of Events and Information	Remarks and references to Appendices
	Oct		Ref. WARVED sheet 27.	
WIPPENHOEK	4		Billets of the Company were transferred into farm at L.34.b.5.3.	
	5		2/Sgt G. Blunden with 1 Sgt & 38 O.R. detached from Company for duty on Frontier post under A.P.M. V Corps	
	6	4.45 AM	1/Sgt NEMYSS with 28 men started off for POPERINGHE to entrain for BETHUNE to ride back the cycles belonging to the casualties of 25th–27th Sept.	
			BETHUNE was reached at 11.30 AM. Of the cycles which were brought to the store house by a the motor lorry on 29th Sept only 26 were now left, several had been removed and those that were left were stripped of their tools, lamps, some bells, & brakes & mudguards before a guard had been put on them. The mens packs on the cycles had also been opened and numerous article extracted. The party arrived back at 7.30 PM.	
			One of the two 2/Cpls at D.H.Q. as clerks returned to the Company for duty as Orderly Room clerk.	
	9/10		1 2/Cpl & 3/private join Company from H. HOUNSLOW. All ranks reported arriving on 28th Sept now accounted for as in the [illegible] or wounded except Lijt. CAMPBELL.	

Army Form C. 2118.

WAR DIARY
or
INTELLIGENCE SUMMARY.

(Erase heading not required.)

3.

Place	Date	Hour	Summary of Events and Information	Remarks and references to Appendices
	Oct			
WIPPENHOEK	12	9 A.M.	Company was inspected by Major-General W.T. Furse C.B., D.S.O. Comdg 9th Div. Between 3rd & 12th the 2 Officers & 40 O.R. sent off on 1st inst. returned to Coy for duty as soon as the camps were occupied. All available Officers & N.C.Os since the 12th inst.	
	17		were out every day studying roads and works in their area. When ever possible men not on fatigue went as well. This work is done in accordance to G.O.C.'s instructions that every man in the Company must be able to guide troops by day and by night to any point of tactical importance in the Corps area. 2/Lts H. R. Alexander, G. Abbott, H.N. Crowe & S.M. Gillett join the Company for duty from HOUNSLOW. Reinforcement of 19 O.R. arrives from Havrelow N.C.Os & men not on fatigue taken out each day	
	22			
	25		from 11 & inst. learning roads & field work. 4 O.R. casualties of 25th = 2) "Left" return to Company	
	27	11 A.M.	1/Lt Ferreira & 26 O.R. formed up on RENINGHELS—HERSKEN [Road	

Army Form C. 2118.

WAR DIARY
or
INTELLIGENCE SUMMARY.
(Erase heading not required.)

Instructions regarding War Diaries and Intelligence Summaries are contained in F. S. Regs., Part II. and the Staff Manual respectively. Title pages will be prepared in manuscript.

Place	Date	Hour	Summary of Events and Information	Remarks and references to Appendices
WIPPENHOCK	27	11 AM	Paraded in G.34.c (Sheet 28 14000) with the other detachments of the II Div and were inspected by H.M. The King.	
	28		3 O.R including 2 casualties of 25th - 27th Sept returned to the Coy.	
	30		14 O.R join company for duty from HOUNSLOW.	
	31		All available NCOs & men have been going round roads & went since 22nd inst. During the month the men of the Company have been principally employed in fatigues. From 8 to 20 men going daily to the Germany for building, thatching & paving their stables. On several days parties of from 12 to 20 were required for coal fatigues at POPERINGHE station & the Div.l Coal Dump. Thawing fatigues were also required during the last week at the billet on account of the mud. The only guard furnished outside the Coy was the usual one at D.H.Q.	

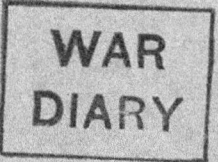

9 th. DIVISION

9 th. CYCLIST COMPANY

NOVEMBER 1915

9th Burann

9th Cyclist Coy.
Vol: 6

121/7795

Nov 15

War Diary

of

9th Division Cyclist Company

From 1st November 1915   To 30th November 1915 (inclusive)

Volume no 6.

(Absolutely) Walker (Capt.)
O/c 9th Div. Cyclist Coy

Army Form C. 2118.

WAR DIARY
or
INTELLIGENCE SUMMARY.

(Erase heading not required.)

Instructions regarding War Diaries and Intelligence Summaries are contained in F. S. Regs., Part II. and the Staff Manual respectively. Title pages will be prepared in manuscript.

Place	Date	Hour	Summary of Events and Information	Remarks and references to Appendices
WIPPENHOEK	Nov 1		2/Lt GILBERT, 1 Sgt & 1 Pte go to Divl. Bomb School for a week's course.	D.R.L.L.
	3		2/Lt McCOURT HILL & ALEXANDER with two N.C.O's each carry out a reconnaissance and report on all roads in the Divl. Area E. of OUDERDOM so far as the line broken for the Storps.	M.D. L.L.
	8		2/Lt CROWE detailed as Officer in charge of Lewis Machine Guns of all the Brigade in the Divl. Area in rear of and including the 2nd Line trenches.	M.R.L.L.
	17		One N.C.O. & 7 men start a bombing course under 2/Lt GILBERT.	D.R.L.L.
	18		The bombing squad which commenced on the 17th inst finished the course.	P.O.S.S.
	21		A 2nd N.C.O. & 7 men start a bombing course under 2/Lt GILBERT.	P.D.L.L.
	22		2/Lt Mc NESS & one O.R. go to Divl. Bomb School for a week's course.	P.D.L.L.
	24		2/Lt GILBERT goes into the trenches for instruction with the 12 R.S.	P.D.L.L.
	25		2/Lt GILBERT returns from the trenches.	P.R.L.L.
	26		The 2nd Bombing squad finished the course.	P.R.L.L.
	27		A 3rd Bombing squad under 2/Lt GILBERT commenced a course.	P.D.L.L.
	30		2/Lt WEMYSS & one O.R. returns from Divl. Bomb School.	P.D.L.L.
			The 3rd Bombing squad under 2/Lt GILBERT finished the course.	P.D.L.L.
			During Nov 2/Lt BLUNDEN & 79 O.R. were employed at Siraha Lines. Memoranda of daily detail at Siraha & at Divl. Y.M.L.L. Dug outs.	Y.M.L.L.

1577 Wt. W1079/1773 500,000 1/15 D. D. & L. A.D.S.S./Forms/C. 2118.

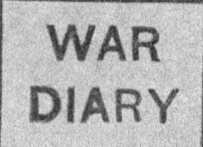

9 th. DIVISION

9 th. CYCLIST COMPANY

DECEMBER 1915

9th Cyclist. Corps
Vol. 1

D/
7928

War Diary
of
9th Division Cyclist Company

From 1st December 1915 — to 31st December 1915 (inclusive.)

Volume. 7.

(Aberchbath) Walker
Capt
Commanding 9th Division Cyclist Company.

Army Form C. 2118.

WAR DIARY
or
INTELLIGENCE SUMMARY.
(Erase heading not required.)

Instructions regarding War Diaries and Intelligence Summaries are contained in F.S. Regs., Part II. and the Staff Manual respectively. Title pages will be prepared in manuscript.

Page I

Place	Date	Hour	Summary of Events and Information	Remarks and references to Appendices
MAPLEWOOD	Dec 1		NCOs 7pm. A 4th Bombing Squad under 2nd Lt GILBERT start a course.	
	2		2nd Lt D. McCOWAN HILL & One NCO go to Divl Bomb School for a week's course.	
	4		2 Lt WEMYSS goes to Divl Officers Class for a weeks course.	
	5		4th Bombing Squad finish the course.	
	6		A 5th Bombing Squad of One NCO & 27 men start a course under 2nd Lt GILBERT.	
	11		2nd Lt D. McCOWAN HILL & One NCO return from Divl Bomb School.	
	11		2 Lt D. McCOWAN HILL & One NCO finished its course.	
	12		The 5th Bombing Squad finished its course. 2nd Lt O.L. WEMYSS returns from Divl Officers Class.	
	15		The Coy was ordered to supply guides for guiding the Batts Inf Bde from the stations where they detrain to go into rest billets. Coy Coys commencing on 17th inst. The following parties were detailed:	
			2nd/Lt FERREIRA, Sgt WALKER, 8 NCOs and 20 men for 28th Bde & 9 Seaforths	
			2nd Lt WEMYSS, Sgt SMITH, 5 NCOs and 16 men for 5 Inf Bde.	
			2nd Lt McCOWAN HILL, Sgt TORNER 5 NCOs and 16 men for 27 Inf Bde	
	16	7AM	The guides moved off to their respective Bde billeting areas to meet troops.	
		7.30AM	The remainder of the Coy moved to meet KIBE & MERRIS who were detained from 9.0 to... G.C.	

Page 2

Army Form C. 2118.

WAR DIARY
or
INTELLIGENCE SUMMARY

(Erase heading not required.)

Place	Date	Hour	Summary of Events and Information	Remarks and references to Appendices
MEERIS	Dec 16th		The Party of guides arrived at MEERIS during the afternoon. On arriving at 23rd Inf Bde HQ 2nd Lt P.D.F.FERREIRA found that the Billets had been allotted with the exception of 6 K.O.S.B. The 9th S.R. moved from W.16.A.4.8 SHEET 27 to X.13.a.9.1 SHEET 27.	9 K.T.H.
			10th H.L.I. " W.29.A.6.8 " " W.28.3.10 "	
			11th H.L.I. " W.22.b-3.10 " " W.16.A.4.P "	
			9th SEAFORTHS " X.13.a.9.1 " " W.29.a.9 "	
	17th		An order came in from 23rd Inf Bde that the billets should be allotted as follows.	R.S.M.
			9th S.R. to W.29.a.6.8 Sheet 27	
			10th H.L.I. to X.13.a.9.1	
			11th H.L.I. to W.29.a.6.8	
			9th SEAFORTHS to take up billets at BAILLEUL.	
		2.30 PM	9 Seaforth 9th S.R. and 6 R.S.F. Transport were out at FLETRE and guided to their respective transport lines.	
		3 PM	8th BLACK WATCH " " " METEREN " " transport lines.	
		10.15 PM	8th BLACK WATCH arrived at STEENWERCK Station and were guided to their billets by Coy.	
		10.30 PM	6th R.S.F. arrived at BAILLEUL STATION	

Army Form C. 2118.

Page 3

Instructions regarding War Diaries and Intelligence Summaries are contained in F. S. Regs., Part II. and the Staff Manual respectively. Title pages will be prepared in manuscript.

WAR DIARY
or
INTELLIGENCE SUMMARY.
(Erase heading not required.)

Place	Date	Hour	Summary of Events and Information	Remarks and references to Appendices
MERRIS	DEC			
	17th	11.15 PM	9th S.R. arrived at CAESTRE station and were guided by guides to their billets.	
	18th	3.30 PM	10th H.L.I. and 11th R.S. Transport arrived at No. regulating transport	
		4. P.M.	5th CAMERONS " " " " " transport lines	
	19th	3.50	11th R.S. detrained at BAILLEUL station and were guided to their billets by G.S.	
		4 AM	5th CAMERONS detrained at STEENWERK station and were guided to their billets by G.S.	
		4.10 AM	10th H.L.I. " " " " " " " "	
		4.30 PM	11th H.L.I. and 12th R.S. transport arrived at FLETRE and were guided to transpulation transport lines	
		5.10 PM	9th GORDONS " " " METEREN " " " " transport lines	
	20th	3.50	12 R.S. detrained at BAILLEUL station and were guided to their billets by G.S.	
		4 AM	8th GORDONS " " STEENWERK " " " "	
		4.40 AM	(1st H.L.I. too Ag.) " STRAZEELE " " " "	
		4 P.M.	6th KOSB. transport arrived at FLETRE and were guided to their transport lines.	
		4.10 PM	7th SEAFORTHS " " METEREN " " " "	
	21st	1 AM	10th Arg & S. Hrs arrived at their transport lines	
		3.50 AM	10th Arg & S. Hrs, 5 H.L.I. detrained at BAILLEUL and were guided to their billets by G.S.	
		4 AM	7th SEAFORTHS " " STEENWERK " " " "	

Army Form C. 2118.

WAR DIARY
or
INTELLIGENCE SUMMARY.
(Erase heading not required.)

Page 2

Instructions regarding War Diaries and Intelligence Summaries are contained in F.S. Regs., Part II. and the Staff Manual respectively. Title pages will be prepared in manuscript.

Place	Date	Hour	Summary of Events and Information	Remarks and references to Appendices
MERRIS	Dec 21st	4.10AM	# KOSB's and A&11th arriving at STRAZEELE station and were guided to their billets by hill by	M.V.V.
	23rd 24th 26th		All the Battalions and transport were guided to their billets successfully. The men who were not acting as guides overhauled cycles.	
	27th		A draft of 1 Offr & 2 Rifles & 78 arrived from the Base. NCO's acted as guides to various carrying parties carrying bricks from the brickfield at HAZEBROUCK to various dumps in the Divl Area. 2nd Lt WEMYSS & Sgt SMITH go to Divl Bomb School as instructors. 2nd Lt D. McC.HILL & 2nd Lt S.M.GILBERT start a squad of 8 men each on a bomb course.	P.D.V.V. P.D.V.V.
	29th 30th		2nd Lt BLUNDEN 25 O.R. Commence carrying all the works in the # 2 Corps Area. 2nd Lt BLUNDEN & 25 O.R. continued works in 2 Corps Area. Squad under 2nd Lt D. McC.HILL & S.M.GILBERT finished the course.	O.D.V.V. M.V.V.
	31st		L/Cpl POWER acts as guide to lorries taking bricks from HAZEBROUCK to 27th Divl Area. L/Cpl PURSER acts as guide to lorries taking bricks from HAZEBROUCK to 28th Divl Area.	M.V.V.

Gd Div. Cyclists
Yr. 6
Van

War Diary
of
9th Division Cyclist Company.
From 1st January 1916 to 31st January 1916.

Volume 8.

G Blunden 2/Lt for Capt
Commanding 9th Division Cyclist Company.

Army Form C. 2118.

WAR DIARY
or
INTELLIGENCE SUMMARY.

(Erase heading not required.)

Instructions regarding War Diaries and Intelligence Summaries are contained in F. S. Regs., Part II. and the Staff Manual respectively. Title pages will be prepared in manuscript.

Page I

Place	Date	Hour	Summary of Events and Information	Remarks and references to Appendices
MERRIS	Sept 1st		1/Cpl POWER acts as guide to lorries carrying bricks from HAZEBROUCK Brickfield to units in the 9th Div.	P.D.Y.Y.
	3rd		2nd Lt D. McCOWAN HILL & one N.C.O. goes to BAILLEUL to attend a LEWIS machine gun course. 2/Lt. H.R. ALEXANDER & two N.C.O.'s commence a week's tactical course at the Brit. Grenade school.	P.D.Y.Y.
	4th to 8th		2nd/Lt. BLUNDEN & 25 O.R. continue to learn the works in the 2nd Corps Area. 2nd/Lt. S.M. GILBERT & 2 N.C.O.'s commence instructing 16 O.R. in bombing. 2nd/Lt BLUNDEN & 25 O.R. continue to learn the works in the 2nd Corps Area. One/Cpl acts as guide to lorries carrying bricks from HAZEBROUCK Brickfield to units in the 9th Div.	P.D.Y.Y. P.D.Y.Y.
	7th 10th		2nd/Lt R.D. FERREIRA & 1 Asst. go to BAILLEUL for a four day course in the LEWIS automatic rifle. 2nd/Lt D. McCOWAN HILL, G. BLUNDEN & S.M. GILBERT make a road reconnaissance from BAILLEUL towards the northern sector of the Corps line to find out which roads were available for bringing up guns.	P.D.Y.Y. P.D.Y.Y.
	11th		2/Lt CROWE goes to Brit. Bomb School for a week's course. 2nd/Lt D. McCowan Hill & 1 Cpl Ast start instructing 24 O.R. in a four day grenade course.	P.D.Y.Y.

WAR DIARY
INTELLIGENCE SUMMARY

Army Form C. 2118.

Page 2

Place	Date	Hour	Summary of Events and Information	Remarks and references to Appendices
MERRIS	15/1/16		Extract from message to O.C. from 9th Divn. "I am directed to inform you that the guard found by your unit to-day was particularly smart and well turned out, and would have done credit to a Guards Bttn."	P.B.4.4.
	17th		CP 3149 Pte LIDDELL awarded the DCM for bravery on 26th Sept 1915. The boy was inspected by Gen Sir H. PLUMER commanding 2nd Army on a route march	Off. 4.4. P.B.4.4.
	20th		2nd Lt P.D.F. FERREIRA takes over the road posts from the 25th Divn. 4 men 9000 observers under an Officer of the Glasgow Yeomanry.	
	21st		2nd Lt D. McCavan Hill appointed temporary instructor at Divisional Bomb School vice 2nd Lt C.L. Wemyss to Hospital	L3.
	24th		Boy left rear billets at Merris & moved to took over billets of 25th Divn. Cycle Boy at Trois Arbes (Map 36 X. B.13. Cent.)	L3.
Trois Arbes	31st		2nd Lt H.N. Crowe given command of the 9th Divn Salvage boy to complete establishment. Three other ranks sent to Salvage boy to complete establishment. Boy employed in carrying on its training, particular attention being paid to bombing, smoke helmet drill & musketry.	L3.

Confidential.

9th Cyclists
Vol: 9

War Diary
of
9th Division Cyclist Company

Volume 9.

From 1st February 1916. to 29th February 1916.

J M Conzurikel
2nd Lieut for Capt.
Commanding 9th Division Cyclist Company.

Army Form C. 2118.

WAR DIARY
INTELLIGENCE SUMMARY.
(Erase heading not required.)

Instructions regarding War Diaries and Intelligence Summaries are contained in F. S. Regs., Part II. and the Staff Manual respectively. Title pages will be prepared in manuscript.

Place	Date	Hour	Summary of Events and Information	Remarks and references to Appendices
TROU ARBRES STEENWERCK.	Feby 1916 1.		1 N.C.O. and 20 men report to Officer i/c 9th R.B. from ARMENTIERES at 7.45 a.m. then return at 10.45 p.m. by 1 N.C.O. and 20 men.	Sheet.
	2.		1 N.C.O. and 20 men report to Officer i/c 9th R.B. from ARMENTIERES at 9.45 a.m.	
			10 men occupied in constructing new stabling.	
			The Coy hands parties report to their several destinations: -	
	3.		Coy hands ordered cycle route march.	Sheet.
	4.		Coy training. Roadmaking Musketry drill.	Sheet.
	5.		Coy training.	Sheet.
	6.		Church parade.	Sheet.
	7.		Coy parade. Route March.	Sheet.
	8.		Coy training. Lewis & Vickers Machine Gun Rifle & Bomb & bayonet.	Sheet.
	9.		Coy training.	Sheet.
	10.	6 p.m.	2nd Lieut. D. Blunden, 2nd Lieut. Gilbert and 53 O.R. proceeded to take up part of the line relative to 2nd Canadian Mounted Troops at C.14 a central Sheet 36. 1/20000 (Nth of south sector. App. I.)	Sheet.

1577 Wt.W10791/1773 500,000 1/15 D. D. & L. A.D.S.S./Forms/C. 2118.

Army Form C. 2118.

WAR DIARY
or
INTELLIGENCE SUMMARY.
(Erase heading not required.)

Instructions regarding War Diaries and Intelligence Summaries are contained in F.S. Regs., Part II and the Staff Manual respectively. Title pages will be prepared in manuscript.

Place	Date	Hour	Summary of Events and Information	Remarks and references to Appendices
TROIS ARBRES STEENWERCK	1916 Sept 11		Routine. Cycle [illegible] cleaned, oiled and tipped in Bleuet.	Sund
	12		Routine. Casualty: one killed, one wounded at half.	Sund
	13		Shoot parades at 6 p.m. 1 Sergt & 30 O.R. relieves garrison of FORT ROMPU and RESERVE FARM the garrison of these places relieving garrison of Trois Arbres. The latter returned to Bleuet at 9 p.m.	Sund
	14		Routine. Work on the trenches. Special attention was given to strengthening parapet and wiring. The parapets are being [illegible] from the [illegible]. Steelhits are also being [illegible] Smith shields on [illegible] – these offer too large a [illegible] when [illegible] and endanger [illegible] being [illegible] and endanger[?].	Sund
	15		Routine	
	16		2 Officers & 23 O.R. joined, 1 Officer & 11 O.R. to 2 Sqn, Royal Glasgow Yeomanry joined, 2 Officers & 21 O.R. and 1 Officer & 11 O.R. Glasgow Yeomanry. The [illegible] of [illegible] party were taken on by return to HQ towards hills.	Sund
	17		Routine. Reinforcement 1 O.R. from Base.	
	18		Routine.	
	19		1 Sergt & 30 O.R. carried out the usual trench Relief. Casualty: one wounded.	Sund

Army Form C. 2118.

WAR DIARY
INTELLIGENCE SUMMARY.
(Erase heading not required.)

Instructions regarding War Diaries and Intelligence Summaries are contained in F. S. Regs., Part II and the Staff Manual respectively. Title pages will be prepared in manuscript.

Place	Date	Hour	Summary of Events and Information	Remarks and references to Appendices
TRIP ARABES STEENWERCK	1916 Feb 20		Rations and Chalk parties	Dull
	21		Rations	Dull
	22		2 Officers & 23 O.R. party detailed from Company carried out Trench Relief. The remainder of the Company furnished parties to assist Spires - Clayporo movement	Dull
	23		Rations	Nil
	24		Rations. Casualty. Drowning	Dull
	25		1 Sergt & 30 O.R. carried out Trench Relief	Dull
	26		Rations. One Car Headlight. One in Sailor. Casualty. One died of wounds	Dull
	27		Reinforcements from Base. 7 O.R.	Dull
	28		2 Officers and 23 O.R. provided by which forming company carried out Trench Relief. Remainder of the Trench party took rations under Lt Evens	Dull
	29		Rations	Dull
	1-29		Lt Wayne attacked from M.E.F.	Died
	1-29		Lt Evans in command Rear Echelon in Divisional area	Still
	1-29		Lt Crow in command of Selling Coy (Divisional)	Med.

Army Form C. 2118.

WAR DIARY
INTELLIGENCE SUMMARY.
(Erase heading not required.)

Instructions regarding War Diaries and Intelligence Summaries are contained in F. S. Regs., Part II. and the Staff Manual respectively. Title pages will be prepared in manuscript.

Place	Date	Hour	Summary of Events and Information	Remarks and references to Appendices
TROIS ARBRES STEENWERCK	1916 Feb 3-29		Capt. E.A. Mackintosh walker attached Coen (Suffolk)	
			2nd D.W.Cameron Hrs returned from 3rd Grenade School as instructor and	
			took command of the Company.	
	1-29		Fatigues & 1 NCO and 7 men on fatigue duty (unloaded coal at Div. Dumps)	Pers
	1-29		1 Corpl & 3 O.R. at Grenade Division HQr	Pers
	1-29		1 Sergt & 9 O.R. on command. (Various attachments)	Pers
	1-29		Hard Stf Sparks 2 O.R.	Pers
	1-29		Trench Garrison 1 Corpl & 4 O.R.	Pers

Appendix 1.

DIVISIONAL MOUNTED TROOPS ORDER

by

Major Macfarlane, O/C Divn. Mounted Troops.

1. The Divisional Mounted Troops will take over 10 Bays of No. 102 Trench from B. Coy. 10th H.L.I. with 60 Men on the night of 10th/11th Feby.

2. O.C. Lieut. Jackson.

3. Details of Relief

    (A) Sergt. Ferguson (Acting Quartermaster) will meet Lieut Jackson at GASOMETER CORNER at 2 p.m. and will proceed in advance and take over stores etc.

    (B) The Party for the Trenches will rendezvous at TROIS ARBRES ROAD JUNCTION at 3 p.m. O.C. Lieut. Blunden.

    They will be at GASOMETER CORNER immediately after dusk, where they will be met by 3 Guides.

    One guide for Party (30 Men) for Trenches.
    One Guide for Party (15 Men) For Fort Paul.
    One Guide for Party (15 Men) for Reserve Farm.

4. R.Q.M.S. Swan will be at GUNNER'S FARM with Ration Limbers, Men's Blankets and Officers' Mess Cart, at 6-30 p.m. and will be met by Ration Party.

5. All indents for R.E. Stores etc, will be sent by Ration Party to the Qr.Mr. at rationing time and brought to H.Q. Divn. Mtd.Troops that night.

6. Indents for Ammunition will be Wired direct to 228th Brigade H.Q. by O.C. Party.

(Sgd.) Walter Macfarlane.
Major.

Divn. Mtd. Troops.
9/2/16.

9 Div Cyclists Vol 10

War Diary
of
9th Division Cyclist Company

Volume 10.

From 1st March 1916.   To 31st March 1916.

Chacksfield Wall Capt
Commanding 9th Division Cyclist Company.

Army Form C. 2118.

WAR DIARY
or
INTELLIGENCE SUMMARY.
(Erase heading not required.)

Instructions regarding War Diaries and Intelligence Summaries are contained in F. S. Regs., Part II. and the Staff Manual respectively. Title pages will be prepared in manuscript.

Place	Date	Hour	Summary of Events and Information	Remarks and references to Appendices
TROIS ARBRES	1/3/16		1 O.R. killed, 1 O.R. wounded	P.D.Y.Y.
STEENWERCK	2/3/16		1 O.R. from hospital in Scotland.	P.D.Y.Y.
	3/3/16		1 O.R. from base.	P.D.Y.Y.
	5/3/16		2/Lt. D.F. FERREIRA, H.R. ALEXANDER and 23 O.R. from the trenches.	P.D.Y.Y.
			2/Lt. G. BLUNDEN, S.M. GILBERT, aged 22 O.R. to the trenches	
	7/3/16		2 O.R. Killed in Action. 1 O.R. [struck through] wounded	P.D.Y.Y.
	8/3/16		3 1 O.R. to the trenches, 28 O.R. from the trenches. 1 O.R. accidentally wounded	P.D.Y.Y.
	10/3/16		3 O.R. wounded. 1 O.R. from base.	P.D.Y.Y.
	11/3/16		2/Lt. D. McCOWAN HILL, H.R. ALEXANDER and 20 O.R. to the trenches.	P.D.Y.Y.
			1/Lt. G. BLUNDEN, S.M. GILBERT and 17 O.R. from the trenches.	
	13/3/16		1 O.R. Wounded.	P.D.Y.Y.
			1 O.R. Wounded.	P.D.Y.Y.
	14/3/16		29 O.R. to the trenches. 28 O.R. from the trenches	P.D.Y.Y.
	15/3/16		1 O.R. Died of Wounds. 1 O.R. Wounded.	P.D.Y.Y.
	16/3/16		1 O.R. Killed in Action.	P.D.Y.Y.
	17/3/16		2/Lt. P.D. F. FERREIRA & G. BLUNDEN and 20 O.R. to the trenches	P.D.Y.Y.

Army Form C. 2118.

WAR DIARY
or
INTELLIGENCE SUMMARY.
(Erase heading not required.)

Place	Date	Hour	Summary of Events and Information	Remarks and references to Appendices
TROIS ARBRES	19/3/16	2PM	D. McCOWAN HILL, H.R.ALEXANDER and 19 O.R. from the trenches.	R.O.S.S.
STEENWERCK.	20/3/16		31 O.R. to the trenches. 27 O.R. from the trenches.	R.O.S.S.
			1 O.R. Killed in Action. 1 O.R. Died of Wounds. 1 O.R. Wounded.	
	23/3/16	2PM	D. McCOWAN HILL, S.M. GILBERT and 20 O.R. to the trenches.	R.O.S.S.
		2PM	P.D.F. FERREIRA, G. BLUNDEN and 20 O.R. from the trenches.	
	26/3/16		31 O.R. to the trenches. 31 O.R. from the trenches.	R.O.S.S.
	27/3/16	2PM	P.D.F. FERREIRA & H.R. ALEXANDER to the trenches.	R.O.S.S.
		5PM	D. McCOWAN HILL & S.M. GILBERT from the trenches.	
	29/3/16		3 O.R. Wounded	R.O.S.S.
			1 O.R. Reinforcement from the Base	
	30/3/16		1 O.R. Reinforcement from the Base	R.O.S.S.
		9.15PM	The Coy is relieved from the trenches by the 9th Scottish Rifles.	

9 Div
Cyclists
Vol II

War Diary

of

9th Division Cyclist Company

From 1st April 1916 to 30th April 1916.

Volume II.

(Checked) T. L. Belcher Capt
Commanding 9th Division Cyclist Company.

Army Form C. 2118.

WAR DIARY
or
INTELLIGENCE SUMMARY.
(Erase heading not required.)

Instructions regarding War Diaries and Intelligence Summaries are contained in F. S. Regs., Part II. and the Staff Manual respectively. Title pages will be prepared in manuscript.

Place	Date	Hour	Summary of Events and Information	Remarks and references to Appendices
TROIS ARBRES	1st to 10th		Overhauling cycles and route marching.	A.S.Y.
STEENWERK.				
EBBLINGHEM	11th		The Coy moves to EBBLINGHEM and is inspected by G.O.C. Div on leaving STEENWERK	O.A.S.Y.
EBBLINGHEM	12th	9 A.M.	Coy move to HARLETTES from EBBLINGHEM to carry out a course of training with the Glasgow Yeomanry under the supervision of G.O.C. 2nd Cav Div, who laid down in attacks by Cabers.	O.A.S.Y.
HARLETTES			The main idea of the training was the meaning of kind of Gelant that of horsemen for a patrol. The horsemen doing work which was unsuitable for Gelant such as patrolling woods & across country, work where Gelant would have to dismount. The section of Gelant doing the road work to cover the horses.	
HARLETTES to EBBLINGHEM	27th	9 A.M. – 12 P.M.	Coy move from HARLETTES to EBBLINGHEM.	O.A.S.Y.
EBBLINGHEM to TROIS ARBRES STEENWERK	30th	9 A.M. 12.15 P.M.	Coy move from EBBLINGHEM to the same billets at TROIS ARBRES, STEENWERK	O.A.S.Y.

APPENDIX A.

DATE OF COURSES.

Division.	March to Area.	Duration of Course.	Return March.
6th) 21st) 50th)	Friday March 24th and Saturday March 25th.	Sunday March 26th to Saturday April 8th.	Sunday April 9th and Monday April 10th.
Guards) 3rd.) 9th.)	Tuesday April 11th and Wednesday April 12th	Thursday April 13th to Wednesday April 26th.	Thursday April 27th and Friday April 28th.
17th) 20th) 1 Can)	Saturday April 29th and Sunday April 30th	Monday May 1st to Sunday May 14th.	Monday May 15th and Tuesday May 16th.
24th) 2 Can) 3 Can)	Monday May 15th and Tuesday May 16th.	Wednesday May 17th to Tuesday May 30th.	Wednesday May 31st and Thursday June 1st.

APPENDIX B.

Sketch of proposed Syllabus of Training for Divisional Squadrons and Cyclists -- Second Army.

March 25th	Saturday.	Squadrons march in.
1st Day.	Sunday.	A.M. Inspection of Horses by G.O.C. Division to ascertain if stable arrangements are satisfactory. P.M. Short lecture by G.O.C. on general duties of a Divisional Squadron and Cyclists.
2nd Day.	Monday.	A.M. March of three Squadrons as a regiment with instructions in march discipline. P.M. Problem on Map. (In control School.) Instructions for a Patrol. Conduct of a Patrol. Collection of information and reports.
3rd Day.	Tuesday.	A.M. Exercise with troops on ground. Conduct of a Patrol. Map reading and writing of reports. P.M. Problem on Map. Mounted Troops and Cyclists with an advanced Guard and orders for them.
4th Day.	Wednesday.	A.M. Exercise with troops - a Squadron and Cyclists acting as Mounted Troops with an Advance Guard. P.M. Problem on Map. Protection by day and night and for same.
5th Day.	Thursday.	A.M. Exercise with troops. Squadrons and Cyclists assisting Infantry in protection by day and night. P.M. Problem on Map. Rear Guard Mounted Troops and Cyclists
6th Day.	Friday.	A.M. Exercise with troops. Rear Guard Mounted Troops and Cyclists. P.M. Exercise on Map. Duties of Mounted Troops with a flank guard.
7th Day.	Saturday.	A.M. Exercise with troops. Squadron and Cyclists with a flank guard. P.M. Problem on Map. Action against a defeated enemy and seizing and holding ground in front of Infantry.
8th Day.	Sunday.	H O L I D A Y.
9th Day.	MONDAY.	A.M. Exercise with troops. Action of Mounted Troops and Cyclists against defeated enemy and seizing and holding ground in front of Infantry. P.M. Problem on Map. "Observation" of a River line, or line of Country. Preparation for delaying if necessary.
10th Day.	Tuesday.	A.M. Exercise with troops. Above, with troops on ground. P.M. Problem on Map. Dismounted attack on locality and wood fighting and hasty defence of them.
11th Day.	Wednesday.	A.M. Exercise with troops. The above with troops on the ground. P.M. Problem on Map. Intercommunication between parallel columns and liaison duties.
12th Day.	Thursday.	A.M. Exercise with troops. The above on the ground with troops. P.M. Problem on Map. Co-operation with other arms in open battle.
13th Day.	Friday.	A.M. Resumé, and preparation for return march. P.M. Short lecture by G.O.C. on tactics of Machine Gun and Hotchkiss Guns with Mounted Troops.
14th Day.	Saturday.	Squadrons return to Divisional Areas.

9 Div Cycle vol. 12

WAR DIARY
OF
9th DIVISION CYCLIST COMPANY

FROM 1st MAY, 1916. TO 31st MAY, 1916.

Volume 12

A. Winchester Hall Capt.
Commanding 9th Division Cyclist Company

WAR DIARY
or
INTELLIGENCE SUMMARY.
(Erase heading not required.)

Army Form C. 2118.

Place	Date	Hour	Summary of Events and Information	Remarks and references to Appendices
TROIS ARBRES STEENWERCK	May 1st		2/Lt S. McC. HILL assumed the duties of Claims Officer to 9 Div. The Coy carried out with training. Relay posts for carrying verbal messages in morning. In the afternoon individual instruction by platoon commanders in theory of advance Rear Guard Patrols, communication and local protection. So over our maps at about	
	2nd		A scheme one half of Coy v the other in advance. I inspect with umpires. Afternoon Platoon commanders go over moving scheme with their platoons & point them out.	
	3rd		Morning Grenade throwing & Signalling. Afternoon. Map reading, Signalling and go over scheme for no 4.	
	4th		Morning. Since the rains so much the 2nd half rests covered. Afternoon Cleaning and repairing trenches.	
	5th		Morning Combined scheme with Glasgow Yeomanry team acts as Enemy. The working together of the two arms.	
	6th		Afternoon Cleaning & clean & arms. Officers conference in evening. Inspection of Bicycles. Kit details.	
	7th 8th 9th		The Coy continues training. 5.0 men for Div fatigue daily till further notice	

Army Form C. 2118.

WAR DIARY
or
INTELLIGENCE SUMMARY.
(Erase heading not required.)

Place	Date	Hour	Summary of Events and Information	Remarks and references to Appendices
STEENWERCK	Aug 26		The long route cycle corps forming the II Corps Cyclist Battalion total strength 320. The ninetten men from this Coy are transferred to the 9th Scottish Rifles. Lt WEMYSS is appointed adjutant. 2/Lt H.R. ALEXANDER being surplus to establishment proceeds to 3rd IB Base Depot	RP/S RP/S MK
	19th			

175113

9TH DIVISION

50TH BDE R.F.A.

MAY 1915 - ~~DEC 1916~~ 1919 SEP

HEADQUARTERS

~~50th 66 BRIGADE 6666 R.F.A.~~
50th BRIGADE R.F.A.

(9th DIVISION)

MAY — SEPTEMBER

1915

Army Form C. 2118.

WAR DIARY
or
INTELLIGENCE SUMMARY.

(Erase heading not required.)

Instructions regarding War Diaries and Intelligence Summaries are contained in F.S. Regs., Part II and the Staff Manual respectively. Title pages will be prepared in manuscript.

Hour, Date, Place	Summary of Events and Information	Remarks and references to Appendices
	CONFIDENTIAL WAR DIARY of The 50TH Brigade, Royal Field Artillery. From May 9th 1915 to Sept 30th 1915. VOLUME I	D.R.O. Blue D.R.O. Caphets Adj: 50 Bde

Army Form C. 2118.

WAR DIARY
or
INTELLIGENCE SUMMARY.
(Erase heading not required.)

Instructions regarding War Diaries and Intelligence Summaries are contained in F.S. Regs., Part II. and the Staff Manual respectively. Title pages will be prepared in manuscript.

Hour, Date, Place	Summary of Events and Information		Remarks and references to Appendices
3pm. 8th May. 1915. BORDON CAMP.	Orders received for 50th Brigade R.F.A. to proceed by rail to SOUTHAMPTON to embark for active service.		
9th May.	B/50 entrained at BORDON STATION at 8pm and 9pm. The remainder of the Brigade following, 1 hour between trains.		
	Strength of Brigade, Officers 24; o.r. 700; horses 650; mules 73.		
	H.Q.S.	Lt. Colonel C.C. van Straubenzee, R.F.A.	Reg.
		Lt. G. Snelling R.F.A., Adjutant.	Reg from Ranks
		2Lt H.H. Gardiner R.F.A., Orderly Officer.	Reg from S.R.
		Lt. A. Stephen R.A.M.C. M.O.	Temp.
	A/50.	Major J.M.R. Harrison, R.F.A.	Reg. I.E.F., Nov'14 - Jan'15.
		2Lt R.S. Gaisford R.F.A.	Reg.
		2Lt C.V. Snart	Temp.
		2Lt H.A. Russell	Temp.
	B/50.	Major C.A.H. Campbell R.G.A.	Reg.
		Lt D.R.D. Fisher R.F.A.	Reg. 2nd Div B.E.F. Aug - Nov '14.
		2Lt W. Surenden	Temp.
		2Lt G.B. Troll	Temp.

Army Form C. 2118.

WAR DIARY
or
INTELLIGENCE SUMMARY.
(Erase heading not required.)

Instructions regarding War Diaries and Intelligence Summaries are contained in F.S. Regs., Part II and the Staff Manual respectively. Title pages will be prepared in manuscript.

Hour, Date, Place	Summary of Events and Information	Remarks and references to Appendices
May 9th	C/50. — Major V. E. Pringle	Temp. R.O. late S.R.
	2Lt G. C. Mc Ewan	S.R.
	2Lt W. W. Brown	Temp.
	2Lt W. L. F. Browne	Temp.
	D/50. — Major Hon H. E. Thellusson R.F.A.	Reg. 3rd Div B.E.F. Aug'14–Feb'15.
	2Lt A. E. H. Boulton	Temp.
	2Lt E. A. B. Hollam	Temp.
	2Lt J. H. Laidman	Temp.
	B.A.C./50. Captain C. E. Morgan	Temp
	2Lt A. R. Kenworthy	Temp
	2Lt A. M. G. Cooper	Temp
	2Lt W. Roe	Reg. from Rawls
10.5. SOUTHAMPTON.	The Brigade detrained at the Docks from 10pm 9th onwards, and embarked at about 10am 10th as follows :—	
	S.S. ARCHIMEDES: H.Q.S.: D/50 less 70 m.m.: A/50 less 70 m.m.: part B.A.C.	
	S.S. COURTFIELD: B/50 less 70 m.m.: C/50 less 70 m.m.: part B.A.C.	
	S.S. EMPRESS QUEEN: about 280 m.m. 4 officers, no horses &c.	
	Sailed about 6pm. Crossing uneventful. Escort, reputed to be two t.b.ds. Calm night. No casualties.	

DF.

Army Form C. 2118.

WAR DIARY
or
INTELLIGENCE SUMMARY.
(Erase heading not required.)

Instructions regarding War Diaries and Intelligence Summaries are contained in F.S. Regs., Part II. and the Staff Manual respectively. Title pages will be prepared in manuscript.

Hour, Date, Place	Summary of Events and Information	Remarks and references to Appendices
11th HAVRE.	Disembarkation began about 7 a.m. Brigade less B/50 + A.C. marched at 12 noon to No 4 Rest Camp till 9 p.m. when units marched to different points to entrain. B/50 + A.C. marched to entraining points direct. Travelled by ABBEVILLE - BOULOGNE - CALAIS - ST. OMER and detrained at ARQUES and WIZERNES starting with B/50 at about 3 p.m. — Time in train 23 hours.	
12th HELFAUT	Each unit on detraining marched to billets at HELFAUT. B/50 did a second detrainment at ARQUES — arrival to march out 45 minutes.	
13th "	By about 8 a.m. all units of the bde. were settled into billets at HELFAUT, horse lines and gun parks all on the common, men mostly billeted in barns. Casualties on journey Nil. In train in France several minor injuries. One gunner fell out of the train at ÉTAPLES and injured his leg seriously — struck off the strength, One gunner broke a leg on the docks at HAVRE. There were no serious casualties among the horses.	
14th "	Spent in billets at HELFAUT.	
15th "	Orders received to be prepared to move.	
16th "	Marched out of HELFAUT for CASSEL at 12 noon. At 1 p.m. orders received for 1 officer per battery to proceed to NIEPPE at once to report to C.R.A 48th SOUTH MIDLAND DIVISION to take over positions from	

WAR DIARY
or
INTELLIGENCE SUMMARY.
(Erase heading not required.)

Army Form C. 2118.

Hour, Date, Place	Summary of Events and Information	Remarks and references to Appendices

The CANADIAN R.F.A. who were attached to that Division.
The following officers were sent:—

    Major J.M.R. Hanram R.F.A.   A-50
    Lt D.R.D. Fisher R.F.A.   B-50
    Major V.E. Pringle   C-50
    Major the Hon: W.E. Thellusson R.F.A. D.S.O.

They rode to BAILLEUL, turned on to NIEPPE and motored to H.Q. 3. C.R.F.A. (composite) Bde; at PLOEGSTEERT from which they proceeded on foot to batteries as follows:— A-50; 11th Bty.; B-50; 10th Bty; C-50; 7th Bty.; D-50; 8th Bty.; where they arrived about 10 p.m. 16th. Meanwhile the Brigade marched to ST. MARIE CAPELLE where they went into billets at 8 p.m.

17th STEENWERCK Brigade marched at 5 a.m reaching STEENWERCK at about 12 noon; and went into billets here. At 2 p.m. the subaltern bn battery and three telephonists were sent on to take over F.O.O. stations telephone wire, etc. 2/Lt Bansford A-50, 2/Lt Swarder B-50. 2/Lt McEwan C-50, 2/Lt Bantow D.S.O.

18th PLOEGSTEERT Colonel van Straubenzee inspected the positions to be taken over by 50th Bde. At 5 p.m the Bde left

WAR DIARY
or
INTELLIGENCE SUMMARY.
(Erase heading not required.)

Army Form C. 2118.

Hour, Date, Place	Summary of Events and Information	Remarks and references to Appendices
18th PLOEGSTEERT	STEENWERCK and took positions at 10 p.m. from the C.R.F.A. as previously detailed. The B.A.C moved into position at LE VEAU by STEENWERCK. The exchange was carried out without a hitch of any kind. The positions of the Batteries was as follows :—	
	GUNS — F.O.O — WAGON LINE	
	A. 50 C.1.a.4.4 C.3.t.7.0 B.10.b.4.2	
	B. 50 C.1.a.0.7 ,, B.11.a.4.10	* Ref Sheet 28.S.W.
	C. 50 B.6.d.6.6 U.21.a.7.1* B.10.a.5.0	
	D. 50 B.6.b.2.6 ,, B.5.c.3.2	
	Bde: H.Q. C.1.b.1.2 — C.1.c.9.8	
	Sde: A.C. B.14.c.8.5	
	Reference 1/20,000 map (B series) Sheet 36 N.W.	
19th ,,	Spent in settling in and registration. 1st shot fired at 2 p.m by C.50 on trenches	
20th ,,	First casualty in Brigade: Gr Lewis B.50 Telephonist at F.O.O station, wounded in arm and leg by shrapnel bullets apparently from anti-aircraft guns: evacuated.	
21st & 22nd	Nothing of moment occurred.	
23rd	As our infantry had been unduly wounded by machine guns, orders were received to retaliate. Consequently	DF/

Army Form C. 2118.

WAR DIARY
or
INTELLIGENCE SUMMARY.
(Erase heading not required.)

Instructions regarding War Diaries and Intelligence Summaries are contained in F.S. Regs., Part II. and the Staff Manual respectively. Title pages will be prepared in manuscript.

Hour, Date, Place	Summary of Events and Information	Remarks and references to Appendices
29th	At 3.30 a.m D/50 opened fire on the BIRD CAGE O.21.d.7.4 + C/50 opened fire on the German trenches in their zone just south of this (Sheet 28 S.W.). In all 350 rounds were fired: neither A effective.	
31st	We blew up BIRD CAGE at 10 a.m, D/50 fired 50 rnds + C/50 100 rnds at it immediately after. A/50 gun position shelled, part of billets alongside burnt down, 1 Sergt + 1 Gr wounded.	
June 1st	Little shelling — Rev: B.R. de Pine joined as Chaplain, & D.R.D Fisher B/50 to be temporary captain d/- 28.5.15 in Gazette of that date.	
3rd	First man killed in Brigade — Gr. Jackson – B/50 by H.E. shell in PLOEGSTEERT VILLAGE	
4th	B/50 withdrawn at 9 a.m to relieve D/51. I.21.2.B (28 S.W); 51st Bde withdrawn to rejoin IX Division and relieved by B/50 and 1st S MIDLAND BDE RFA (T) 3 batteries under which B/50 came tactically; their wagon lines remained unchanged — F.O.O? During the day C/50 gun position was shelled, one shell 5.9" How" wounding the B.S.M and 3 N.C.O's who were evacuated.	
7th	Following transfers approved by G.O.C., R.A :— Capt D.R.D Fisher B/50 to be Adjutant.	

WAR DIARY
or
INTELLIGENCE SUMMARY.

(Erase heading not required.)

Army Form C. 2118.

Instructions regarding War Diaries and Intelligence Summaries are contained in F.S. Regs., Part II. and the Staff Manual respectively. Title pages will be prepared in manuscript.

Hour, Date, Place	Summary of Events and Information	Remarks and references to Appendices
	Lt. Lt. Snelling from adjutant to B.A.C. 2nd Lt. A.R. Kenworthy from B.A.C. to B/50. These transfers were carried out this day. Lt. Col. Short – 63rd Bde. R.F.A. 12th Dvn. with his adjutant & 4 B.C.'s came to inspect positions with a view to taking over. These officers met Lt. Col. van Straubenzee and B.C.'s at 50 Bde: at C/50 gun position at 12 noon.	
8th	B/50 was relieved by B/63 at 10 p.m. and went into reserve. billets at LE PETIT MORTIER.	
9th	C/50 was relieved by C/63 at 10 p.m. and joined B/50 at LE PETIT MORTIER. D/63 came into action near A/50's position	
10th	At 7 a.m the Germans blew up a trench nearly opposite to the BIRD CAGE and started shelling PLOEGSTEERT WOOD and VILLAGE. Communication with F.O.O at LE GHEER (U.21.d.7.1 – 2B.5.w) interrupted. C-63 fired 50 rnds at trenches in their zone. Damage done, by mine – NIL, by enemy's rifle fire – 2 infantrymen wounded. At 10 p.m D/50 was relieved by A/63 and marched to LE PETIT MORTIER.	
11th	At noon Bde: H.Q.S handed over control to O.C 63rd Bde. and proceeded to join B.C + D/50 at LE PT. MORTIER.	
12th	Bde: A.C. handed over to 63rd Bde: A.C. and marched	

Army Form C. 2118.

WAR DIARY
or
INTELLIGENCE SUMMARY.
(Erase heading not required.)

Hour, Date, Place	Summary of Events and Information	Remarks and references to Appendices
June 13th LE PT. MORTIER	to LE PT. MORTIER at 9 a.m. At 10 p.m. A/50 was withdrawn to the same place.	
14th	Orders received from G.O.C., R.A. 48th S.M. DIVN. to proceed to rejoin 9th Division as early as possible on 14th via SAILLY sur LYS & LA GORGUE to MERVILLE. Billet here 14th/15th, march at 8 a.m. 15th via CALONNE SUR LYS, ROBECQ, L'ECLEME, LILLERS to billets in 26th Bde. area. At FERFAY; warned by G.S.O. 9th Division that we might be held up by ammunition lorries passing through ROBECQ along ST VENANT-BETHUNE road. Marched at 12.5 a/m, reaching billets on outskirts of MERVILLE at 3.30 a/m. At 10 a/m orders received to march to not to FERFAY but to ECQUEDECQUES by same route. Day spent in billets.	
15th	Marched at 8.10 a/m, halting 11 a/m - noon head of column at L'ECLEME; no lorries encountered. Met in LILLERS at 1 p/m by 2/Lt. Gardiner (who had gone on with the billeting party) with orders from G.O.C., R.A. to proceed to BOURECQ, as there was not a sufficient water supply in ECQUEDECQUES.	

(73989) W4141—463. 400,000. 9/14. H.&J.,Ltd. Forms/C. 2118/10.

Army Form C. 2118.

WAR DIARY
or
INTELLIGENCE SUMMARY.
(Erase heading not required.)

Hour, Date, Place	Summary of Events and Information	Remarks and references to Appendices
15th	Reached exceedingly good billets in BOURECQ at 11.45 pm. At 5 pm orders received from 9th Div DHQ that the Divn was to be ready to move at 1 hour's notice, starting from 6 am July 16th. B.C.s warned confidentially of this.	
16th	Orders received at 8 bm to draw from the Div. A.C. at HAM-EN-ARTOIS H.E. shell at the rate of 9 per gun in the battery and 4 per gun in B.A.C at 7 am 17th in exchange for shrapnel made surplus.	
17th	Exchange of shell completed with D.A.C.	
18th	At 9 am orders received from H.Q. 9th Division that the 1 hour's notice had been increased to 3 hours, as from 6 am 18th — B.C.s informed. Lt D Campbell R.A.V.C. joined, i/c us + 26th Inf. Bde.	
BOURECQ 21st	Message received at 2 bm from H.Q.5 9th Division "Orders for Div: to be ready to move at short notice cancelled" 2 Lt Russell to hospital sick. Telephone wire laid to HQS 51st Bde: at LE CORNET BRASSART thence through to R.A.M.Q.s at BUSNES.	
23rd	Three distant explosions heard between 3 + 5 pm. Rumoured later that a French powder factory at MEISNIL about 10 m SW of here had been blown up causing great damage.	

DF.

Army Form C. 2118.

WAR DIARY
or
INTELLIGENCE SUMMARY.
(Erase heading not required.)

Instructions regarding War Diaries and Intelligence Summaries are contained in F.S. Regs., Part II. and the Staff Manual respectively. Title pages will be prepared in manuscript.

Hour, Date, Place	Summary of Events and Information	Remarks and references to Appendices
24th	At 4.20 p.m. orders received from 9th Div. H.Q. that the Divn came under the command of 1st Corps from 6 p.m. 23rd inst: and will be in Corps Reserve (less 26th Inf. Bde. + 9th Seaforths) W. of R. LAWE. The Divn less 50th Bde: R.F.A. ordered to shift billets on 25th and 26th into the ST. HILAIRE – LILLERS – CHOQUES area. 50th Bde: being already on the fringe of this area, left in peace. At 10.15 p.m. orders received from 9th Divn for Bde: to be ready to move at 4 hours notice.	
25th	Our billets now in 27th Bde: Area. Brig. Genl. Bruce – 10th Bn Argyll + Sutherland Highlanders marched into billets in BOURECQ.	
27th	C -- 50 moved to X. good billets at FME DU MALENOY, 2 m N.W. of BOURECQ, in order to make room for infantry.	* 28th 2/Lt J.H. Keidman D.S.O. detached to School of French Montars at ST VENANT for instruction. 2/Lt C.C. Carstairs joined Also from 9th Divl Park R.
29th	Orders received at 6.30 a.m. for C.O., 2 B.C.s + 2 F.O.O.s to meet Bde: Major at GORRE by BETHUNE at 11 a.m. (15 miles) two this would probably be wanted that night in action; cavalcade composed of Colonel, O.O., Majors Harrison (A) + Campbell (B) 2/Lts Snatt (A) + Sounden (B) started at 9 a.m. and returned at 8 p.m. with orders that no Hys were required,	*

WAR DIARY
or
INTELLIGENCE SUMMARY.
(Erase heading not required.)

Army Form C. 2118.

Hour, Date, Place	Summary of Events and Information	Remarks and references to Appendices
RUE D VACHES	29th But that Brigade was to march next day to billets at RUE DES VACHES by CALONNÉ S/LYS in its own time.	
	30 Brigade marched as ordered — "A" starting at Dnoon, "B" at 12.30 p.m, etc. Orders received that A/50 was to go into action in relief of "T" R.H.A. (7th Div.) at 10 p.m 1st July.	
July 1st.	Colonel + Adjutant rode to see C.R.A. at LOCON, starting at 8 a.m. It is decided to move up Bde H.Q.S. to GORRE that day at 9 p.m into billets vacated by 4th Bde: R.H.A. (F+T) (7th Divn) M.Q.S. B + C Btys are to come into action during night 2nd + 3rd in relief of C + D/51 — D/50 + B.A.C to remain at RUE DES VACHES — Move of H.Q.S & A/50 completed without incident — Chaplain + V.O. attached to B.A.C for the time being.	
GORRE 2nd	Move of B + C successfully carried out — B.A.C moved under direct orders from C.R.A. to billets at ÉCLUSE D'ESSARS.	
3rd	Day spent in registration, laying + digging in of telephone wires, making of fresh dug outs and improving old ones, and above all in steaming	

Army Form C. 2118.

WAR DIARY
or
INTELLIGENCE SUMMARY.
(Erase heading not required.)

Hour, Date, Place	Summary of Events and Information	Remarks and references to Appendices
2nd	wh drainage and general sanitation. Lines everywhere very bad, mosquitos fairly so; conditions been improved. Positions of units now as follows:- (Reference - 40.000 BÉTHUNE contoured sheet). Bde H.Q.S. Office, mess rc F.4.c.5.6. Horse lines X.28.a.4.7. A/50: guns F.4.d.4.8. wagon line X.25.d.4.5. F.O.O. A.B.a.4.7 and A.i.d.6.6. B/50: guns X.3o.c.0.8. wagon line X.25.d.2.7. F.O.O. S.25.d.8.7 and A.2.c.8.0. C/50: guns F.5.c.8.4. wagon line X.25.d.2.8. F.O.O. A.2.c.8.0 D/50: B.A.C: in billets at RUE DES VACHES (9 miles) at ÉCLUSE D'ESSARS X.19.c.4.9 General zone covered, German trenches from CHAPELLE	

WAR DIARY
or
INTELLIGENCE SUMMARY.
(Erase heading not required.)

Army Form C. 2118.

Hour, Date, Place	Summary of Events and Information	Remarks and references to Appendices
July 6th	ST. ROCHE to RUE D'OUVERT. R.A.H.Q. at LOCON – X.7. central. D-50 moved into billets at CROIX DE FER F.1.f.8.4. Still in reserve; they laid out a wire to Bde: H.Q. as there was none to the wagon lines. 2/Lt. Massey joined D/50 from D.A.C.	
11th	B-50's gun position shelled from 5:30 to 6:30 pm Objective supposed to be a farm where their L-xm guns were concealed. These guns shifted to night of Hy during the night – no damage done.	
12th	D-50 came into action at X.28.c.2.B. in relief of A/51 who moved to the left of the Dw9. wagon line at CROIX DE FER. F.O.O at 5.20 et 5.1. No outstanding event occurred during July The daily expenditure of ammunition averaged 4 rounds per gun – an index to the quietness of the times.	
22nd	2/Lt. A.G.S. Leggatt joined from Base and attached to A-50	
Aug 1st	The horses allotted to the Div9 was altered and are now off to the N.B.C + D. Bris remained in position but A moved to X.22 a 7.7 in relief of C-51 who went North	

DF.

Army Form C. 2118.

WAR DIARY
or
INTELLIGENCE SUMMARY.
(Erase heading not required.)

Instructions regarding War Diaries and Intelligence
Summaries are contained in F.S. Regs., Part II.
and the Staff Manual respectively. Title pages
will be prepared in manuscript.

Hour, Date, Place	Summary of Events and Information	Remarks and references to Appendices
Aug 2nd LOISNE	Bde. H.Q.s moved from GORRE to a small farm at LOISNE X.22.d.3.3 where 51st Bde Q.s had been prior to their move to LE TOURET - X.16.b. The wagon line and B.A.C. were also moved as ESSARS was now in the 2nd Divn area. The position of the wagon lines was:- Bde: H.Q.S. - X.22.d.3.3 in H.Q.S farm. A-50 X.19.b.8.6 sharing with D/50 B-50 X.20.b.3.5. C-50 X.20.a.4.6 D/50 X.20.a.0.4 sharing with A-50 B.A.C X.14.c.7.3 LES GLATIGNIES. D/53. 4.5" Hows (Major Hon. H. Scarlett) were now added to our tactical group. They had been in action all July at X.14.a.B.6 and remained there. Our general zone though shifted a little northwards remained much the same. Are covered the right battalion (C.1) and most of the next one (C.2) of the right brigade (C) of the 4th Division. Our co-operation arrangements with the infantry went as follows:-	

WAR DIARY
or
INTELLIGENCE SUMMARY.

(Erase heading not required.)

Army Form C. 2118.

Hour, Date, Place	Summary of Events and Information	Remarks and references to Appendices
Aug 2nd	1. To C.1 were allotted B, C & D 55 and to C.2 went A & D 50. 2. One officer from each of these sub groups and a telephonist per battery were always at the H.Q.S of the battalion returning they allotted subsection; they lived in a dug out provided by the Infantry and changed daily at 7.30 p.m. 3. Each of these dug-outs was connected by telephone with each battery in its own sub-group and to B.H.Q direct. The dug-outs were not connected direct to each other, but could talk on the Infy trench telephone. 4. In each dug out was kept a tracing of the German lines showing the zone allotted to each battery of our group. It was the duty of the R.A officer at the B.H.Q.S. to communicate to the battery concerned any request by the Infantry for RETALIATION. If the retaliation did not succeed in stopping the enemy's fire, or in any	

WAR DIARY
or
INTELLIGENCE SUMMARY.
(Erase heading not required.)

Army Form C. 2118.

Hour, Date, Place	Summary of Events and Information	Remarks and references to Appendices
2nd	other case where it seemed to him desirable he reported the facts to Bde. H.Q. Retaliation was normally but not always directed on the German fire trench opposite to the portion of our trench which the enemy were shelling. The Infantry also sometimes asked for other fire — e.g. on transport heard on the RUE DU MARAIS at night — and the R.A. officer instructed the battery concerned accordingly. In the event of any emergency his orders were just to warn the battery of his sub-group and decimally to warn H.Q.S. Throughout, he DIRECTED but did not OBSERVE the fire, as from the support trenches where the BN. H.Q.S were only a small portion of the German line was visible. F.O.O.s were employed in the usual manner. 5. Our Bde: H.Q.S was connected direct by telephone to Inf.y Bde H.Q.S (C Section) at LOISNE X.2B.a.5.9. and to 7th Bde. R.G.A. (6" Hows) so that at a pinch we could get a heavy gun turned on quickly, but as a rule this was done through R.A. H.Q.S. We were also connected to the 36th Bde: — 2nd Division on our right and to the 52nd Bde: on our left, and had with them the usual	

WAR DIARY
or
INTELLIGENCE SUMMARY.
(Erase heading not required.)

Hour, Date, Place	Summary of Events and Information	Remarks and references to Appendices

arrangements for mutual support. We had also a line to our R.A.C. which allowed the batteries to communicate fairly easily with their wagon lines roughly 20 miles of Bde: H.Q.S. were not of course including the 3 F.O.O lines on the R.A. wire, which belonged to SIGNALS.

During the last fortnight in July and the first one in August, the energies of the batteries were mainly devoted to the making of rear gun positions for the VILLAGE & LE TOURET LINES.

In all — 8 – 4 gun positions were prepared by the 5 batteries of the group and two observing stations for each selected. In addition to this, considerable work was done in trenching on ditching all works running in front of Bde: H.Q.S.

12th G.O.C., R.A. 7th Division inspected gun positions with a view to taking over; his being 6-gun batteries, some juggling was necessary as not all positions had 6 emplacements.

13th At 5 a.m. orders received that R.A. of 4th Division would be relieved by R.A. of 7th Division during

WAR DIARY or INTELLIGENCE SUMMARY.

Army Form C. 2118.

Hour, Date, Place	Summary of Events and Information	Remarks and references to Appendices

the night 14th – 15th and that we would march by certain roads to billets near L'ÉCLÈME, Y3., R.A. orders gave detail by batteries so no arrangements were left for Bde: H.Q.S. to make. "F" R.H.A. relieved C/50 – "T" R.H.A relieved A_50 – 12th Bty R.F.A – D/50. A/50 was not replaced, and D/53 was handed back to 53rd Bde: and relieved by a Bty of the 27th (Hows) Bde: Bde: H.Q.S were taken over by 14th Bde: R.H.A. and at 9.0 p.m. Colonel Shautenger handed over responsibility for C 1 and C 2 sub sectors to Col: Tudor R.H.A.

Aug 15th
L'ECLÈME All units of the Brigade were settled into their billets by 7 am – B.H.Q.S. could not be accommodated in the 50th Bde: Area and were given a small farm at V.11.d.9.9.

23rd Lt: Colonel C.C. Van Shautenger R9 a. left the 50th Brigade R.9. A. on appointment to 18th Division (near ARRAS) as G.O.C. R.A. The Command of the Bde: devolved temporarily upon Major Campbell Major Pringle being on 7 day's leave to England &: Colonel E. Harding Newman posted to Bde: – and not yet joined.

WAR DIARY or INTELLIGENCE SUMMARY.

Army Form C. 2118.

Hour, Date, Place	Summary of Events and Information	Remarks and references to Appendices
Aug 23rd	Major Campbell Command'g 9/50th Bde goes out to CUINCHY to reconnoitre battery positions.	
LECLEME — 24th	Battery commanders and adjutant with one subaltern per battery ride to CUINCHY to select Battery positions from the six suggested by G.O.C. R.A. Positions selected as follows:—	
	A-50 at A.13.A.q.B. at present occupied by 54th Bty - 1st Division.	
	B-50 at A.14.c.1.3 in Orchard behind GIRLS SCHOOL — new position.	
	C-50 at A.14.c.2.7 position not used since January — requiring to be rebuilt.	
	A-50 at A.14.c.5.B. new position, guns all in houses, sheds etc.	
	Bde. H.Q. S temporarily at 54th Bty billet A.14.c.1.9 Rel Trench map sheet 36c N.W (1) wagon lines and O.P. not yet Allotted arrangements made to send out working parties of B, C + D 50 at once to get on	

50 b.e R.7u.

Aug 30 | both positions.
A-50 & C-50 march into action at CUINCHY,
starting at 4 h.m.; A-50 to come under 61st bde;
9th Div: for defensive purposes. C-50 under 34th
bde, 2nd Division.

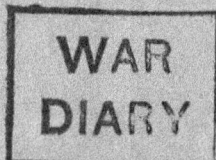

Headquarters,

50th BRIGADE, R.F.A.

(9th Division)

S E P T E M B E R

1 9 1 5

WAR DIARY
INTELLIGENCE SUMMARY
50th Brigade, R.F.A.
September 1915

Place	Date	Hour	Summary of Events and Information	Remarks and references to Appendices
CUINCHY	Sept 1st		50th Bde: H.Q. marched into CUINCHY — Major V.E. Pringle returned from leave and assumes command → B/50 + D/50 come into action.	
	2nd		BAC march to BEUVRY — wagon lines all in BELLENVILLE WOOD. The role of the 50th Bde: at this time was purely registration with a view to wire cutting and enfilading MADAGASCAR TRENCH — FOSSE TRENCH — FOSSE ALLEY — etc. A/50 + C/50 skill rem am. detached. The 50th Bde: was not in communication with any infantry, and as a brigade, had no defensive duties.	
	3rd		Observation stations allotted as follows :—	

INTELLIGENCE SUMMARY.

(Erase heading not required.)

Hour, Date, Place	Summary of Events and Information	Remarks and references to Appendices
COINCHY 3rd	A, 50: FOSSE No 9 de BETHUNE (18). B, 50: Cottage A.21.a.0.0. C-50: CORNER HOUSE A.20.d.7.9. D-50 BRICKSTACKS A.20.d.5.6. to which new wires were laid. Observation also done from advanced trenches. It is decided to move the Bde: H.Q.S for battle purposes to a fortified cellar at A.14.c.9.5. This is too far up, being in front of 3 batteries, but there is no suitable place close in rear, and as it is understood that active operations will soon begin – Bde: H.Q.S must be near the batteries in order to make all telephone wires to be Dutcher. and buried in time. The Brigade zone is from Cross Roads at A.22.6.9.9. inclusive to the toe of the HOHENZOLLERN REDOUBT and all suitable trunks in the area are reqused. from day to day. 4th 1st Contls consider wagon lines are too far forward. They are therefore moved back to 5th Major & Brevet Lt: Colonel E.W.S. Brooke R.F.A joins	

INTELLIGENCE SUMMARY.
(Erase heading not required.)

Instructions regarding War Diaries and Intelligence Summaries are contained in F.S. Regs., Part II and the Staff Manual respectively. Title pages will be prepared in manuscript.

Hour, Date, Place	Summary of Events and Information	Remarks and references to Appendices
6th.	From 6th July 3rd Division and assumes command of the 50th Bde: it is not known why Lt. Col. Harding Newman's posting was cancelled. Following targets registered by aeroplane:— C-50 × rds —— A. 22, b. 9.9 D-50 × rds —— A. 22, d. 9.8 A-50 × rds —— A. 30, b. 8.9 —— A. M, b. 8.7 It was understood that these targets were registered with a view to night firing — D-50 were therefore not given one, as their position was so near the creek that it was thought their flashes would be visible to the enemy.	
7th/21st.	This fortnight was spent in preparation and was in itself uneventful. The following work in particular was carried out. 1. All telephone lines both Bde to Bty and Bty to O.P. were either trenched, ditched or buried. The only air-lines were portions of A-50's lines observation wires to Posn 9 which were so far back as to run little risk of cutting by shell fire; they	

INTELLIGENCE SUMMARY.

(Erase heading not required.)

Instructions regarding War Diaries and Intelligence Summaries are contained in F.S. Regs., Part II and the Staff Manual respectively. Title pages will be prepared in manuscript.

Hour, Date, Place	Summary of Events and Information	Remarks and references to Appendices
	remained intact throughout the operations. 2. Much work was done in strengthening gun positions. All gun pits and dug outs were double roofed with a 9 inch airspace. An unlimited supply of sandbags was procured and nails and sleepers were taken from the BETHUNE – LA BASSEE railway. This latter practice was finally put a stop to by C.R.E. 9th Div'n but not before our fortifications were complete. These double roofs were supposed to keep out a direct hit from a 5.9" Howitzer, — fortunately they were never put to the test. 3. Each battery also prepared one or two cellars close to the guns as funk pits to which to withdraw the battery detachments if the position was heavily shelled. The procedure generally adopted was to leave a look out above the existing floor of the ground floor room and then on a framework of railway rails shoved through holes in the wall to make a solid platform of sleepers crossed by a double layer of sandbags. These cellars were normally used	

INTELLIGENCE SUMMARY.

(Erase heading not required.)

Hour, Date, Place	Summary of Events and Information	Remarks and references to Appendices
	for officers & telephonists — dug out huts they were also required. 4. Each battery built me on two bridges for crossing banks. Chief bridges raised a good deal. Some were made in sections to carry on ammunition wagons. Others were built up solid on the fore carriage of a country cart & toned behind a wagon, to drop wholesale into a trench so :—	
	[sketch of bridge cross-section]	
	The average span was 12 feet — unfortunately no experience was gained with these bridges.	
20th	Orders were received at 8pm that the bombardment would start at 6am on the 22nd.	
	Bde. H.Q.S into cellar previously mentioned where the telephone exchange had already been set up.	
21st	Move Bde. H.Q.S into cellar at at 9.0 a.m. Backs for first day's bombardment are as follows:— A — 50 — — 100 H.E. } MADAGASCAR B — 50 — — 200 H.E. } COTTAGES	

INTELLIGENCE SUMMARY.

(Erase heading not required.)

Hour, Date, Place	Summary of Events and Information	Remarks and references to Appendices
	C/50 --- 100 H.E. MADAGASCAR COTTAGES D/50 --- 500 S were cutting on MAD POINT. Very little retaliation from the enemy. From 6 p.m. to 6 a.m. 22nd — A, C — D/50 fired 12 rounds an hour at MAD POINT — FOSSE TRENCH & HAISNES CROSS ROADS 22nd Tasks for 2nd day's bombardment were as follows:— A — 50 B — 50 100 } MADAGASCAR C — 50 50 } COTTAGES D — 50 500 were cutting on MAD POINT. Night tasks 22nd/23rd as before. Very little artillery fire from the enemy. 23rd 3rd day of bombardment. The only task for 50th Bde: was wirecutting on MAD POINT by D/50 but as they did not requiring all the rounds allotted for this purpose — B — 50 & C — 50 were given some to assist the 7th Division in wire cutting along MADAGASCAR TRENCH.	

INTELLIGENCE SUMMARY.

(Erase heading not required.)

Hour, Date, Place	Summary of Events and Information	Remarks and references to Appendices
	Two Bombardiers of B.50 (telephonists) were killed whilst working in forward trenches with O.C. "B" 50 who was observing the fire. Enemy's artillery rather more active but not by any means overwhelming. Night tasks 23/24th were doubled — i.e. A-C+D/50 each made 288 rounds between 6am and 6am	
24th/25th day of bombardment. Tasks as for 2nd day. The only tasks for which 50 H.Bde. was responsible during the whole bombardment were 1. The taking of MADAGASCAR COTTAGES. To the time of 400 H.E. the visible effect was good, but as it was known that the majority if not all of these Ken cottages had fortified cellars it was impossible to tell what real damage had been done. 2. The cutting of wire at MAD POINT. This appears to have been carried out effectively both from observation and from reports of the infantry, but MAD POINT itself was a nest of machine guns emplacements requiring heavy artillery to knock out, and as sufficient heavy artillery was	

INTELLIGENCE SUMMARY.

(Erase heading not required.)

Hour, Date, Place	Summary of Events and Information	Remarks and references to Appendices

24th apparently not available for this purpose. MAD POINT though divested of its wire, remained too strong a nut to crack.

8.50 was withdrawn at 8 h.m to SAILLY LABOURSE with a view to advancing with the 62nd Brigade R.F.A at a suitable phase of the operations of the 9.25th. The remainder of the brigade had orders to be ready to concentrate at SAILLY LABOURSE at an early stage on the 25th, there to come under the direct orders of G.O.C. R.A. It was hoped that the Brigade would be able to advance in the neighbourhood of FOSSE 8.

A road was reconnoitred from SAILLY LABOURSE to our front line trenches opposite to BIG WILLIE and forward of that our portable bridges were to be used for crossing the enemy trenches. All teams were saddled up and gun emplacements prepared as far as possible to allow of the rapid removal of guns & wagons. At about 9 h.m an order was received to the effect that if weather conditions were suitable to the use of ACCESSORY (the official euphemism for GAS) the hour of Zero would be 4.50 A.m and the bombardment would start at 4.15 A.m; if not only a small attack would be made on the toe of HOHENZOLLERN REDOUBT.

INTELLIGENCE SUMMARY.

(Erase heading not required.)

Hour, Date, Place	Summary of Events and Information	Remarks and references to Appendices
25th	and no artillery support would be required from us. At about 2/m orders were received that the full programme would be carried out. The oft-piece bombardment was over at 6.10 a.m. and the order to concentrate at SAILLY LABOURSE was awaited. It did not come, as we were an Infantry Brigade pure & simple, working with no particular Infantry but covering the whole 9th Division front. We had no forward officers with the Infantry advance, but depended on instructions & information from G.O.C. R.A. until 9E nurse Bde advanced & and got into touch with 27th Infantry Brigade to which we were to be affiliated. We kept up a slow fire on HAISNES TRENCH - etc for a time, but as no information as to the progress of the Infantry was obtainable at 8 a.m. 2/Lt A.E.H. Barton with two telephonists was sent forward to pick up what information he could. He and one of his telephonists were killed other having cut their line. By 9.0 a.m. the wet had cleared a little and we obtained some information from our observing stations — & so came into action	

INTELLIGENCE SUMMARY.

(Erase heading not required.)

Instructions regarding War Diaries and Intelligence Summaries are contained in F.S. Regs., Part II and the Staff Manual respectively. Title pages will be prepared in manuscript.

Hour, Date, Place	Summary of Events and Information	Remarks and references to Appendices
	Near HOHENZOLLERN REDOUBT under the 2nd. Bde: they were withdrawn to VERMELLES during the night 25th-26th and came into action there still in Bde: until we were finally withdrawn on Oct 2/3rd. They lost 1 gunner killed and 2 wounded in their advance. On the night 26th/27th Major Campbell comdg B/50 and Lt: Ainsworth took 2 limbers into the FOSSE 8 cottages to remove 2 captured guns — they were however able to remove one only the other being so buried under débris that it was impossible to extricate it.✻ From the 25th to our final withdrawal on 23rd October we were continually firing, sometimes at bodies of Germans which could be seen between HAISNES + the CORONS DE PEKIN but usually forming barrages by orders of the G.O.C. R.A. One most useful task was the enfilading of FOSSE ALLEY + PEKIN ALLEY; no record of targets was kept.	✻ The captured gun was last seen on the HORSE GUARDS PARADE labelled (no doubt for some good reason) "captured by the 9th Division at hoog" — LOOS — FOSSE 8 being a matter of miles! DF.

INTELLIGENCE SUMMARY.

(Erase heading not required.)

Hour, Date, Place	Summary of Events and Information	Remarks and references to Appendices
17th	2/Lt H.R. GARDINER - Orderly Officer, was sent forward to HOHENZOLLERN REDOUBT with a signalling lamp, to signal back to FOSSE 9 any news which he could obtain but owing to the conditions then prevailing not much information was forthcoming. He had and 2/Lt GARDINER was chiefly employed under orders of a STAFF OFFICER in rallying the infantry of a high division which had recently arrived and appeared to be short of officers of experience.	
28th	2/Lt GARDINER laid out a wire to central BOYAU to Infantry HdQ: M.G.S. and for the remainder of the observations at RElE an other here through a series of Infantry HdQs of the 9th, 24th + 28th Divisions and there obtained news, but there was laid across the open. NOT once was the only wire working, as the communication trenches were in a wretched condition through rain, shelling and constant passage of troops.	

INTELLIGENCE SUMMARY.

(Erase heading not required.)

Hour, Date, Place	Summary of Events and Information	Remarks and references to Appendices
	Our wire was therefore frequently used by the infantry brigadier as this was the only way of communication with Bgd HQ with whom we were always in touch. On this day one man of D/50 was killed & one man wounded by shrapnel near the gun position which was continually being shelled as the road by PONT FIXE was just behind it and appeared to attract a g[er]m. (org. field gun battery) which was supposed to be behind AUCHY-LEZ-LA BASSÉE about A.25.a. FC H.A.R. Group at our request turned a counter battery on to their square and after that we had very little trouble from this direction.	
29/1[2]	We were told that the 9th B[riga]de infantry were being sent by rail to POPERINGHE that the 51st, 52nd & 53rd Bdes were being relieved by the 20th Division, but that we were to hi[old] the strand on train to 28th Division for an indefinite period.	

INTELLIGENCE SUMMARY.

(Erase heading not required.)

Hour, Date, Place	Summary of Events and Information	Remarks and references to Appendices
30th The 9th Dn H less 50th Bde: depart for the North.		
	Ammunition Expended & Casualty and Ammunition returns for September are attached. Appendix.	
	From Sept 1st to 20th Shrapnel 556 HE. 12	
	" " 21st to 25th " 6719 " 1561	
	" " 26th to 30th " 5870 " 2201	
	Casualties :—	
	1 Officer & 6 other ranks killed	
	7 other ranks wounded.	

Appx 50B 1/A/1 9.11.15
OR.D.TS/w R.F.A.
R.D. Capt 508 R.F.A.

HEADQUARTERS

50TH BRIGADE R.F.A.

(9th DIVISION)

OCTOBER

1915

Army Form C. 2118.

WAR DIARY
or
INTELLIGENCE SUMMARY.

(Erase heading not required.)

Instructions regarding War Diaries and Intelligence Summaries are contained in F. S. Regs., Part II and the Staff Manual respectively. Title pages will be prepared in manuscript.

Hour, Date, Place	Summary of Events and Information	Remarks and references to Appendices
	CONFIDENTIAL WAR DIARY OF The 50th Brigade. Royal Field Artillery. 9th (Scottish) Divn October and November 1915.	

WAR DIARY
INTELLIGENCE SUMMARY

Army Form C. 2118.

Hour, Date, Place	Summary of Events and Information	Remarks and references to Appendices

October 1st
CUINCHY

Orders received from 28th Div. R.A. that the 50th Bde. will be relieved on 2nd by 36th Bde. R.F.A., 2nd Divn. and march to rejoin the 9th Divn. in the neighbourhood of YPRES. As the relief is to take place in the middle of (more or less) active operations, guns are to be handed over, so as to obviate the necessity for fresh registration by the incoming batteries. Targets: junctions of Dump Trench & Mark Face in sq. A.I.9. – also enfilading Essex Alley. Batteries search PEKIN ALLEY from 8pm to 8.30 pm. Adjutant of relieving Bde. arrives.

2nd

Quiet day. Whiz-bangs (77mm.) at D/50 and C/50 at midday. Move by Bde. Hdqrs. to B.A.C. after Lt.Col. BROOKE had handed over to Lt.Col. WARD. A/50, C/50 and D/50 were relieved by Batteries of 36th Bde. at 4 pm. B/50 were withdrawn to their wagon line at 6 pm. All Batteries spent the night in their wagon lines. As the 36th Bde. had handed over their guns to the Batteries of MEERUT Div. by whom they had just been relieved, A/50, B/50, and D/50 took over MEERUT Div. guns in place of their own ones – old pieces dating from 1905 and unfitting in every joint and gear. B/50 retained their own guns. At 6 pm others were withdrawn, retained their own guns, that 50th Bde. with one section of D.A.C. which received from 9th D.A. had been left behind were to march on 3rd to LE PETIT MORTIER

Army Form C. 2118.

WAR DIARY
or
INTELLIGENCE SUMMARY.
(Erase heading not required.)

Instructions regarding War Diaries and Intelligence Summaries are contained in F.S. Regs., Part II and the Staff Manual respectively. Title pages will be prepared in manuscript.

Hour, Date, Place	Summary of Events and Information	Remarks and references to Appendices
(1914) October		
POPERINGHE	and STEENWERCK, billets there, and march next day (4th) to billets in the neighbourhood of POPERINGHE.	
3rd	Marched 9am and billeted at STEENWERK 4pm.	
4th	Marched 9am on BAILLEUL to billets on BOESCHEPPE – POPERINGHE road, about 2 miles from POPERINGHE.	
5th	At rest. One man per Bty (telephonist) left 11.45am for attachment to 52nd Bde. Also a working party under an officer from 13 A.C.	
6th – 7th	At rest.	
8th	B/50 attached to 23rd Bde R.F.A. 3rd Div. and moved into action south of YPRES	
11th	(between ROUKERS and COURTRAI railway)	
12th	F.S.C.M. on B.S.M. KNEEFE (C/50), Br. PERRY (Bde. H.Q.) and D. SHARPE (B.A.C.) – President – Maj. HARRISON.	
13th	Telephonist from each unit south of D.A.C. for course. Reconnaissance of routine to the station up by 50th Bde. By Adjutant.	
14th	Reconnaissance continued.	
15th	Working party to prepare A/50 gun positions. BAC supply transport. Orders received for 50th Bde. to move up into position. C/50 and D/50 to send up gun – detachments only. One action night of 17th – 18th, other section night of 18th – 19th. Bde H.Q. to relieve 42nd Bde. H.Q. on night of 18th – 19th (Major M.T. FURSE) to	2/Lt. A.H. GARDINER (Ord. Off.) left for 18th Div. Artig. H.Q. as A.D.C. to Br. Gen. C.C. VON STRAUBENZEE.
16th	Telephonists under Adjutant go forward. G.O.C. 9th Divr.	

Army Form C. 2118.

WAR DIARY
—or—
INTELLIGENCE SUMMARY.
(Erase heading not required.)

Instructions regarding War Diaries and Intelligence Summaries are contained in F.S. Regs., Part II and the Staff Manual respectively. Title pages will be prepared in manuscript.

Hour, Date, Place	Summary of Events and Information	Remarks and references to Appendices
October.		
SOUTH OF YPRES–ZILLEBEKE RAILWAY	17th Visit 50th Bde. wagon lines during the day; visit did not take place.	
	18th Adjutant and Major HARRISON go up to batteries. B/50 returns to 50th Bde. right section in position 100x SW. of RIENS. B/50 (A.C. & D/50) moves off 1.30 pm.; Billets taken over by batteries of 51st Bde. moves other sections a number. 51st Bde. Batteries of 51st Bde. relieved by 50th Bde. Wagon lines near OUDERDOM.	R.S.M. RAWSON posted to 9th D.A.C.
	19th 7am. 50th Bde. H.Q. moved to H24 a.9.9. arrived 10.45am. Batteries did not fire till afternoon. 50th Bde. carried front of 28th Infde. – Transfer A1 to A3.	R.S.M. DAWSON posted to 50th Bde. H.Q. from A/50.
	20th Communications – Single wire (D5) from B.H.Q. to each Battery.	
	21st D.A.C. unable for arrived to dig in telephone wires.	
	22nd Re-arrangement of Bde. Groups. – B/63 (Hav) takes place of D/50 in 50th Bde. B.A.C. to consist of 3 18 pdr. sections, 1 4.5" How section and 1 S.A.A. section. Change to take effect at noon on 25/10. Pilgrimage of wagons of Div. Artly. into YPRES to fetch bricks and wattle for horse standings; dump formed near Bde. H.Q. and guard of 1 n.c.o. and 3 men set over it.	
	23rd 52nd Bde. find guard over dump from 12 noon. B/50 decide to change position owning to length of range. One section moved at night to an old position near B/53.	
	24th Direct hit by 4.2" How shell on dug out of B/50 old position, just on the remaining section was about to move out. 1 Sgt., 1 qt fitter and 3 men killed; 2 men wounded. Six 4.2" Hows. shell fell near Bde. H.Q.	

Army Form C. 2118.

WAR DIARY
—or—
INTELLIGENCE SUMMARY.
(Erase heading not required.)

Instructions regarding War Diaries and Intelligence Summaries are contained in F. S. Regs., Part II. and the Staff Manual respectively. Title pages will be prepared in manuscript.

Hour, Date, Place	Summary of Events and Information	Remarks and references to Appendices
October 26th – 29th.	Catapling transport of 81st — 1 man killed 2 wounded. Nothing noticeable. Normal expenditure of ammunition.	
29th	52nd Bde in rest – relieved by 51st Bde.	
30th	Continuous Bombardment.	
31st	Bombardment continued. Quilloeflorene Road, rifle mines & hang guns.	Casualties during October. 5 other ranks killed. 2 " " wounded. Ammunition Expenditure. About 1000 rounds 18 pr. " 100 " 4.5" Hows.

HEADQUARTERS

50th BRIGADE R.F.A.

9th Division

N O V E M B E R

1915

30 Septr. 1874.
Vol: 2

121/7678

J. Kwain

Octr Nov 15.

50 Bde R.F.A.
Army Form C. 2118.

WAR DIARY
INTELLIGENCE SUMMARY.
November 1915

(Erase heading not required.)

Instructions regarding War Diaries and Intelligence Summaries are contained in F.S. Regns. Part II and the Staff Manual respectively. Title pages will be prepared in manuscript.

Hour, Date, Place	Summary of Events and Information	Remarks and references to Appendices
November		
SOUTH OF YPRES – ZILLEBEKE RAILWAY	1st – 3rd Nothing unusual occurred.	
	4th Opened very quietly. Enemy aeroplane (FOKKER) brought down by one of ours at 11.30 a.m. near VERBRANDEN MOLEN. Pilot and observer killed. Activity by 10 cm. Jsans in evening; retaliation by 6 inch Hows.	Lt. J.F. BLIGH joined Bde. H.Q. from 6th Bty, 40th Bde. as Orderly Officer. 2Lt. W. BAINBRIGGE attached c/50 from 9th D.A.C.
	5th Quiet till 11.30 a.m. Then artillery duel.	
	6th Bombardment by 17th Div.; assisted by 1st Group, which fired 120 18pr, 20 4.5" How. and 15 6" How. shell. Over at 6.30 a.m. Germans retaliated.	Capt. C.E. MORGAN left 50th Bde A.C. to take up duties as Claims Commission.
	7th Foggy day. Over KRUISTRAAT and towards VLAMERTINGHE. Lt. Col. BROOKE, Maj. HARRISON and Ord. Off. reconnoitred various defiladed siting fronts between ZILLEBEKE and U60.60 for preparation of Defence Scheme. Trenches knee deep in slush.	
	8th Registration of 1st Group Btys. by aeroplane observation. Wireless instrument too yellow at Bde H.Q.	
	9th Quiet day.	Capt. D.D.R. FISHER posted to 50th Bde A.C. Lt. J.F. BLIGH appointed Adjutant.
	10th c/50 Rawling shelled by 15 cm and 10 cm. Hows. 2.30 p.m. Detachments withdrawn. No casualties to men or equipment. Guns withdrawn at night and ridden in horses, preparatory to taking of new position.	
	11th Aerial registration completed (C/53 – A/50). c/50 close new position	

Army Form C. 2118.

WAR DIARY
INTELLIGENCE SUMMARY.
(Erase heading not required.)

Instructions regarding War Diaries and Intelligence Summaries are contained in F.S. Regns. Part II and the Staff Manual respectively. Title pages will be prepared in manuscript.

Hour, Date, Place	Summary of Events and Information	Remarks and references to Appendices
November		
12th	in Ridge 150x N.W. of that evacuated by B/50 on 25.10.15. Zone of 1st Group extended to the East owing to 9th Div. taking over more trenches from 17th Div. All Infantry + Arty Bdes of 9th Div. now in action at same time. 1st Group still own trenches held by 28th Inf. Bde. (48 to A 6) D/50 (4th Group) relt. by o.c. 4th Group to own part of 1st Group front until c/50 had completed new position. A very wet day c/50 prepare new position.	
13th	During night 12th-13th c/50 occupied new position with 2 guns. Did not register owing to wet and bad prepared condition of gun platforms. Two Germans in blue uniforms and flat caps retired near BLAUWE POORT FME at dusk. They resembled into space. A Cat. R BROOKE went to transfer minor operation by 9th Div. Arty. German rent fire system of trenches from YPRES - COURTRAI Railway to 500x N.W. thoroughly plastered from 8.30am - 8.35am. Detached gun (A/50) at LA CHAPELLE enfiladed front-line trenches with shrapnel at short range and fired 42 rounds in 3 mins	(x) A/50 and B/50 fired 45 rounds each o/c c/50 did not take part in operation
14th	A.O. (x): Other 18 hrs fired 50 rounds per fifty, 75% H.E.; B/63 50 rounds H.E. Very little retaliation. c/50 Group fired third gun into position during night 13th-14th 5pm: 2nd H.A.R. shelled German Transport. On retaliation from Germans 17th Div sent up 3 rockets – a prearranged signal — and 9th Div. Arty. fired on selected points on roads behind German lines, 10 rounds at each point. c/50 left fire post with one gun. 4 pm. Gn. FORSTER (Bde Staff) killed by a German Arty A/50 wire along canal with 2 other men whilst retiring A/50 wire along canal with 2 other men	Maj. J.A.R. HARRISON left A/50 to take up duties of Brigade Major to 17th Div. Arty. Capt. O.R.D. FISHER posted to A/50 from 50th B.A.C.
15th		

WAR DIARY
INTELLIGENCE SUMMARY.
(Erase heading not required.)

Army Form C. 2118.

Instructions regarding War Diaries and Intelligence Summaries are contained in F.S. Regs., Part II and the Staff Manual respectively. Title pages will be prepared in manuscript.

Hour, Date, Place	Summary of Events and Information	Remarks and references to Appendices
November 16th	20th Siege (8 m/L Htrs) attacked to 9th Div. for retaliatory purposes vice 3rd Siege (6 in How). Tariff for retaliation for various natures of German projectiles. Laid down by F.O.C. 9th Div. YPRES shelled in evening - retaliation fr 15th C/50 completed registration of 3 guns and covered rain nr ZOO, and D/50. Lt COL BROOKE F.G.C.R.A. on Dr. ROBERTS (50th B.A.C.). Frosty day.	
17th	C/50 took over detailed guns at LA CHAPELLE from A/50. Gun lift there to await eventualities.	2/Lt. G.B. TRAILL posted to Bde H.Q. from B/50 as Ord. Off. 2/Lt. R.M. BONNIN posted to B/50 from 9th D.A.C.
18th	3 German aeroplanes over Bde H.Q at 7.30am, on return from raid on POPERINGHE	
19th	4.15pm. C/50 fired shoot B/g, L Group & 41st Trench Mort. Bty. Retaliation on ZILLEBEKE.	
20th	Friday. German aeroplane very persistent over YPRES 10am - 10.30 am. 2.15 am German retaliation fr 19th with minenwerfer. B/50 and C/50 re-retaliated. 3pm. 20th Siege did time registration through 1st SNO ORDER (B/50) in the trenches.	
21st 22nd 23rd	Fine & frosty. Quiet day. 7.30am Burst of rifle & mg. fire at Hill 60. B/50 & C/50 Sufts. & Group. Quiet day. Lt Col BROOKE invalided Duties A.C. just taken over. Hoar. Very foggy morning. 2" H.A.R. fired at chart Retaliation with 10 cm Hows near Bde H.Q. 7 prs and 9 prs - many splinters.	
24th	Lt Col BROOKE visited trenches with Maj. CHAPPELL + Capt USSBOURNE. Strong front at 1.30 & 4.9 the dealt with B/9, 12th Siege (9.2 How) & noon - rapt. ranging through B/50. 2" H.A.R. fired in evening: 15cm + 10 cm retaliation near Bde H.Q. 9-10pm.	2/Lt. C.N. ANDREW posted to 50th B.A.C. from 9th D.A.C.

WAR DIARY
or
INTELLIGENCE SUMMARY.
(Erase heading not required.)

Army Form C. 2118.

Hour, Date, Place	Summary of Events and Information	Remarks and references to Appendices
November 25th	12th Siege ran telephone wire to F.O.O. & B.A.C. & sent 2 officers to trenches with B/50 F.O.O. to register T30 A 4.5. But too misty to observe.	
26th	Gr. BROWN (Gunner of B/50) had both feet removed by 77cm shell in ARMAGH WOOD and died on 26th. Bn. Gen. UNIACKE (Arty. adviser to 5th Corps) visited R.H.Q. 12mm. — 12.30am 2nd H.A.R. fired heavily in retaliation. Germans replied with 10cm., 1am — 2am, in close proximity to R.H.Q. 12th Siege (9.2 How.) fired at T30 A 4.5 (per B/50 F.O.O.) Snowstorms in morning	
27th	Continued shoot by 1st Group & 47th Trench Mortar Btty. planned for 28th to destroy suspicions looking work (at T30 2 4.0) of unknown quality. Our trenches shelled at 9pm by 15cm. items. 20th Siege retaliated. 60pm. 4.7" guns also fired; replied by 10 cm shots. damaging 28th Gp. F.Rle. H.Q.	
28th	Foggy day. 3.25pm B/53 dealt with machine gun emplacements (15 rounds) — 3 direct hits. No retaliation F.G.I.M. on 2nd Battn Hall and Dr Sharpe (B.A.C.) 2/Lt. W. ROE (A/60) hit in shoulder & about upon discounting position of single gun against trenches. 1.30pm Germans retaliated on A3 — A6 for our bombardment	
29th	Warm & rainy. Artillery duel ensued till 4.30pm. — 20th Siege & Trench of 28th Motors. Busy.	2/Lt. W. ROE (wounded) left A/50. 2/Lt. C. W. ANDREW posted from 50 B.A.C. to A/50
30th	Quiet day.	

Army Form C. 2118.

WAR DIARY
INTELLIGENCE SUMMARY.
(Erase heading not required.)

Hour, Date, Place	Summary of Events and Information	Remarks and references to Appendices
		Casualties during November. 2 other ranks Killed. 1 officer wounded. Ammunition Expenditure About 1600 rounds 18pr " 300 " 4.5" How

5/12/15.

[signature]
for
LT. COLONEL R.F.A
COMMANDING 50th BRIGADE R.F.A

HEADQUARTERS

50th BRIGADE   R. F. A.

9th Division

DECEMBER

1915

J. H. Stream(?)

50 Khas. R.F.C.
Vol: 3

121/7834

WAR DIARY
or
INTELLIGENCE SUMMARY.
(Erase heading not required.)

Army Form C. 2118.

Instructions regarding War Diaries and Intelligence Summaries are contained in F.S. Regs., Part II and the Staff Manual respectively. Title pages will be prepared in manuscript.

Hour, Date, Place	Summary of Events and Information	Remarks and references to Appendices
Near YPRES	December	
	1st Lt. Col. BROOKE and ord. officer walked to trenches with Maj CAMPBELL and Capt. USBORNE. Clear, east showery. Night was firing parties shelled	
SOUTH OF YPRES-ZILLEBEKE RAILWAY	By A/50, B/50 & C/50.	
	2nd Cloudy morning. Then Bde. Fit. Adjt. & Ord officer walked to telephone wires. 11.30am A/50, B/50, C/50 combined with 47th Trench Mortar Bty against machine gun emplacement. Very successful: 15 direct hits by B/53 out of 24 rounds — emplacement & something near A/50 detonated well. Man wounded (B/50). By stray bullet	
Bde. Hdqrs at KRUISTRAAT in artillery-positions	3rd Artillery to be over entire responsibility for telephone from Regts. to Bn. Hdqrs. – owing to difficulties was divided contact with Infantry. Germans shelled YPRES and KRUISTRAAT with 77cm shrapnel and 13.5 cm high velocity gun from 7pm till 11pm. Several 77cm shells close to Bde. H. Qrs. All windows broken. 15cm Hows (H.E.) 12 midnight till 2am.	
	4th Strenuous day. Bombardment of small salient in German trenches at I.30.d. planned. C.R.A. at Bde H. Qrs. Quiet evening.	
	5th Lt. Col. BROOKE walked to trenches with B.G.O.C. 2nd Inf. Bde. Co-operation with 9.2" Hows. against strong point at I.30.d. 4.5	

WAR DIARY
INTELLIGENCE SUMMARY
(Erase heading not required.)

Army Form C. 2118.

Instructions regarding War Diaries and Intelligence Summaries are contained in F.S. Regs., Part II. and the Staff Manual respectively. Title pages will be prepared in manuscript.

Hour, Date, Place	Summary of Events and Information	Remarks and references to Appendices
	Planned Bt. proposed moves to match up of aeroplanes to Poane. F.S.C.M. on Farr St. (Sgt) COCKER J.W. (reduced to Corp Sgt) and Sgt. JKNIGHT R.G. (reduced to Corpl) both of R.A.C. F. down Rennes. Maj. CAMPBELL president.	
6th	Clear, windy. KRUISTRAAT shelled from 8 p.m. to 11 p.m. By 10 cm. 16 cm. (H.E.)	
7th	Bright morning; wet evening. 17th Div. shelled STIRLING CASTLE. 9th Div. ready for retaliation. E.R.A. visited Bty. and ordered at Bde. H.Qrs.	
8th	New flat 9th Div. to be relieved by 50th Div. before 21st Dec. 12.30 pm Bombardment of I.30.d.4.b. by A/50 (20 rounds), B/53 (20 rounds) and B/50 (40 rounds) together with 47th Trench Mortar (no known effect enemy retaliated) Bty. YPRES shelled heavily, some A2 ms. fell (3 Pd). Btn. YPRES.	Ord. Officer acted as Adjutant in place of letter on leave 9th till 18th.
9th	13 cm. near Bde. H.Qrs. in evening. Shelling round KRUISTRAAT started at about 3 a.m. & was fairly continuous round the farm. Also on VLAMERTINGHE - YPRES road & district. A 15cm. shell fell near C/50's position causing 4 casualties (2 Killed 2 wounded.) The rest of the day was normal. Weather, dull and wet.	

Army Form C. 2118.

WAR DIARY
INTELLIGENCE SUMMARY.
(Erase heading not required.)

Hour, Date, Place	Summary of Events and Information	Remarks and references to Appendices
Dec. 10th	Lt. Col. E.W.S. BROOKE walked to Trench with Maj. CAMPBELL, and was slightly wounded by a Rifle-Bullet below shoulder. He was able to walk back to Bde. H.Qrs and was sent to Base Hospital at BOULOGNE that evening. Maj. C.A.H. CAMPBELL (in absence of Maj. V.E. PRINGLE) assumed command of Bde.	Lt. Col. E.W.S. BROOKE wounded and sent to Base Hospital. —— Maj. C.A.H. CAMPBELL took over command of 1st Group.
11th	Quiet day.	
12th	Orders received for 9th Div. to move out of action. The Artillery to move on 20th/21st and 21st/22nd to training area near WATTEN.	2/Lt W. BAINBRIGGE (4/50) on course at 3rd Army School BEATHEN.
13th STEENVOORDE	To relieve C/B, D. Artry of 50th Division. Bde H.Qrs & vicinity heavily shelled in morning. Direct hit on artery-pavilion. Lt. outspanned dumflt not successfully. Left out 10 cm. S.E. shell. Officers servant (Pte WEST) killed. Area made out by pleas, otherwise unhurt.	
14th	C/50 together with 2 Btys from 3rd & 4th groups taken out of action and spent night at wagon lines. D/51 came under command of O.C. 1st Group and covered zone of C/50. — 1st Group H.Qrs moved to action north of ROULERS railway. Situation normal.	Maj. H.T. BELCHER D.S.O. (4th Gp.) assumed command of 1st Group.
15th	Verbal orders received from Bde. Major that in view of the possibility of a gas attack by the enemy, the enemy's front line	

Army Form C. 2118.

WAR DIARY
INTELLIGENCE SUMMARY.
(Erase heading not required.)

Instructions regarding War Diaries and Intelligence Summaries are contained in F.S. Regs., Part II and the Staff Manual respectively. Title pages will be prepared in manuscript.

Hour, Date, Place	Summary of Events and Information	Remarks and references to Appendices
Dec		
	parapet was to be engaged by all Batteries with a view to doing as much damage as possible. C/50 mentioned to STEENVOORDE.	
16th	Bombardment of enemy's parapets continued – daily allowance of ammunition (about 20 rounds per 18 pr. Bty & 10 4.5" How.) not exceeded. Enemy retaliated on our trenches & futher back. Several shells in vicinity of Bde H. Qrs.	
17th	Enemy's parapet shelled again. Telephonist wounded in B/53. Bombardment of enemy's parapet discontinued.	
18th		
19th	Bright & sunny. 1am. Some shell near Bde H. Qrs. 3am rapid rifle fire in fact of 2nd. 5-30am Rifle gas attack on 6th Div. front. ½ mile E of ROULERS railway. No Infantry attack. Gas fired at KRUISTRAAT and wagon lines first in O.P.s. Smoke helmets (Vermorel sprayers) effective. Much shelling of entire salient & YPRES all day. Bde H. Qrs. had a warm time. Wires all futher except to A/50. Enemies out all day in trenches in 15t Group. 8pm Zeppelin reported over YPRES and POPERINGHE. Quiet in trenches in our No casualties. Zone. B.A.C. (Bn 4.5" How Sec.) relieved By 50 of Div. R.A.C.	Lt. C.V. SNATT evacuated to Base Hospital sick – (Pott–shock). Later to England.

Army Form C. 2118.

WAR DIARY
or
INTELLIGENCE SUMMARY.
(Erase heading not required.)

Instructions regarding War Diaries and Intelligence Summaries are contained in F. S. Regs., Part II and the Staff Manual respectively. Title pages will be prepared in manuscript.

Hour, Date, Place	Summary of Events and Information	Remarks and references to Appendices
Dec.	and marched via POPERINGHE, which was being shelled at the	
20th	time to billets near CAESTRE. C/50 marched to BOLLEZEELE. Quieter day. Officers of 1st & 4th Northumbrian Bdes. present to look round camp. 4 p.m. KRUISTRAAT Shelled by 10 cm. How. (H.E.) — Salvoes of 3. Midway of Bde. H. Qs. Postau. a despatch rider flash off his motorcycle into the ditch. 1 Section of B/53 retired at 8 p.m. By a section of 5th "Q" Bty. (5"How') Bty. 10 pm. Stray shells caused 4 casualties (1 Pdr.) to latter detachment.	1 man (B/53) wounded (D. PEACOCK) died in hospital.
21st	Sec. of B/50 Spent night at Rugen Farm. of 1 Sec. of B/53 & D/51 relieved	Wagon lines A/50, B/50 & D/51 marched to STEENVOORDE area at 12 noon.
	Misty rain. Very quiet day. 8 p.m. remainder of B/53 came out of action. Detachments of 1 Sec A/50 and remainder of B/50 and D/51 relieved by 1st Northumbrian Bde. Guns handed over complete. Gun detachments (18 pr.) travelled to STEENVOORDE by motor 'bus.	
22nd	Fine morning: wet afternoon. Relief of A/50 completed and 1st Northumbrian Bde. took over from 1st group at 10 a.m. Remainder of gun detachments (18 pr.) proceeded to STEENVOORDE by motor 'bus. Bde. S. O. & B/53 marched. n arr. Refilled at farms. Bde H. Qs., A/50,	Major H.T. BELCHER D.S.O. returned to 4th group. Major V.E. PRINGLE assumed temporary command of 1st group.
23rd	4·5" Jeen Sec. of 50 = B.A.C. marched to CAESTRE. Bde H Qs., A/50, B/50 & B/53 marched in order named via STEENVOORDE, and ARNEKE	

Army Form C. 2118.

WAR DIARY
or
INTELLIGENCE SUMMARY.
(Erase heading not required.)

Hour, Date, Place		Summary of Events and Information	Remarks and references to Appendices
BOLLEZEELE	Dec. 24th	To BOLLEZEELE in WATTEN Training area. Good billets: men in farms, escort B/53 & H.Qrs. in School; Officers in houses in the town. The fields were very water-logged, but in most cases horses-lines were on Bye-roads. 9th Divt. leaves VCorps & comes under II Corps.	
	Xmas 25th	Cleaning harness etc. Practice of firing for Xmas Dinner. Church Parade in School at 9.30 A.M. Xmas dinners — (oxt. plumpudding & beer) N.C.O.s	10 am Dr. BUNNIN (B/50) on course at 2nd Army School, BERTHE M.
	26th to 31st	Bty. training: gun drill, dummy drill (dismounted), baths, concerts etc. etc. to driving, signalling classes,	2/Lts. W.R. BROWNE W. SWORDER C.V. SNATT W.L.F. BROWNE L.H. JACOBSON } promoted Lt. (8th Dec.)
	26th		
	29th	9th Divn. in Army Reserve : to be ready to move at 9 hours notice.	Casualties during December. 1 Officer wounded 2 other ranks killed 1 " " died of wounds 7 " " wounded Ammunition Expended About 1500 rounds 18pdr. 250 " 4.5" How.

W.F.B.R.A
Lt. R.F.A.
ADJUTANT 50th BRIGADE R.F.A.
31/12/15.
for LT. COLONEL R.F.A.
COMMANDING 50th BRIGADE R.F.A.

9th Division.

Artillery.

50th Bde ROYAL FIELD ARTILLERY.

JANUARY 1916

CONFIDENTIAL

WAR DIARY.

50th Brigade R.F.A.

for

January 1916

J.F.Rhys Lt.
for
LT. COLONEL, R.F.A.
COMMANDING 50th BRIGADE R.F.A.

1/2/16

Army Form C. 2118.

WAR DIARY
—or—
INTELLIGENCE SUMMARY.
(Erase heading not required.)

Instructions regarding War Diaries and Intelligence Summaries are contained in F.S. Regs., Part II. and the Staff Manual respectively. Title pages will be prepared in manuscript.

Hour, Date, Place	Summary of Events and Information	Remarks and references to Appendices
BOLLEZEELE January 1916		
1st	Bde. Staff had Telephone from R.A. Hdqrs at BOLLEZEELE to VOLKERING. G.O.C. 9th Div. expected to inspect Btys; but didn't. 1st Grp. Btys. 1st Grp. Wag. Move	
2nd 3rd	Training as usual.	
4th	G.O.C. 9th Div. (Maj Gen W.T. FURSE) inspected 1st Grp Btys; and expressed his satisfaction. Advance parties under O.O. (5 per unit) marched to CAESTRE area to disinfect and prepare billets.	
5th	Packed up.	
6th	9 am. 1st Grp marched via ROUBROUCK, MAISON ROUGE and STAPLE to CAESTRE. Order of march 3rd, 4th, 1st, 2nd Grps.; 1st Grp. Bde H Qrs T Btys B/53, B/50, A/50, R.A. Hqrs., C/50. Tactical scheme for MAISON – 1 Subaltern officer per Bty; Halted in at ROUGE the midday Halt. Billets poor after BOLLEZEELE. Very crowded	
7th	Lt Col. PRINGLE and O.O. looked round for better Btys. billets but found none.	
8th	Search for billets again unsuccessful. A/50 took over a second farm.	
9th	C.O. and Adjt. attended conference at Div. Hdqrs. at MERRIS. Maj. GOODMAN (Bde.Maj. R.A.) lectured on Artillery cooperation with Infantry. Church parade at CAESTRE school. O.O. left for signalling course at 25th Div NIEPPE	

Army Form C. 2118.

WAR DIARY
INTELLIGENCE SUMMARY.
(Erase heading not required.)

Instructions regarding War Diaries and Intelligence Summaries are contained in F. S. Regs., Part II. and the Staff Manual respectively. Title pages will be prepared in manuscript.

Hour, Date, Place	Summary of Events and Information	Remarks and references to Appendices
CAESTRE Jan 10th	Xmas gifts from 50th Bde. distributed to the 4 Battns. of 28th Inf. Bde. Germans another aeroplane bombed BORRE and HAZEBROUCK. F.G.C.M. on 4 men our footballs wft 52nd Divr. wft 52nd (0-0) of A/50 — Arm. Reserve.	
11th	Lecture on F.S.C.M's by Gen't WROUGHTON at Divl. H.Q. for Staff Capts & Adjutants. Bttry training, chiefly interior matters continued whilst at CAESTRE.	
12th	Route march for whole of 9th Divn Artly via HAZEBROUCK (near) SYLVEVES (G.O.C. 2nd Army Commander (Gen PLUMER) especially complimented.	
	CAPPEL & CAESTRE, marched past 2nd Army Commander (Gen PLUMER) especially complimented.	
	A very good showing; 50th & 52nd Bdes beat 52nd (5-3) in football replay.	
13th	Boxing: Bde beats. Honours Lieut. Maj. HARRISON (Lt.e of A/50) and Maj. THELLUSSON (Late of D/50) got D.S.O's	15th Lt. W.W.BROWN transferred from C/50 to B.A.C. *Lt. R.M. NICOLLS transferred from B.A.C. to B/50-D
14th	G.O.C.R.A. inspected the B.A.C. 5 subalterns under Maj CAMPBELL reconnaitred gun positions (anti aircraft defence scheme) S. of NIEUVE EQUISE	2/Lt H.S.J.C. BECHER joined & posted to C/50 A.C. BELL B.A.C. A. IRELAND B/53 D.L. SHEPPERD A/50.
15th	Racing — R.A. beats. Three representations from 1st Gp. defeated. C.O. dined with 11th H.L.I. 4 officers joined Bde. (as far as in) Concert by A.P.M's troupe at school CAESTRE. Canadoel Revue and very good show.	
16th	Nothing unusual. Church Parade at school.	
17th	Lecture at BAILLEUL by Col. HOLLAND (9th Divr) on LOOS. Col. FORBES & Maj. ANDREWS (11th H.L.I) entertained between by Bde Helgn. at Cercle Francaise.	
18th	Wet. Cancel by a few Staffly Columns at school, CAESTRE.	

Army Form C. 2118.

WAR DIARY
or
INTELLIGENCE SUMMARY.
(Erase heading not required.)

Instructions regarding War Diaries and Intelligence Summaries are contained in F.S. Regs., Part II and the Staff Manual respectively. Title pages will be prepared in manuscript.

Hour, Date, Place	Summary of Events and Information	Remarks and references to Appendices
CAESTRE. Jan 19th	Summer-like day. Football officers (50th U.S.I.D.) at D/53 R.F.A.	
	Won 2-1. 2Lt ANDREWS & 2Lt BECHER wicked. Team: 2Lt BAISFORD; 2Lt GLIGH	
	2Lt BONNIN; 2Lt IRELAND, 2Lt BROWNE, 2Lt BROWN; 2Lt CAMPBELL (A.V.C.), 2Lt CRAIG (R.A.M.C.), 2Lt ANDREWS	
	2Lt BAW BRIGGS, 2Lt BECHER. Lecture by Medical Officer to N.C.O.s	
20th	Lecture at BAILLEUL on the new true (Bantam) — from PLOEGSTEERT Lt.	
	ARMENTIÈRES.	
21st	C.O., B.C.s & sub. forward Obs. & Adjt. travelled by motor-bus to NIEPPE	2Lt J.J. O'GRADY joined Bde. posted to B.A.C.
	to reconnoitre gun positions of 111th Bde. R.F.A. & D/113 Bde. (25th Div.).	
	Very quiet. Lecture by Veterinary Officer to officers & N.C.O.s of B.A.C.	
22nd	C.O. attended Lecture at BAILLEUL by Col. POOLE R.A. on Counter Batteries, 11am	2Lt R LIMPENNY joined Bde. posted to A/50.
	Meeting of Gp. Commanders at R.A. HQ, 2pm. Lecture by 2nd Corps	
	Intelligence officer at CAESTRE school. 6pm.	
23rd	11am. Inspection of B.C.s at Bde. HQ in new positions. 11:30am. Church	
	parade at HQ. Hot day. Lecture by V.O. in evening.	
24th	Lecture by V.O. in evening.	
25th	Lt. Col. E.W.S. BROOKE returned from NICE convalescent home. Bde. dinner	Lt. Col. E.W.S. BROOKE resumed command of 1st group.
	at café Francaise.	
26th	B.C.s, F.O.O.s & Telephonists made up to new positions. Lecture by N.O. on gas &	Maj. V.E. PRINGLE returned to c/50.
	gas cartouch (Officers' Co.)	
27th	D/50 returned to 1st group. 1 section of each Bty.	
	& B.A.C. of 1st group took over from 111th Bde. & D/113, WEST OF PLOEGSTEERT.	

WAR DIARY
or
INTELLIGENCE SUMMARY.

(Erase heading not required.)

Army Form C. 2118.

Hour, Date, Place	Summary of Events and Information	Remarks and references to Appendices
Nr. PLOEGSTEERT. Jan. 28th	Bde. HeadQrs. & remaining sections of Btys & B.A.C. took over from 111th Bde & D/113 Bde. Considerable shelling by 10cm. of Ploegsteert Wood from N/50. Relief successfully completed.	Supporting 27th Inf. Bde. 26th I.Bde on right; 28th on left. 51st Bde R.F.A on right; 52nd on left.
29th	Misty. 10am. O.C. 1st Group took over from O.C. 111th Bde. Quiet day. Registered. Eastwind.	Lt. W.W. BROWN left for England to resign commission & qualify for R.A.M.C.
30th	Cold & foggy. Quiet. G.O.C. 9th Div. walked round 1st Group Btys.	
31st	Cold & foggy. Very quiet.	

(signature)
LT. COLONEL R.F.A.
COMMANDING 50th BRIGADE R.F.A.

Army Form C. 2118.

WAR DIARY
or
INTELLIGENCE SUMMARY.
(Erase heading not required.)

Instructions regarding War Diaries and Intelligence Summaries are contained in F. S. Regs., Part II. and the Staff Manual respectively. Title pages will be prepared in manuscript.

Hour, Date, Place	Summary of Events and Information	Remarks and references to Appendices
	Addenda to WAR DIARY of OCTOBER 1915.	
	Officers of B/53 (on joining 50th Bde.)	
	Temp. Capt. A.J. USBORNE	
	" 2Lieut L.H. JACOBSON	
	" 2Lieut J.N.G. DUTHY	
	" Lieut G.H. SMITH	
	Temp. Lieut. R.M. NICOLLS (attached).	

9th Division.

Artillery.

50th Bde. ROYAL FIELD ARTILLERY

FEBRUARY 1916

CONFIDENTIAL WAR DIARY

OF

50th Brigade, Royal Field Artillery

9th (Scottish) Division

for

February 1916.

[signature]
LT. COLONEL R.F.A.
COMMANDING 50th BRIGADE R.F.A.

29.2.16.

Army Form C. 2118.

WAR DIARY
50th Bde. R.F.A.
INTELLIGENCE SUMMARY.
(Erase heading not required.)

Instructions regarding War Diaries and Intelligence Summaries are contained in F.S. Regs., Part II. and the Staff Manual respectively. Title pages will be prepared in manuscript.

Place	Date	Hour	Summary of Events and Information	Remarks and references to Appendices
near PLOEGSTEERT	Feb. 1916			
	1.		Nothing of interest. Registration. 2 Bombs dropped west of PLOEGSTEERT. U27d. and 28a shelled (shelling Le GHEER)	
	2.		G.O.C. 9th Div. visited gunpositions. Registration. B/53 retaliated on the BIRDCAGE (U21.6.) for trench mortars.	
	3.		B Gen. TUDOR the new C.R.A. visited Bde Hdqrs. Registration. C.O. reconnoitred new position for D/50	Reor CN. deVINE C.F. attd Bt 50th Bde
	4.		C.R.A. visited batteries. Enemy shelled ST. YVES, and LE GHEER (1sec) near CALVAIRE.	Lt. R. LIMPENNY transferred from A/50 to 50th B.A.C.
	5.		1st Othrank B/50 slightly wounded. Suspected O.P. fired on by D/50.	
	6.		Some shells fell 150x to right of A/50's position. DEULEMONT church shelled by B/53	
	7.		C.O. selected position for D/50 (1sec) at CALVAIRE, to fire S.E. into 21st Div. zone	2/Lt J.T. O'GRADY on course Trench Mortar School
	8.		Nothing of interest. Registration.	
	9.		NIEPPE shelled in retaliation for fire of our 6" guns.	BERTHEN
	10.		Nothing of interest. Working parties fired on	
	11.		Very wet.	
	12.		Bright day. C.R.A. visited Hdqrs. Also shelled the monastery U24 c.77	
	13.		C.R.A and C.O. round O.Ps. Great aeroplane activity. A/50 shelled Battalion Hdqrs. U.22.d.2.2.	A/50 and B/50 fired
	14.		2.30pm. Strafe by 41st Siege Bty. (6" How.) on our Rt at U 28 & 5.6. A/50 and B/50 fired.	

Army Form C. 2118.

WAR DIARY
INTELLIGENCE SUMMARY.
(Erase heading not required.)

Place	Date	Hour	Summary of Events and Information	Remarks and references to Appendices
	Feb.			14.
			on communication trenches round the work. Considerable damage appeared to have been done.	C.O. on leave
		3 p.m.	Retaliation on A/50's O.P. at AB GHEER.	Major PRINGLE C/50
	15.		Great gale till 11 a.m. Very quiet.	in command of Bde.
	16.		Tremendous gale. Little firing.	
	17.		Meeting of Battery Commanders at Bde.H.Qrs. Also tested failure for wire cutting on ST. YVES ridge. B/53 fired 93 rounds at the BIRDCAGE (U22) to test various types of shell, Lyddite and Amatol with and without No.2 fuze. C.R.A. present at the O.P.	17. Lt. W. SWORDER attached to B.A.C. via 2/Lt. AC. BELL to Bde.
	18.		Stormy. Fired about 250 rounds. 'Strafe' by B/53. D/50 at OBSERVATION HOUSE and wireless station in LA BASSEVILLE. C/50 and A/50 searched the road running North and South from this point, firing 9 salvoes each at irregular intervals. Effect difficult to observe as light poor. Group concentration test, 1 round per Bty on the last gun ready, at LOOPHOLE FARM (U.21.d.3.A.) C/50 first in 4'15".	
	19.		Considerable artillery activity. PLOEGSTEERT church shelled and twice hit by 5.9" Hows.: the spire fell at 4.40 p.m. Group concentration test at U.28.6.7.: A/50 first in 1'55". B/53 first 55 secs. A/50 shelled Farm NICOLLS	
	20.	3.45	12 rounds per Bty. Fired at DEULEMONT church in retaliation. Fine day. Concentration test U.16.q.92 (TROIS TILLEULS FARM) B/53 first	20. Farm NICOLLS on course of BERTHEN (gunnery)

Army Form C. 2118.

WAR DIARY
or
INTELLIGENCE SUMMARY.
(Erase heading not required.)

Instructions regarding War Diaries and Intelligence Summaries are contained in F. S. Regs., Part II. and the Staff Manual respectively. Title pages will be prepared in manuscript.

Place	Date	Hour	Summary of Events and Information	Remarks and references to Appendices
DEULEMONT	21.		DEULEMONT church, in conjunction with 1st Canadians Heavy Bty.	21st 1st B.group abolished. D/50 returned to 50th Bde. For all purposes. B/63 to 50th Bde except for tactics. 50th Bde + B/53 formed Centre Group.
PLOEGSTEERT			PLOEGSTEERT shelled. Centre Group replied with 20 rounds per gun into DEULEMONT. Group concentration test. B/50 fired 1/5" PETITE HAIE FME (U.23.c.9.9.) Ran aeroplane registration. A/50 on PONT ROUGE. But too dark, so given up.	
	22.		Showed off and on all day. Group concentration test on U.28.d.6.8 (Battln. Hdqrs.) D/50 fired 1/15". Wet Rain [Started] fired on on most days.	
	23.		Fine morning. Snow from 10 am. to 3 pm. "Strafe" by 41st Siege and D/50 on machine gun emplacement at U.22.c.3.3. C/50 fired on communication trenches. Several direct hits.	23. Lt Col BROOKE returned from leave.
	24.		Very bad frost. Snow on ground 23°F.	
	25.		Very heavy snow fall during night. Temperature 23°F. C.R.A. visited wagon lines. B/53 shelled the BIRDCAGE at 2:30 pm. and rounds for transport from 6 to 8 pm. Test concentration U.23.c.6.4. at 5 p.m. A/50 fired 1'.	25. 2/Lt. H.M. PRICE joined Bde. + posted to A/50.
	26.	10:30 am	B/53 replied on DEULEMONT for shelling of PLOEGSTREET.	
		11.AD PM	False gas-alarm - started by 21st Div. on right by mistake.	
		11:45	Combined strafe Pittsweek B/50 and 6th Royal Scots Fusiliers on gap at U.28.a.A.6.	

WAR DIARY
INTELLIGENCE SUMMARY
(Erase heading not required.)

Army Form C. 2118.

Place	Date	Hour	Summary of Events and Information	Remarks and references to Appendices
	27		Stormy day; warmer. Snow disappeared. "Strafe" by B/53, A/50 and D/50 on machine gun emplacement. U.28.a.4½.9. Parapet was much damaged and burst-wire destroyed. 15 hits obtained by B/53. Enemy retaliated on AU GHEER, CONVENT and edge of PLOEGSTEERT WOOD. 9th Div. gave concentration test on TROIS TILLEULS FME. B/50 & D/50 first fire 2'45"	
	28.		C/50 registered with aeroplane. Machine gun emplacement at U.30.c.4.6. fired at.	
	29	9.30 am	11.30 am Aeroplane registration V.30.a.8.9 for B/50 and V.17.d.7.4. for C/50.	
		11–15 am	Test Concentration for whole of 9th Divl. Arty. on DEULEMONT Church. D/50 fire first. 35 secs.	
		2/2pm	D/53 (How) fired on parapet at U.28.a.4.2. and A/50 cut wire in front with a single gun east of PLOEGSTEERT village. At night B/50 continued with machine guns against working parties repairing the damage.	

WAR DIARY

INTELLIGENCE SUMMARY.

Army Form C. 2118.

Place	Date	Hour	Summary of Events and Information	Remarks and references to Appendices
			Ammunition fired during Feb.	Officers in D/50 when the Battery returned to 50th Bde.
		18/pr.	About 1800 shrapnel. 4.5" How. About 700 H.E.	Capt. B.L. MARRINER
			1000 H.E.	Temp/Lt. E.A.B. HOLLAM
			Casualties	" Lt. G.H. MASSEY
			1 other rank wounded.	" Lt. J.M.G. BELL
				" Lt. A.E. CLARKE.
				Capt. DALLOW and 2/Lt LESLIE (2/3 London Brigade R.F.A. T.F.) attached to A/50 and C/50 for a fortnight from 15th.

Wh. Flaworth -
LT. COLONEL R.F.A.
COMMANDING 50th BRIGADE R.F.A.

9th Division
Artillery.

50th Bde ROYAL FIELD ARTILLERY.

MARCH 1916

50 RFA
Vol 2

CONFIDENTIAL

WAR DIARY

50TH BRIGADE R.F.A.
9TH (Scottish) DIVISION
MARCH 1916

WAR DIARY or INTELLIGENCE SUMMARY

Army Form C. 2118.

Place	Date	Hour	Summary of Events and Information	Remarks and references to Appendices
near PLOEGSTEERT	March 1916		Reference to map: Sheet 28.	
	1.	3.45 pm	C/50 retaliated on the BIRDCAGE for aerial torpedoes.	
	2.	9.30 am	Aeroplane registration: A/50 on PONT ROUGE.	
		5 am	S.O.S. alarm; return of a bombardment by Canadian Division on left.	
		1 pm	C/50 and B/53 shelled R.E. dump at U.28.a.1.5 off to m. Germans replied with 15cm. into PLOEGSTEERT wood till midnight. 60hrs replied.	
	3.	10 am	Meeting of Group Commanders R.C.R.A. at NIEPPE.	
		5 pm	Staff of U.22.6½. 3½. by A1st Siege (6" How) and D/50. Meeting of Bty Commanders for C.O. at the Chateau. Wet evening.	
	4.	9.15 am	Snow and rain. 9th Aus. Arty. Test concentration on U.22.c.7.7.	
		6.30 pm	Two rounds for gun in the Air onto DEULEMONT, registration for shelling of NIEPPE.	
	5.		Aeroplane up twice. Lots clouds too low to shoot. German sausage up. List of recommendations for honours sent in. C.O. reconnoitred subsidiary line with O.C. D/50. R.E. dump U.22.c.7.7. Shelled by 6" Hows and D/50.	
	6.	9 am	Aeroplane registered B/53 onto crossroads at C.11.d.8.4. (Sheet 36). DEULEMONT church bright down by 9.2" guns. Aeronauts paid visit in the evening.	
	7.		Snow and sleet all day.	

Army Form C. 2118.

WAR DIARY
INTELLIGENCE SUMMARY.
(Erase heading not required.)

Place	Date	Hour	Summary of Events and Information	Remarks and references to Appendices
	8.		Snow & ice deep: thawed all day, sunshine.	
	9.	10am	Meeting of Group Commanders at R.A. H.Q.rs. Aeroplane up for 5th Bde.	
		12noon	Fine cold. Staff 'C' Right Group - 0/95 on N.E. TOUQUET schent; no patrol let off fire.	
		12.50pm	main Camp B/53 forts B/53 69R front Garage trench C.10.b.9.2 to C.11.c.4.9. (46 rounds) to C.10.b.9.2 to C.11.c.4.9. (Sheet 36)	
		5.35pm	A/50 shelled monastery (V.24.c.7.7).	
	10.		C.O. and O.C. B/50 and S of PLOEGSTEERT village.	
	11.	2.30pm	D/50 shelled R.E. dump at V.22.c.T.8. B/53 retaliated for shelling of PLOEGSTEERT - used on V.Z.1.P.	
	12.		The enemy's artillery was fairly quiet today but we fired about 150 rounds. Divine Service was held at Bae H.Q. at 7.30 a.m. and 6.30 p.m. The Colonel and CRA visited B/50's new position.	[14] AUSTRALIAN (Ayt)
	13.		B/53 and D/50 in conjunction shelled a dump at V.22.c.8.7. with good effect. The vicinity of MOUNTAIN GUN FARM (B/50's O.P.) was shelled today. The enemy's artillery generally has rather active. 93 rounds recorded. 2 Lt G.M. BONNIN from B/50, joined Bde H.Q. as Orderly Officer and Brigade Signal Officer.	Reinforced to 30 Bar Lt G. BYAN (Ayt) Lt G.A. BONNIN (B/50) orderly officer
	14		A beautiful spring day - atmosphere very clear and in consequence	

WAR DIARY
or
INTELLIGENCE SUMMARY

Army Form C. 2118.

Place	Date	Hour	Summary of Events and Information	Remarks and references to Appendices
	14		There was considerable aerial activity. A novel type of German aeroplane was seen today. It appeared to have two fuselages, or a sort of car below the upper fuselage. She was markedly short and thick. The enemy fired about 55 rounds today - chiefly on working parties and registering. Lieut BLIGH, Adjutant, left the Brigade today - posted to the 38th (Welsh) Division. The Colonel visited the 27th Infantry Bde. & D/50 trench lines & the Orderly office tested the Brigade telephone lines.	
	15		Enemy artillery fairly active today - 50-60 rounds. Rounds fell near A/50 but beyond breaking a window aid no more damage. The battery (A/50) retaliated with 28 rounds and B/53 put 5 rounds into DEULEMONT. We first attempted 69 rounds today. The weather has been fine and much warmer but misty early. A German aeroplane was seen today with the figure "5", on the underside of each wing just the cross - a new marking.	

Army Form C. 2118.

WAR DIARY
or
INTELLIGENCE SUMMARY.
(Erase heading not required.)

Instructions regarding War Diaries and Intelligence Summaries are contained in F. S. Regs., Part II. and the Staff Manual respectively. Title pages will be prepared in manuscript.

Place	Date	Hour	Summary of Events and Information	Remarks and references to Appendices
	16.		Fine and warm. Enemy fairly active today. 241 rounds were recorded but a number of "blinds". We fired 208 rounds, chiefly in retaliation. Aeroplanes on both sides were very busy all morning.	
	17		Not so much artillery activity today. Conference of Brigade Commanders with C.R.A. at 53rd Bde H.Q. The Enemy put two 5.9" into B/50's new position which however had only just begun to make.	
	18		62 rounds from the Enemy today. We fired 165 rounds against suspected H.Qs, O.Ps, working parties & movement in his communication trenches. Considerable aerial activity on both sides.	
	19		Artillery action again today. Ammunition Expended for the last 3 weeks noon to day - 556 Shrapnel, 135 H.E.	

Army Form C. 2118.

WAR DIARY
or
INTELLIGENCE SUMMARY.
(Erase heading not required.)

Instructions regarding War Diaries and Intelligence Summaries are contained in F.S. Regs., Part II. and the Staff Manual respectively. Title pages will be prepared in manuscript.

Place	Date	Hour	Summary of Events and Information	Remarks and references to Appendices
	20		Sears has opened again today. 1 hrs before midday. A good deal of shelling on both sides at the usual targets.	
	21		PLOEGSTEERT was heavily shelled today. We retaliated but otherwise did not fire much. D/50's F.O.O. observed a man & pulling with a small mirror, in what seemed his P: Gradeen has able to read it — he seemed keen in Code.	
	22		The Enemy shelled PLOEGSTEERT very heavily again today. We had a visit from Lt. Colonel LEWIS, R.F.C. to discuss Co-operation of Artillery and Aeroplanes. The Division ammunition has altered today to half Shrapnel and half H.E. A quiet day.	
	23		The Colonel visited B.A.C. in the morning to inspect turnouts.	

Army Form C. 2118.

WAR DIARY
or
INTELLIGENCE SUMMARY.
(Erase heading not required.)

Instructions regarding War Diaries and Intelligence Summaries are contained in F. S. Regs., Part II. and the Staff Manual respectively. Title pages will be prepared in manuscript.

Place	Date	Hour	Summary of Events and Information	Remarks and references to Appendices
	24		A heavy fall of snow during last night but a thaw soon set in. A few rounds were fired by the Enemy into PLOEGSTEERT again. The Colonel went into ARMENTIERES in the morning to see O.C. 79th Bde. and round batteries in the afternoon. As a first round of morning & newwork was reported by F.O.O's during the day at LOOPHOLE FARM, 9.50 first found N.E. at it at about 5pm.	
	25		A fine morning. One of our "Morane" aeroplanes came down between PLOEGSTEERT and ROMARIN. 96 Enemy rounds were fired today. Its first 121 in retaliation and for effect on various targets.	
	26		At 2am a minor operation was carried out by the 10th Argyll & Sutherland Highlanders - a raid on the Enemy's trenches. The Artillery (52nd Bde Howitzers) cooperated by putting up a barrage	

WAR DIARY or INTELLIGENCE SUMMARY

Army Form C. 2118.

Date	Hour	Summary of Events and Information	Remarks and references to Appendices
		from 2 am till 2.17 am. A/50 fired 209 Shrapnel and H.E. and C/50 fired 155 rounds, while B/53 fired 102 rounds at a building at U.22.a.2½.3. The barrages were from U.22.a.3½ – 1.3½ and from U.22.a.1.3 to O.4. Retaliation was not heavy and everything was quiet by 2.45 am. The remainder of the day was uneventful – 37 rounds from the Enemy, a few of which were very near to B/53. Ammunition Expended during went ended noon today 566 Shrapnel 433 H.E. Total 999.	
27		A violent bombardment was heard on our left at 4.30 am. The 52nd Bde informed us that they had heard from the Canadians (on our left) that it was taking place on their next Sector but one. It was over by 8.30 am. B/53 moved their rear section further forward today to U.30.d.3.3.	
28		A quiet day. With a strong wind all day. The Colonel 45th	

Army Form C. 2118.

WAR DIARY
or
INTELLIGENCE SUMMARY.
(Erase heading not required.)

Place	Date	Hour	Summary of Events and Information	Remarks and references to Appendices
	29		round batteries in the morning and to R.A. H.Q. in the afternoon. Our fire about 150 rounds today but the enemy artillery was quiet - only 34 rounds recorded.	
	30		A clear day and considerable aerial activity. Observation balloons were also in evidence, 5 being noticed at one time in the afternoon from one O.P. The enemy fired 96 rounds and our 105 in retaliation and on working parties (with fuse 2(f. of) and other targets.	The units mentioned opposite belonging to AUSTRALIAN Field Artillery owing to 3rd & 4th Batteries of his Brigade - Major Durham Capt. Dixon Lt. Luxton Lt. Hon and some
	31		The Enemy were very active today. Some 400 rounds being recorded - hostily fired 139. Weather fine & clear.	

18pdr Ammunition Expended during the month
2494 Shrapnel
992 H.E.

M. Allwork
LT. COLONEL R.F.A.
COMMANDING 50th BRIGADE R.F.A.

9th Division.
Artillery.

50th Bde   ROYAL FIELD ARTILLERY.

A P R I L   1 9 1 6

50 RFA vol 7

CONFIDENTIAL IX

WAR DIARY

50TH BRIGADE R.F.A.

9TH (Scottish) DIVISION

APRIL · 1916.

Army Form C. 2118.

WAR DIARY
INTELLIGENCE SUMMARY
(Erase heading not required.)

Place	Date	Hour	Summary of Events and Information	Remarks and references to Appendices
NEAR PLOEGSTEERT Bⁿ HQ. B.11.d.3.7	APRIL 1916		Map References — A B & C. Sheet 36 } 1/40,000. T U & V. „ „ 28 }	
	1		The Enemy Shelled very heavily all morning near here HQ. 100 rounds all falling about the east of the Avenue, B.18.a central. Our heavies were busy on the suspected hostile battery at V.26.6±9 but fired 141 rounds today. Including an aeroplane shoot by B/50 at a battery position at U.30.d.5.3.	
	2		Conference of Brigade Commanders at Horse HQ at 10 a.m. The Enemy Shelled here and of the avenue again in the morning. Half of the 10th & 11th Australian batteries left in the morning to go to the 34th Divisional Artillery (on our right). Little exception of the Shelling of the Avenue referred to, the day was unusually quiet, from an artillery point of view, on both sides. The 18pdr Ammunition Expended during the week ended	

WAR DIARY
or
INTELLIGENCE SUMMARY.
(Erase heading not required.)

Army Form C. 2118.

Place	Date	Hour	Summary of Events and Information	Remarks and references to Appendices
	3		Noon today amounted to 369 Shrapnel & 291 H.E. The remainder of the 11th Australian Battery left today. The enemy shelled NIEPPE in the evening & put several between us and A.B and C's positions, cutting our telephone lines to all three batteries. This was the first time these communications had been cut by shell fire since they were put up. Similarly put up by the Brigade who took over line before the 111th (25th Division) whom we relieved. A few bits fell in OOSTHOVE FARM and round our billets but without doing any damage. We retaliated for this shelling by firing 2 salvos from every gun throughout the Division into DEULEMONT. Altogether, today the front line has been quite warm. Fired 143 rounds.	
	4		A quiet day, no event of interest occurred.	

WAR DIARY or INTELLIGENCE SUMMARY

Army Form C. 2118.

Place	Date	Hour	Summary of Events and Information	Remarks and references to Appendices
	5		The rest of the 10th Australian Battery left today. There were a fine upstanding lot, officers & men. B/50 had an aeroplane shoot at the same balloon they fired at on the 1st – U30d53. and scored an "O.K." to fire a good deal today at various targets including some transport in the late afternoon. This latter was very successful, the Forward Observing Officer (A Bratton) reporting that he had seen men take to fallops and a cyclist fell into the ditch.	
	6		A Clear day today and balloons prevented much shooting. We fired on some working parties, however, also transport again – 23 rounds – and B/53 (Howitzers) fired at the LES ECLUSES chimney by special order of the C.R.A. We expended 60 rounds from the Enemy.	

WAR DIARY
or
INTELLIGENCE SUMMARY.
(Erase heading not required.)

Army Form C. 2118.

Place	Date	Hour	Summary of Events and Information	Remarks and references to Appendices
	7		The Enemy fired 90 rounds today. The flashes of two batteries were spotted by F.O.O's. We fired 68 rounds. One of our targets was a half finished Concrete dug out in the Enemy's Support trenches which suffered severely. Transport was again successfully dealt with in the Evening. No working parties were observed today - which is unusual. B/50 moved one section in the Evening to D's old position at U.19.c.4.3.	
	8		B Battery moved the other section this evening to above position and after registering took over C's Zone - C Battery taking over B's. D Battery now has no zone of fire responsibility Except in Event of an S.O.S call when they Enfilade trenches opposite our trenches 113-116. A table showing the positions of our Batteries and their zones of fire is appended. We fired 140 rounds today, mostly by B and C Batteries registering their new zones.	Appendix I.

Army Form C. 2118.

WAR DIARY
or
INTELLIGENCE SUMMARY.
(Erase heading not required.)

Place	Date	Hour	Summary of Events and Information	Remarks and references to Appendices
	9		Shooting today was again chiefly confined to "Bank C". Continuing their registration. 2Lt H.M. PRICE (A/50) was hit in the head by a small piece of 4.1" shell while in the O.P. The wound was very slight and he returned to duty. The 18pdr ammunition expended for task Enemy hosni today was 343 Shrapnel & 316 H.E.	
	10		An aeroplane shoot was attempted both morning and afternoon but it was too cloudy to observe in the morning and in the afternoon a balloon stopped us firing. Lot fired 67 rounds howitzers on various targets and the enemy's artillery was active — 167 rounds. A good many shells fell in the vicinity of D's position but without doing any damage.	
	11		A quiet day. Orders received today that for the present	

Army Form C. 2118.

WAR DIARY
or
INTELLIGENCE SUMMARY.
(Erase heading not required.)

Place	Date	Hour	Summary of Events and Information	Remarks and references to Appendices
			No ammunition whatever is to be expended for the "maintenance of the line" - The Enemy fired 46 rounds round LONDON FARM (C3.a.5.6) and CALVAIRE (C2.d.4 C3.C.)	
	12		It rained most of today. In accordance with orders we fired nothing today and only 12 rounds from the Enemy were recorded in our Particular Sector. Leave was stopped today.	
	13		A quiet day. Nothing of interest to record.	
	14		Very heavy Enemy Shelling today but no answerable to reply. D/50 registered their forward Gun (C3C.5.5) with 15 rounds	
	15		The Enemy Shelled very heavily again today. They seem to be taking advantage of their immunity from retaliation	

Army Form C. 2118.

WAR DIARY
or
INTELLIGENCE SUMMARY.
(Erase heading not required.)

Place	Date	Hour	Summary of Events and Information	Remarks and references to Appendices
	16		not only to do a Considerable amount of firing but also to keep about forty of the O.O's kept an exceptional amount of movement at all hours of the day. Lt. G.C. McEWAN (C Battery) left for England today on receiving his Commission in order to continue his Medical training. This officer has been in C Battery since 15/9/14	
			The tall Chimney at LES ECLUSES (U30 d 3.3.) was knocked down by the 12" Howitzers with their third round at 12.15 p.m. The Enemy's artillery was not so active today. Ammunition (18Pdr.) expended during the week ended noon today was 105 Shrapnel & 12 H.E.	
	17		A quiet uneventful day.	
	18		General Lawrie visited Centre Group battery positions with the	

WAR DIARY
or
INTELLIGENCE SUMMARY.
(Erase heading not required.)

Army Form C. 2118.

Place	Date	Hour	Summary of Events and Information	Remarks and references to Appendices
			Colonel into morning. Captain ROWDEN and 2Lt. DONNE of the 2/1st and 2/2nd South Midland Brigades R.F.A. (T.F.) arrived to be attached to A and B batteries respectively. The Enemy's artillery was quiet today and 1st did no shooting. Captain SNELLING (O.C. Ho Column) left for BERTHEN today for a Course in Heavy Trench Mortars.	
	20		The Enemy was fairly active today in our sector. It fired 4 rounds today on some trench holdings at U29 a 6.8. which appeared to have successful results.	
	22		The German artillery was fairly active in white morning, specially in the neighbourhood of LE GHEER and AU GHEER - U21.d. and U27.d.— The restriction on Expenditure of ammunition was removed today. No actual allotment is fixed but a limit of Ground per Gun (18 pdr.) per day Considered sufficient to meet normal requirements.	

WAR DIARY
or
INTELLIGENCE SUMMARY.
(Erase heading not required.)

Army Form C. 2118.

Instructions regarding War Diaries and Intelligence Summaries are contained in F. S. Regs., Part II. and the Staff Manual respectively. Title pages will be prepared in manuscript.

Place	Date	Hour	Summary of Events and Information	Remarks and references to Appendices
	23		it has could be Expended to much his batts. 1st fired 65 rounds today at various targets including a Suspected M.G. Loophole at U.22.c.3.3. Enemy artillery was active again today. Ammunition (18 pr) Expended during the day ended noon today – 17 Shrapnel, 2 H.E. = 19 rounds.	Lt W. L. E. Brown c/s.o. Sick to hospital with jaundice.
	24		There was considerable activity in the air today and at 7.30 am a German Aeroplane was brought down by a direct hit from one of our Anti-aircraft guns. It landed at T.30.c.1.4. & both pilot & observer was killed. It fired a little today chiefly in retaliation. The Enemy again did a good deal of shelling round AUGHEER. U.27.b.8.8.	
	25		A Considerable amount of artillery activity on both sides. LE GHEER and AUGHEER again getting the lions share of the Shelling. Several	

WAR DIARY
or
INTELLIGENCE SUMMARY.

Army Form C. 2118.

Place	Date	Hour	Summary of Events and Information	Remarks and references to Appendices
	26		Aircraft like was obtained to look those O.P's though not sufficient. Enough was done to show to make them untenable. The O.C. 9th Divisional Trench Mortars wished us in the afternoon to arrange a joint shoot on the FORT, a strong point in the Enemy's front line at U.28.a.4.6. The day was quiet and uneventful till about 6 p.m. when a heavy bombardment of our trenches South of the ZYS began. This was kept up for about an hour and a half & then died down but began again an hour or so later with artillery and trench mortars. The Enemy then attacked trench 88 (C.17.c) but only about 20 men succeeded in getting a footing out of a small party of 50 who left the Enemy trenches. These 20 left in a hurry leaving behind them a number of rifle bombs & cartridges. D/50 was the only battery of our group to take a part. The Section Enfiladed the 17th Division trenches (on our right) first	

WAR DIARY
or
INTELLIGENCE SUMMARY.

Place	Date	Hour	Summary of Events and Information	Remarks and references to Appendices
			208 rounds. Our Casualties (as heard) amounted to about 40 and Trenches 88 and 89 were practically obliterated.	
	27		At 1 am this morning there was a gas alarm which afterwards proved to be false. It was stated that the Enemy started the alarm themselves, possibly with the idea of finding out where our barrage would be. One Coy of our Batteries fired (B/50) Coy fot a "GAS BAGS" message from them infantry and fired 33 rounds. All was quiet again by 2 am. Information however was received during the day that, according to histories of two deserters a gas attack was contemplated on a front of 20 Kilometres - including the YPRES Salient and the MESSINES and WYTSCHAETE ridges. The Enemy fired a fire deal today. C2C and C2d were shelled and the CONVENT at U.28.a.22 and the Xr. Nr: Ploerenhoek had 150 rounds of 10.5 cm. Lt fired 100 rounds mainly to forking. The night was quiet	

WAR DIARY
or
INTELLIGENCE SUMMARY.
(Erase heading not required.)

Army Form C. 2118.

Place	Date	Hour	Summary of Events and Information	Remarks and references to Appendices
	28		A minor operation was carried out at 12.30pm in conjunction with Trench Mortars on the FORT in KITCHENER's front line at U 28 a 4.6. Front and support trenches were swept by our 18pdrs as follows:- A/50 .. U 22 c 5.1 to U 28 a 6.5. B/50 .. U 22 c 3.5 .. U 22 c 5.1. C/50 .. U 22 a 6.5 .. U 28 c 8.8. D/50 .. U 22 c 3.7 .. U 22 c 3.10. A/50 also fired 10 rounds on LOOPHOLE FARM. D/179 fired 30 rounds on LOOPHOLE FARM. B/53 fired 10 rounds each on HOSPICE & PETITE HAIE Fms. The Right Group fired on Fme DURIEZ and LONG BARN. The Left -- -- -- -- OBSERVATION HOUSE & SUGAR REFINERY. The operation was successful. Considerable damage being done to the FORT and neighbouring parapet. Retaliation was feeble, & casualties very few. 18pdrs fired 245 + Hows. 54 rounds.	

WAR DIARY
or
INTELLIGENCE SUMMARY.
(Erase heading not required.)

Army Form C. 2118.

Place	Date	Hour	Summary of Events and Information	Remarks and references to Appendices
	29		The day was uneventful but not so the night. At 10.40 p.m we fired a burst of 48 rounds from A B & C batteries on the point U 28 A 4.6 reported to up-to-day. The 6th Royal Irish Fusiliers gave no information. Observer kept patrols reported work going on there & at first the River batteries by water from Bde. H.Q. at the same instant. The Enemy retaliated pretty heavily but replied with a few same shells which silenced them for a while. Just before midnight howitzer were warned by telephone from R.A. H.Q. that the Enemy were expected to attack further North at about N 30 (Sheet 28) with gas. The alarm was heard at 12.45 a.m & the Enemy then began to shell our Group front heavily. The R.I.M and left Groups were not called upon at all but at fired, between 12.45 and 2.30 a.m. 503 Shrapnel 1860s & 150 4.5"How. The Howitzers were also busy. Our Cavalries were slept and by 3 a.m all was Quiet. The rest of the day was normal but in the evening	
	30			

WAR DIARY
or
INTELLIGENCE SUMMARY.
(Erase heading not required.)

Army Form C. 2118.

was again fired a burst (15 rounds) on U.28.a.4.6. which favoured retaliation which at last eventually silenced with a couple more salvos from each battery. Another fire attack was supposed to have taken place further back but this was afterwards contradicted. All was quiet on our front by midnight.

Ammunition (1850) Expended during the month:-
1481 Shrapnel
9. 6 H.E.
2407

Casualties:-
9th 247 H.M. PRICE (A Battery) Sl. ght wound in the head from H.E. Shell - Returned to duty.
30th 247 H. St J. BECHER (C Battery) Bullet in upper right arm - To hospital.

J.W.Burke
LT. COLONEL. R.F.A.
COMMANDING 50th BRIGADE. R.F.A.

WAR DIARY
or
INTELLIGENCE SUMMARY.
(Erase heading not required.)

Army Form C. 2118.

Place	Date	Hour	Summary of Events and Information	Remarks and references to Appendices
			Appendix I.	
			Showing Positions and Zones of Fire of C/50 Group Batteries	
			A/50. C.1.a.1.8. Trenches 109-112. U.28.a.6.4 to U.22.c.3.4.	
			B/50. U.19.c.1½.3. " 113-120. U.22.c.3½.3. to U.21.6.8.4.	
			C/50. B.6.6.2.6. " 103-108. U.28.c.7.3 to U.28.a.6.5.	
			D/50. 1 gun at C.3.c.5.5. " 113-116. U.22.c.3.3 to U.22.a.3½.0.	
			" " C.2.d.2.0. } This Section Enfilades trenches to S. on 17th Divn front.	
			" " C.2.d.3.6. }	
			" " has a roving Commission.	
			B/53 (How) One Section U.26.6.8.6 } Zone:- U.28.c.6.5 to U.21.6.9.8.	
			" " U.20.d.3.7 }	

9th Division
Artillery

50th Bde ROYAL FIELD ARTILLERY

MAY 1916

CONFIDENTIAL IX

WAR DIARY

50TH BRIGADE R.F.A.
9TH (Scottish) DIVISION

MAY 1916

WAR DIARY

(Erase heading not required.)

Army Form C. 2118.

Place	Date	Hour	Summary of Events and Information	Remarks and references to Appendices
PLOEGSTEERT Bde HQ B.11.a.3.7.	MAY 1916		Map Reference - A B or C Sheet 36 1/40,000 T U or V - 28	
	1		Quiet uneventful. Gunner ROO (A Battery) slightly wounded in the leg by a chance shell.	
	2		Normal Shelling of CONVENT and AUGHER and in the evening LE GHEER. G.O.C and C.R.A visited A & B Batteries today.	
	3		We fired about 135 rounds today at various targets.	
	4		Enemy's artillery active today but nothing out of the way occurred.	
	6		A quiet day - little artillery activity.	

WAR DIARY or INTELLIGENCE SUMMARY

Army Form C. 2118.

Place	Date	Hour	Summary of Events and Information	Remarks and references to Appendices
	7		Orders received that one detachment per battery from the 187th Bde 41st Division are to come up tomorrow to be attached to batteries. O.C. 187th Bde (Lt. Col A.E.M. HEAD) and Orderly Officer arrived and visited A, B & C Batteries with the Colonel. Ammunition Expended during the week – 286 Shrapnel, 171 H.E. = 457 rounds.	
	8		Shelling of LEGHEER and 25% of PLOEGSTEERT wood at intervals during the day. Shrunno Pruit Prevented. New detachments and Battery Commanders came up. Instructions re move received.	
	9.10.11		Found nothing noteworthy.	
	12		Artillery active on both sides. LEGHEER & PLOEGSTEERT WOOD Shelled.	
	13		Instructions re move to CAESTRE area cancelled at 6.30pm. 113–130 Enemy bombarded our trenches very heavily and at 8.30 a	

WAR DIARY
or
INTELLIGENCE SUMMARY.
(Erase heading not required.)

Army Form C. 2118.

Place	Date	Hour	Summary of Events and Information	Remarks and references to Appendices
	15		Party of about 60 attempted a raid on "HAMPSHIRE T." Only 15 reached our parapet and they were all killed. 2/Lt Montgomery (Hay) 11 Rifles 1st Rd fired 1100 rounds. The 11th Royal Scots held the trenches raided. Most prisoners taken by (?) Enemy casualties killed 30 wounded 50. Our Casualties 1 Officer wounded	
	18		D/183 (How) Battery came up and occupied B/53's old position at T30 Central.	
			DEULEMENT CHIMNEY was brought down by B/53 at the 29th round. The base was hit at the 21st, the 26th hit the middle & gave it a cant whilst rapid fire through hit the base again bringing it down.	
	20		PLOEGSTEERT village was heavily shelled in the morning. Retired two or three lots of "front Retaliation" in reply. Artillery on both sides was generally speaking active.	

WAR DIARY
or
INTELLIGENCE SUMMARY.
(Erase heading not required.)

Army Form C. 2118.

Place	Date	Hour	Summary of Events and Information	Remarks and references to Appendices
	21		B Battery heavily shelled from 8-10 am by about 80 rounds. One gun hit and three men killed - Serjeant HADLEY, Bombardier SCRIVENER and Gunner RAMSHAW.	
	24		CALVAIRE and neighbourhood of LONDON SUPPORT Farm heavily shelled in the morning. An Officer of his 187th Bde attached to D battery was wounded.	
	25		O.C. 187th Bde arrived.	
	26		One section of re-enforcing batts. so came up and a section of each of our batts. so marched to CAESTRE area.	
	27		The remainder of the Brigade marched to CAESTRE, his Brigade finally handing over to 187th at noon.	

Army Form C. 2118.

WAR DIARY
or
INTELLIGENCE SUMMARY.
(Erase heading not required.)

Place	Date	Hour	Summary of Events and Information	Remarks and references to Appendices
	28		At CAESTRE. B/53 came under the Colonel's command. D Battery found to this 53rd Bgde.	
	29		B/53 became D/50, and D/50 became A/53.	
	30		The M.G. R.A. 2nd Army inspected some of the batteries of the 9th Divl Artillery. B, C and D of this brigade were visited.	
	31		Conference of Brigade Commanders with C.R.A. to discuss programme of training at THEROUANNE area, where we march tomorrow. Ammunition for the month 1051 Shrapnel, 982 H.E.	

R. P. Newbolt
LT. COLONEL R.F.A.
COMMANDING 50th BRIGADE R.F.A.

9th Division.
Artillery.

50th Bde ROYAL FIELD ARTILLERY.

JUNE 1916.

Army Form C. 2118.

WAR DIARY
or
INTELLIGENCE SUMMARY
(Erase heading not required.)

Place	Date	Hour	Summary of Events and Information	Remarks and references to Appendices
THEROUANNE	June 1916			
	1		The Brigade marched from the CAESTRE to the THEROUANNE area for training. Bde H.Q. marched at 5.30 am followed by B Battery at 5 minutes interval and then C D and A in that order at 15 minutes interval. Route HAZEBROUCK – EBBLINGHAM – QUIESTEDE – THEROUANNE. Arrived 11.45 to 12.30. Billets found. Conference of B.Cs at 6.30 pm to settle training programme.	
	2		O.C. and Adjutant reconnoitred training area. A quiet day.	
	3		Training began. Weather fine.	
	4		Conference of Brigade Commanders at 4.30 pm and B.C. at 7pm.	
	5th to 12th		Training continued. included a Brigade Scheme in conjunction with the 27th Inf.f Bde. The Colonel judged hunsour for the Division	

Army Form C. 2118.

WAR DIARY
or
INTELLIGENCE SUMMARY.
(Erase heading not required.)

Instructions regarding War Diaries and Intelligence Summaries are contained in F. S. Regs., Part II. and the Staff Manual respectively. Title pages will be prepared in manuscript.

Place	Date	Hour	Summary of Events and Information	Remarks and references to Appendices
	11		Horse show to take place on the 13th.	
	12		Orders received at midnight to march to LILLERS to entrain. Horse show and Divisional Scheme arranged for 13th cancelled.	
	13		At 3 a.m. detailed orders and march table received. Brigade Staff and A & B Batteries entrained & left for LONGUEAU. S. of AMIENS (Ref map 1/100,000 AMIENS.17) at 12.40 p.m. C and D and HQ rest of B Battery followed by later train. On arrival at LONGUEAU detrained & marched to CORBIE. Headquarters XIII Corps. Fourth Army.	
	14		Units camped at CORBIE on the CORBIE - VAUX SUR SOMME road. The Brigade marched at 9pm for the BOIS DES TAILLES (sheet 62D 1/40,000 Square K) where it arrived at 11pm & bivouacked at about K.23.b.3.8.	

WAR DIARY
or
INTELLIGENCE SUMMARY.

Army Form C. 2118.

Place	Date	Hour	Summary of Events and Information	Remarks and references to Appendices
	15		Batteries were split up among different groups of the 18th Divisional Artillery for the forthcoming offensive against the Germans. The 50th & 51st Brigades being attached to the 18th Division and the 52nd & 53rd to the 30th Division.	
			A/50 to R. Fd. Group (84th Bde - Lt. Col. BROIS)	
			B/50 " Centre " (83rd " SEGRAM)	
			C/50 " Left " (82nd " THORP)	
			D/50 " XIII Corps Heavy Artillery - his 29th H.A.G. for Counter Battery work.	
			H.Q. 50th Bde attached to 84th Bde H.Q. - with the Exception of the Colonel, the Brigade Staff remained at the BOIS de TAILLES till August accommodation could be made at 84th Bde HQ.	
			Battery positions were as under.	
			A. A 20 d 7 8. (Sheet 62 c 1/40,000)	
			B. F 23 d 2 5 (" 62 D ")	
			C. F 22 a 9 5 (" " ")	
			D. F 30 a 9 2 (" " ")	

Army Form C. 2118.

WAR DIARY
or
INTELLIGENCE SUMMARY.
(Erase heading not required.)

Instructions regarding War Diaries and Intelligence Summaries are contained in F.S. Regs., Part II. and the Staff Manual respectively. Title pages will be prepared in manuscript.

Place	Date	Hour	Summary of Events and Information	Remarks and references to Appendices
	16		84th Bde H.Q. at A.25.d.6.5. (Sheet 62c.1/40,000) Batteries commenced work on their positions and the transport of ammunition to the gun positions (600 rounds per battery) was begun.	
	17/20		The Colonel went to 84th Bde H.Q. Batteries busy making their positions & transporting ammunition.	
	21		Orders received to take over positions to be occupied by this Brigade if a move forward is made. Anyone Bde H.Q. A.15.c.2.7. (OXFORD COPSE) (Sheet 62c.) A Battery A.20.a.27.8. (alongside) " B " A.15.c.2.8 " C " A.14.b.4.4 " D " to remain with 29th H.A.G. Or forward position to be at A.9.c.1.5. but to communicate on their present out on communication.	

T2134. Wt. W708-75. 500000. 4/16. Sir J.C. & S.

WAR DIARY
or
INTELLIGENCE SUMMARY.
(Erase heading not required.)

Place	Date	Hour	Summary of Events and Information	Remarks and references to Appendices
	22		80 men of the 2nd South African Regiment were attached to the Brigade to help dig Communications.	
	24		The first day of bombardment. — As the Brigade "our" Brigade, had not been bombarded, Wales intended to attack the position. Proved very difficult to attack. Every battery known, attacked as previously	
	25		"	
	26		"	decided to the hops of the 18 Division did fire.
	27		"	And I was ordered some [illegible] to attack it.
	28		"	The assaulting Infantry on the day of the attack. A/So was Subsequently greatly referred to by O.C. R.E.1 Pers. in this Connection.
	29		The attack was to have taken place to-day at 7.30 a.m. but was postponed for 48 hours. The walks were wet and ground very slippery. Bombardment and wire cutting was further continued.	
	30		Bombardment and wire cutting continued. Communication now established from the Brigade H.Q. at OXFORD COPSE to A, B & C's probable new positions and also to a forward dug-out to the	

WAR DIARY
or
INTELLIGENCE SUMMARY.

(Erase heading not required.)

Army Form C. 2118.

Place	Date	Hour	Summary of Events and Information	Remarks and references to Appendices
Trenches at about A9a4.3 (Sheet 6.S.c)			Appendix	

Honours & Awards.

Lt. W. SWORDER, R.F.A. "B" Battery, was awarded the Military Cross for his work as forward observing officer during the raid on the trenches in front of PLOEGSTEERT WOOD last month.

Bombardier G.W. SMITH, "B" Battery, was awarded the Military Medal for Excellent work as lineman on the 19th December last during the gas attack in the YPRES Salient.

Casualties (wounded in action)
A. Battery. NIL

Army. Form C. 2118.

WAR DIARY
or
INTELLIGENCE SUMMARY.
(Erase heading not required.)

Place	Date	Hour	Summary of Events and Information	Remarks and references to Appendices
			B Battery. No. 85227 Gunner Colley L.A. Died of wounds	
			96547. " Scallion D. Wounded	
			95801. " Turnbull J. "	
			95191. " Stapple J.S. "	
			C. Battery Nil	
			D Battery. No. 96015. Bomb.r Hexshall O. Killed	
			41807. Gunner Ryan J. Wounded	
			94643. " Sutton G.J. "	
			95890. " Creek A.G. "	
			91318. " De la Rue "	
			95906. Driver Gascoigne S. "	
			94489. B.Q.M.S. Gibbs R.S. "	
			66368 Bomb.r Loch W. "	
			94658. " Alliston H. "	
			57128. Gunner Wilson A. "	

John F. Burke
Lt. Col. R.G.A.
Commanding 50th Bde R.G.A.

9th Div.
XIII.Corps.

Division transferred
to IV.Corps, First
Army, 25.7.16.

WAR DIARY

Headquarters,

50th BRIGADE, R.F.A.

J U L Y

1 9 1 6

EK 121

Brigade Major
9th Divl Artillery.

Herewith Original WAR DIARY
of the 50th Brigade RFA.
for July.

G B Scaill
for LT. COLONEL R.F.A.
COMMANDING 50th BRIGADE R.F.A.

3/8/16.

Confidential 4th July

S O R F A
Vol 10

War Diary
50th Brigade R.F.A.
9th Scottish Division
July 1916

WAR DIARY or INTELLIGENCE SUMMARY

Place	Date	Hour	Summary of Events and Information	Remarks and references to Appendices
MAI MONTAUBAN Ref. Sheet MONTAUBAN 1/20,000	July 1		The attack on the front of the 18th & 30th Divisions was launched at 7.30 a.m. The 7th Division was on the left of the 18th & the 30th to the Right of the 18th. It was a misty morning and observation was difficult until about 8.30 a.m. The front fifteen Septems of trenches were gained with apparent ease though the 18th were checked at the Craters (A8a&c) and again later on at the LOOP (A2c). The enemy were eventually dislodged from the latter by Stokes mmr & about 300 of them took prisoner. The line was successfully cut all along the line. MONTAUBAN was entered at about 10.15 a.m. and the line held in the evening on the result of the days operations was approximately that the 18th & 30th Divisions had gained their objectives but the 7th on the left had not progressed so quickly.	
	2		Counter attacks by the enemy in bivouacing on MONTAUBAN and the BRIQUETERIE were repulsed. Telephone line established from our forward defenses in front line to Bde.	

WAR DIARY
or
INTELLIGENCE SUMMARY.

Army Form C. 2118.

Place	Date	Hour	Summary of Events and Information	Remarks and references to Appendices
	3		K.T.K. Corner of MONTAUBAN. The latter place was shelled during the day but not heavily.	
	4		Quiet on our front. Brigade H.Q. moved up to OXFORD COPSE (A15 c 3.7) Positions previously chosen for batteries to move forward to were not all occupied, but positions were chosen for six 18 pdr batteries in Ad. D/50. Still under Capt. Heavy Artillery, moved to a position near the TRONES BOIS.	
	6/7		Batteries moved forward during the night of the 6/7th and came under the brigade again for both batteries and administration on the 7th.	
	8		Mr RITCHIE (B/50) was wounded in the back, also Lt IRELAND (D/50) Infantry parties deploying at morning. One cutting forward	
	9		Very heavy shelling all morning. One cutting forward satisfactory during the day. However enemy's shellfire rendered shooting possible. Lt JACOBSON wounded in the foot	

WAR DIARY
or
INTELLIGENCE SUMMARY.
(Erase heading not required.)

Army Form C. 2118.

Place	Date	Hour	Summary of Events and Information	Remarks and references to Appendices
	10		and one other rank killed. D/50 moved back to A3c 6.3. During the afternoon. A, B & C batteries were heavily shelled again today & during the evening moved back to positions about as under. A. A3d 15.60. B. A3d 70.45. C. A3d 35.35.	
	11		D remaining at A3c 6.3. Wirecutting much interfered with today owing to enemy's shellfire, and his true difficulty of preventing any sort of communication intact. Orders received that XIII Corps. with the XV Corps on the left and the French on the right would attack the French system of trenches after ten orbit 73. preliminary bombardment to commence today - on Brigade 1858n to continue wirecutting, D battery to keep communication	

WAR DIARY or INTELLIGENCE SUMMARY

Place	Date	Hour	Summary of Events and Information	Remarks and references to Appendices
	12		Trenches under fire. Satisfactory progress with the wire cutting but communication continually cut. Causing difficulty and delay. Conference of Brigade Commanders with C.R.A. Tomorrow's attack seems likely to be postponed. Wire cutting proceeded with. Battn. put some 4.5 shell into it to make heavy wire stakes.	
	13		The whole plan of attack was altered today and orders were received that the 9th Division would attack on the front LONGUEVAL to WATERLOT FARM. Battn. is cut own on part of this zone today in conjunction with the 40th Brigade. Operation Orders were issued in the afternoon and the zero time was 3.25 a.m. on the 14th. Colonel and Orderly Officer went up to MONTAUBAN to Battle HQrs. of the 27th Infantry Brigade.	

WAR DIARY
or
INTELLIGENCE SUMMARY.

(Erase heading not required.)

Army Form C. 2118.

Place	Date	Hour	Summary of Events and Information	Remarks and references to Appendices
	14		At 3.05 am the Infantry Advanced. Fighting continued all day & by the evening LONGUEVAL, the whole of TRONES WOOD and, on our left, the village of BAZENTON le PETIT were in our hands. Two counter attacks made by the Enemy during the day were successfully repulsed. British Cavalry came up during the morning & bivouaced near our Battery Position.	
	15		Batteries firing continuously all day. The Colonel returned late at night from Infantry Bde HQr. in MONTAUBAN.	
	16 to 18		Our Batteries were barraging practically continuously, during these three days, in points round the Southern portion of LONGUEVAL & DELVILLE WOOD. The Enemy Shell kept pressing on the Northern parts of these places. During the night of the 18th/19th orders were received for the attack on LONGUEVAL and DELVILLE WOOD from the road by the 3rd Division.	
	19		At 3.35 am to day this attack took place. Our Batteries	

WAR DIARY
or
INTELLIGENCE SUMMARY.

Army Form C. 2118.

Place	Date	Hour	Summary of Events and Information	Remarks and references to Appendices
	20.		Supporting with Lewis gun fire. The Colonel was with the 76th Infantry Brigade HQ. The morning was fairly quiet but after 11am firing became more continuous again - towards GUINCHY, reports full of German were searched to also the battalion HQ of DELVILLE WOOD. Communication very poor today from 76th Infantry Brigade HQ. Right line were relaid from S.12.c.0.2. to d.0.y. when line were kept under fire throughout the night by one battery at a time firing bursts of fire at irregular intervals. The night was quieter than usual.	
	21.		Today was much quieter - firing was continued by our batteries at a time as during last night. Battalion was unable to do some reported communication being much better. A counter attack on LONGUEVAL at 10.30 p.m. was easily repulsed.	

WAR DIARY
or
INTELLIGENCE SUMMARY.
(Erase heading not required.)

Army Form C. 2118.

Place	Date	Hour	Summary of Events and Information	Remarks and references to Appendices
	27		At 2 am today the trenches between the railway at S2 & S.9 and WATER LOT FARM were attacked by the 3rd Division from the N.W. It supported with 18 pdr barrage, fire and D Battery bombarded houses in GUINCHY. It was fired from 1.55 am till 3.15 am on three barrages.	
	28		The Northern part of LONGUEVAL and DELVILLE WOOD were again attacked today by the 3rd Division in conjunction with the 5th operating on its left. An attack from GUILLEMONT Simultaneously on GUILLEMONT station by the 3rd Division in Conjunction with an attack by the 30th Division on GUILLEMONT. We took no part in the latter attack.	
	29		Orders rec'd that the 2nd Division will relieve the 9th on 26th & 27th. A Section per Battery at a time. B-Battery had a Boche hit on a gun today.	

Date	Hour	Summary of Events and Information
26		One section fire battery of the 36th Bde 2nd Division relieved a section of such B/XXX battery so arrived this morning and repitched. Orders received today for another attack on LONGUEVAL and DELVILLE WOOD by 2nd & 5th Divisions.
	18p.m.	Enemy broke into and made heavy and very fierce fire salvos on one battery at a time on their SOS line beginning at
	11 p.m.	D Battery was firing all day on new trenches in the vicinity of GUILLEMONT.
27		The attack on LONGUEVAL & DELVILLE WOOD took place this morning batteries opening fire at 6.10 a.m., our final barrage remaining north of this wood which was taken & held by our infantry, as also the northern part of the village. Our remaining section of the 36th Brigade relieved during the afternoon a Lt. Col NEWCOMB with his Brigade staff arrived. Our Brigade staff, with the exception of the Colonel Adjutant & 4 telephonists, moved down to bivouacs lines

Army Form C. 2118.

WAR DIARY
or
INTELLIGENCE SUMMARY.
(Erase heading not required.)

Place	Date	Hour	Summary of Events and Information	Remarks and references to Appendices
	28		The Enemy made an unsuccessful counter attack in the evening about 10 p.m. Battn. fired Salvos during the night on S.O.S. line. 1st hauled out at 9 am & the 36th Brigade and marched to VAUX Sur SOMME, Battn. 20 starting at 10 am from their bivouac lines.	(AMIENS 1/100,000 map)
	29		Marched at 4 p.m. for ARGOEUVRES where we arrived about 9.45 p.m.	
	30		Left ARGOEUVRES at 9 am & marched to COCQUEREL which we reached at 3 p.m. A very hot day.	(ABBEVILLE 1/100,000 map)
	31		Battn. 20 left COCQUEREL to entrain for at PONT REMY for 1st Army Area - A at about 6 p.m. B " " 10 p.m. C " " 1 am (1st) D " " 4 am (1st) Bde H.Q. remained till 3 am on the 1st August.	

WAR DIARY or **INTELLIGENCE SUMMARY.**
(Erase heading not required.)

Army Form C. 2118.

Place	Date	Hour	Summary of Events and Information	Remarks and references to Appendices
			Casualties during the operations on the Somme.	
			Killed (or died of wounds) wounded	
			A. Officers — 1	1
			Other ranks — 14	15
			B. Officers — $4	$4 Officers
			Other ranks 5 21	26
			C. Officers — 1	1
			Other ranks 2 8	10
			D. Officers 1 1	2
			Other ranks 2 17	19
			TOTAL Officers 1 6	7 Officers
			Other ranks 10 60	70

Army Form C. 2118.

WAR DIARY
or
INTELLIGENCE SUMMARY.
(Erase heading not required.)

Instructions regarding War Diaries and Intelligence Summaries are contained in F.S. Regs., Part II. and the Staff Manual respectively. Title pages will be prepared in manuscript.

Place	Date	Hour	Summary of Events and Information	Remarks and references to Appendices
			Number of rounds fired:-	
			Shrapnel H.E.	
			A. 15,261 6,332 = 21,593	
			B. 11,959 4,883 = 16,842	
			C. 13,208 3,723 = 16,931 (18pdr)	
			40,428 14,938 55,366	
			✻D. 121 11,599 = 11,720 (4.5 How.)	
			✻ also fired 279 THERMITE	

J.W. Clarke
LT. COLONEL R.F.A.
COMMANDING 50th BRIGADE R.F.A.

9th Division
Artillery.

ROYAL
50th Bde/FIELD ARTILLERY

AUGUST 1916

EK 139.

2th Divl. Artillery.

Herewith original War Diary
of the 50th Brigade R.F.A.
for August 1916.

[signature]

1/9/16.

LT. COLONEL R.F.A.
COMMANDING 50th BRIGADE R.F.A.

Vol II
SOFIA

CONFIDENTIAL
WAR DIARY
OF THE
50TH BRIGADE. R.F.A.
9TH (Scottish) Division.
AUGUST - 1916.

WAR DIARY
or
INTELLIGENCE SUMMARY

Army Form C. 2118.

Place	Date	Hour	Summary of Events and Information	Remarks and references to Appendices
	AUGUST			
	1st		The Brigade Staff entrained at 4.40 a.m. at LONGPRÉ for BRYAS in the 1st Army Area (Sheet 36B 1/40,000) later HQ arrived via ABBEVILLE and ST POL at 12.15 p.m. and marched to billets at CALONNE RICOUART.	
	2/12		On arrival at CALONNE RICOUART. The IOM inspected lines on the 2nd and the D.D.V.S. inspected lines on the 7th. On the 10th orders were received to be prepared to relieve the 37th Division in the line on the nights 13/14, 14/15th. Orders B. March order were received.	Sheet 36B.
	13th		The Brigade moved at 7 a.m. HQ 6 Bois de la HAIE (SC7 a.1.1) A & D to Support line near CAUCOURT and B.C. to Support line near GAUCHIN LEGAL. The Section for taking relieved during the night.	
	14th		The remaining Section relieved this Evening, Batteries taking over from the corresponding batteries of the 124th Bde (37th Division) 8 Exchanging guns.	
	15th		Brigade & Battery Commanders took over at 6 a.m. Tactical are as follows	

Place	Date	Hour	Summary of Events and Information	Remarks and references to Appendices
			Bde HQ. X 7 d 1.1	Shed 36 B.
			A Battery X 22 b 0.9½	
			B " X 16 c 28.45	
			C " X 16 c 15.5	
			D " X 4 c 7.3	
	16		A little repairing & rectifying of initial lines &c was done. The situation was reported very quiet.	
	17		Situation unchanged. Aeroplane targets to be registered were arranged.	
	18	10 am	A quiet day. Conference of Brigade Commanders at DA HQ at which 100 men of the South African Infantry Brigade were allotted to the Brigade for work on communications. Trench ladders were taken extensive use made for use of us.	
	19		Retaliated: a little repeating was also done. No enemy activity – Registration.	
	20		The day was normal. In the evening information was received that	

Place	Date	Hour	Summary of Events and Information	Remarks and references to Appendices
	21		The Enemy was expected to blow a mine near KENNEDY CRATER (Sq.c.1.) and batteries were ordered to be alert. The shower did not come off. The 63rd Division on our left changed a cloud of gas at 11.15 p.m. accompanied by artillery bombardment. Airmen guided by moonlight. A Balloon reported two troops by aeroplane. Our Trench Mortars were active at 4.30 p.m. opposite IRISH CRATER (Sq.a.9.8½) hrs retaliated with 4 rounds for E.O.S.M. thrown into the barrage. Enemy again bombed at 8 p.m. and 12 feet over 6 rounds from mortars. D/50 fired a mason gun emplacement at Sq.a.5.4 obtaining a direct hit and two rounds into his trench near.	
	22		Very quiet all day. A little Trench Mortar activity in the Evening but no retaliation called for.	
	23		High altitude and battalion working on T.M.'s Shelled to Enemy line near IRISH & KENNEDY CRATERS. Retaliation feeble.	

WAR DIARY or INTELLIGENCE SUMMARY

Army Form C. 2118.

Place	Date	Hour	Summary of Events and Information	Remarks and references to Appendices
	24		Quiet day again. Hd fired nothing all day. The 60th Division on our right carried out a small "Enterprise" at 11pm with half an hour artillery bombardment.	
	25		The Enemy has now active today with his artillery - CARENCY, ABLAIN & SOUCHEZ all being shelled during the day. 6th K.4.2. A/50 repeated 3 targets by aeroplane In answer at 8.50pm the Right Battalion (6th K.O.S.B.) called for 40 rounds retaliation for T.M.'s. Battn's bay with work on alternate posts, rest of the night. Enemy fairly quiet.	
	26		Our Enemy fired 16 Y.Men. into CARENCY today at 2.45pm. We retaliated at 4pm & 6pm for T.M's and returned K.S front line between IRISH & KENNEDY Craters, back to alternate posts continued.	
	27		A quiet day. Hd repeated S15 a.22. and S9c.22. T.M.'s near action between 12 and 1pm. Observation was bad owing to heavy rain & mist.	

WAR DIARY or INTELLIGENCE SUMMARY

Army Form C. 2118.

Place	Date	Hour	Summary of Events and Information	Remarks and references to Appendices
	28		C. Battery cut wire today from S.15.c.2½.9. – S.15.a.1.2½ in conjunction with T.M's. The wire was successfully cut by them official B.K. with the expenditure of 334 rounds. The day was otherwise quiet with no returned fire. A little enemy T.M activity at 10 am & 2 pm started S.15.a.1.4½	
	29		A very hot day. No activity on Battery side. D Batty moved their position in the evening to X.22.a.9.8	
	30		9th Divl Artillery Operation Order in connection with impending operation by the 26th Infantry Brigade was sent out to Batteries.	
	31		Rest following – no activity on Battery side. B & D Batteries registered by Kite balloon during the afternoon. Our trenches at S.8.a.4.4 were shelled started 4.45 pm & this was a little T.M activity near IRISH CRATER at about 6 pm	

Army Form C. 2118.

WAR DIARY
or
INTELLIGENCE SUMMARY.
(Erase heading not required.)

Instructions regarding War Diaries and Intelligence Summaries are contained in F. S. Regs., Part II. and the Staff Manual respectively. Title pages will be prepared in manuscript.

Place	Date	Hour	Summary of Events and Information	Remarks and references to Appendices

Ammunition Expended (from 15th)

19pr.
4.5" How.

1036 Shrapnel   111 H.E.
 188 H.E.

1224

Casualties None

Honours While in rest at CROUAY, B.S.M. C.F. Hunter of D/50 Bty was awarded the D.C.M. for conspicuous gallantry and devotion proved under shell fire on 30th June last.

D.V.F. Brooke
LT. COLONEL R.F.A.
COMMANDING 50th BRIGADE R.F.A.

9th Division.

Artillery.

50th Bde ROYAL FIELD ARTILLERY.

SEPTEMBER 1916

vol/2

CONFIDENTIAL WAR DIARY

OF THE

50TH BRIGADE RFA

9TH (SCOTTISH) DIVISION

SEPTEMBER 1916

WAR DIARY

INTELLIGENCE SUMMARY

Place	Date	Hour	Summary of Events and Information	Remarks and references to Appendices
	September			
Near CARENCY.	1st		The Enemy put a few "4.2" about 200 yards in front of B and C+ positions. A little Trench Mortar activity on our trenches S15a.6-0.5	
X to Sheet 36B S.E.	2nd		1st and some Repairing.	
36 c S.W.	2nd		Afterwards, much hoeing in S8.6 between 9 and 10 a.m. Trench Mortars, Lakismes & Kitcheners Wire; being all day near the PIMPLE (S9a 1.5) D Battery replied to front line from S9a and also S15 a.4.7. D Battery bombarded the front line from S9a 0.4½ to 2.9; firing 400 rounds. This was in accordance with Operation orders from our against a hostile Sap at S9a.1.9½. Our bombplace at midnight + firing ceased at 12.28 a.m. Enemys retaliation feeble.	
	6		The Enemy was a little livelier today. ZOUAVE VALLEY, S8a and C and S14d all came in for attention ask 4.7 cm trench 4.2".	
	7		Registered Enemy's wire about S15a 1.2. The Hours repaired S15a 2½.3. Enemy Quiet.	
	8		There was a fair amount of firing by his Trenches at various times during the day. but freed by some retaliation in his morning	

WAR DIARY
or
INTELLIGENCE SUMMARY

Army Form C. 2118.

Place	Date	Hour	Summary of Events and Information	Remarks and references to Appendices
			3 rounds per gun throughout at SgcH.8, Sgc 9.2, Sgc 5.4, & Sgc 5.2.2. The concentration of his Artillery (18 pdrs) & gun batteries was lifter to-day. A section of B/53 formed A/50, the other section formed B/50 and a section of C/53 formed C/60 - 9/50 moved its position to B/53's position & came under the 63rd Division tactically, A & B dividing our present Zone concentration - A on the right with K.6 guns & B on the left with K.6 guns.	* This Division was received later on in the month by the 37th.
	9	12.2 am	At 12.2 am we received a request for retaliation for minenwerfers. This was fired at 12.10 am. During the day there was some shelling & trench mortaring by the Enemy but no further retaliation called for. B Battery Reported S/5 a 82.Y & aeroplane bracketed except for retaliation for minenwerfer. This minenwerfer is thought to come up along rails & our fire is reported by our infantry to have the effect of usually putting a temporary stop to its activity.	
	10/11			
	12		A & B Batteries cut wire between IRISH & KENNEDY craters, with	

WAR DIARY
or
INTELLIGENCE SUMMARY.

Army Form C. 2118.

Place	Date	Hour	Summary of Events and Information	Remarks and references to Appendices
	13		only four craters so far as could be observed, these were in places still appearing to be thick. The Enemy fired a few 10.5 cm shell into X 11 a & b - near A & D's positions. During no barrage - a trap was put up marked "H Z 14 VORST S.W N 15" - wire cutting was continued by A & B between S 9 c 1.4 & 1.5 6.	
	14		A raid on the Enemy's trenches at about S 9 c 1.5.5 was carried out at 4 am by the 2nd S.A. Infantry Regt. The raiders were very successful. 5 prisoners taken & 12 Germans killed in their trenches besides that casualties which must have resulted from the bombing of 5 dugouts. No fires a barrage in support of the operation & this was reported to be very accurate. During the day A & B tried to cut wire between S 15 a 2.3 and S 15 a 2.5 - practically nothing of this however could be seen. At 10.9 pm the 26th Infantry Brigade, Black Watch & Cameron raided the enemy between S 15 c 5.4 & 5.3, taking	

WAR DIARY
or
INTELLIGENCE SUMMARY.

Army Form C. 2118.

Place	Date	Hour	Summary of Events and Information	Remarks and references to Appendices
			Our Batteries & Cavalry many casualties & considerable damage to the trenches. We barraged outpost lines in rear & the operation. In the afternoon the Corps Commander (Lt. Gen. Sir H.H. Wilson K.C.B. D.S.O) presented medal ribbons to the following:-	
			A Battery 51866 Dr. S.Sgt. N. Bramall. Military Medal. 20.6.16	
			96145 Gunner H. Burnley " 3.8.16	
			96195 " A. Garratt " 3.8.16	
			B " L/Sjt. W. Swores Military Cross 8.6.16	
			54920 Bdr. G.W.Smith Military Medal 20.6.16	
			64938 a/Bdr. C.A. Ison " 5.9.16	
			C " 79940 Sergt. P. Jackson D.C.M. 11.9.16	
			D " 34124 B.S.M. C.J. Hunter " 13.8.16	
15			Two hostile batteries engaged with aeroplane observation to-day. Infantry by B/50 with good effect and a battery in action by B/50. Some retaliation attempted by aeroplane but few rounds were	

WAR DIARY
or
INTELLIGENCE SUMMARY.

(Erase heading not required.)

Army Form C. 2118.

Place	Date	Hour	Summary of Events and Information	Remarks and references to Appendices
	16		Heavy du heavy Artillery & T.M's were very busy today. The enemy was apathetic. Wire cutting apron heavy between S15a 2.3 and 2.5. Sandbags and stakes were seen to be blown away & a loopholes was	
	17		Lt Caswell an Explosion. A & B Battery attempted to wire-cut between S21.6 2.9i and S15d2.1 (about 150 yds) but had to give it up on account of the impossibility of observation. The enemy put a few shells into ABLAIN and ZOUAVE VALLEY but otherwise maintained his passive attitude.	
	18		Very wet. Lt Rhelicka fir minenwerfer at 11.20 am	
	19		A + B Batteries did some registration by aeroplane - 1st rehearsal for minenwerfer at 5.30 am and again at 11.00 pm After enemy shells into CARENCY today but 80% of them were blind. No damage was done	
	20		Fewer Trench Mortars were built action today. We were	

WAR DIARY or INTELLIGENCE SUMMARY

Army Form C. 2118.

Place	Date	Hour	Summary of Events and Information	Remarks and references to Appendices
	22		Called upon three times for retaliation. A Battery cut wire today from S.15.a.2.2½ to 2.5. The shooting was good. Hostile Artillery again conspicuous by its absence as it and a little retaliated.	
	23		12 Blind shell fell into A8.c.1.1.1 today. Otherwise today was quiet as usual.	
	24		Enemy very quiet again.	
	25		At 4.15 a.m. the 29th Left Brigade carried out a raid on the Enemy's trenches between S.15.a.0.3 and 2.0. The line was found to be unoccupied. Two prisoners were taken. The bombard support line in rear.	
	26		Enemy Trench Mortars were here active today. S.8.d. 9½.3.6. 9½.1½, S.8.6.5.5. and S.14.6.7.8. all being shelled. Our T.M's retaliated but artillery fire was not called for.	
	30		A Battery repeated S.15.a.8.4 by aeroplane in the morning. Hostile artillery displayed its usual inactivity. On leaving	

WAR DIARY
or
INTELLIGENCE SUMMARY.
(Erase heading not required.)

Army Form C. 2118.

Place	Date	Hour	Summary of Events and Information	Remarks and references to Appendices
			Bombarded points behind hostile front line during the afternoon and also fired 30 rounds H.E. in salvos at irregular intervals during the night at S.15.a.9.4. to keep junction Flers Lane – Aeroplane in the morning.	
			Honours awarded. In addition to those previously mentioned:–	
			A. Battery. 82140 Corporal H. Pickles. 24.9.16. Military Medal	
			B. " 90417 Sergt. J. Hulton – " –	
			C. " 33226 Bmdr. J. Montague – " –	
			Ammunition Expended. 18 pdr. Shrapnel 3195	
			H.E. 1794 4989	
			How. H.E. 1230	
			Incendiary 168 1398	
			6387	
			Casualties None	

Jh.P.Clarke
LT. COLONEL R.F.A
COMMANDING 50th BRIGADE R.F.A

9th Division.
Artillery.

50th Bde ROYAL FIELD ARTILLERY.

OCTOBER 1916

EK151

H.Q. / R.A. 9th Division

Herewith Original War Diary
of the 50th Brigade R.F.A. for
October 1916.

1/11/16.

[signature]
for O.C. 50th Bde R.F.A.

vol 13

CONFIDENTIAL WAR DIARY

OF THE

50ᵀᴴ BRIGADE R.F.A.

9ᵀᴴ (SCOTTISH) DIVISION

OCTOBER 1916

WAR DIARY
INTELLIGENCE SUMMARY

Army Form C. 2118.

Place	Date	Hour	Summary of Events and Information	Remarks and references to Appendices
October 1916.				
Mt. CARENCY (VIMY RIDGE)	1		Orders received for our relief in the line by the 107th Brigade, 24th Divn. on night of 3/4th and 4/5th October. D battery registered S.11.b.2.1 and	
Aptx.X to 36.B.S.E.			S.10.c.4½.8 by balloon. Enemy artillery NIL.	
S. 36.C.S.W. (1/20,000)	2		Ret. and Grand B Battery fired on Infantry at S.10.d.5.4 in reply to an aeroplane call. Result O.K. Wire to be relied by 108th Bde. instead of 107th. Enemy quiet as usual.	
	3		O.C. 108th Bde. cams. up and 15th round Batteries with the Colonel. One section of each Battery relieved during the night. No artillery activity on either side.	
	4		Remainder of Batteries relieved during the afternoon. Relief complete at 6pm. Batteries at 7pm for Track nature on R. pd. Batt. front	
	5		Marched at 9am for HOUVELIN and ROCOURT (O.29 + 33. 1/40,000 36B) HQ, A and C billeted at the former and B and D at the latter.	
	6/7		at HOUVELIN and ROCOURT.	

Army Form C. 2118.

WAR DIARY
or
INTELLIGENCE SUMMARY.
(Erase heading not required.)

Instructions regarding War Diaries and Intelligence Summaries are contained in F. S. Regs., Part II. and the Staff Manual respectively. Title pages will be prepared in manuscript.

Place	Date	Hour	Summary of Events and Information	Remarks and references to Appendices
	8		Marched again for REBREUVE SUR CANCHE. Good billets. Brigade HQ billeted in a Chateau for the first time since coming to France.	
	9		Marched again for LUCHEUX. Billets at LA FOLIE farm.	
	10		Marched 7.15 am for TALMAS via DOULLENS.	
	11		Colonel, Adjutant, BCs of A C & D with 2 NCO's and 2 Telephonists (his battery head by motor bus to FRICOURT (9th Division HQ) return to HQ 237th Bde (47th (London) Division) when we are to relieve on the 13th.	
	12		He attacked his enemy trenches on M17c. Scheme not successful. Lt KINNEAR came up to before lines with an advance party.	
Ref. 1/20,000 57c SW	13		Batteries came up during the afternoon and took over as follows	
			A from A/237 M35 c.4.4.	
			B B/235 S 9 b.2.8	
			C B/237 M 36 a.1.7	
			D D/236 S 9 c.2.3 (M&f S10 c.4.6)	

Army Form C. 2118.

WAR DIARY
or
INTELLIGENCE SUMMARY.
(Erase heading not required.)

Place	Date	Hour	Summary of Events and Information	Remarks and references to Appendices
Near HIGH WOOD & BAZENTIN le GRAND. B Battery Map 57c S.W. 1/20,000.			Relief was completed at 6.30 p.m. Battery fired during the night 70 rounds per hour on Barrage from M17.a 9½.5 to M11c 1.1 and 30 rounds per hour on the BUTTE de WARLENCOURT.	
	14		Repetition of the BUTTE and of S.O.S. lines was done. D/50 repeated M17c 6.4 and 2.5 and bombarded from 2 p.m - 6 p.m M17c 3.6 - 1.8. Enemy Artillery fairly quiet - M35 c.3 > EAUCOURT and vicinity of HIGH WOOD bombarded.	
	15		Enemy artillery more active today - 59 and 42 intermittently at S9b, M36, M33, M23 and S10, also HIGH WOOD as usual. We bombarded for 10 minutes at 1 p.m with guns to BUTTE and trenches SE of it. Enemy aeroplane active.	
	16		Bombardment for 10 minutes at 1 p.m and 3.45 p.m from M17c 3.5 to 1.8 and northward towards BUTTE. B/50 fired during the night 100 rounds from M17c 8.6 to M17a 8.6. D/50 repeated M17a. Enemy activity normal.	

WAR DIARY or INTELLIGENCE SUMMARY

Army Form C. 2118.

Date	Hour	Summary of Events and Information	Remarks
17		Bombardment of enemy trenches at DEWDROP, BOVY SPUR. 120 rounds were fired on SOS lines and GIRD LINE during last night. 0/50 bns heavily shelled 16/9.S.9. 2/Lt KINNEAR was killed and 4 other ranks wounded (one afterwards died) About 6 rounds from a 4/2 Gun killed 2 men of A/50	
18		Attacked the SNAG TRENCH at 3.40 a.m. The attack was carried out in co-operation with the 30th Division its line on the right and of our Infantry, the 26th. I Bde were on our right and the South Africans on the left. Objectives were M18c2.5 to M17 c.0.3. The Enemy (named to be between the MILL and Battalion HQ (S.A.Inf.) at about M22 a.6.4. 2/Lt LEWIS (B/50) was found on 9.0.O with the Infantry and was wounded on its front lines in trench M36a and was heavily shelled and C/50 had 3 casualties.	
19		Bombardments and barrages were carried out in accordance with orders from D.A.H.Q. It failed to fol	

WAR DIARY or INTELLIGENCE SUMMARY

Army Form C. 2118.

Place	Date	Hour	Summary of Events and Information	Remarks and references to Appendices
	20		We took of our object of yesterday and Enemy are still in possession of TAIL TRENCH (M17C 4.4. 6.0.9.) The Enemy's artillery was active on our front and support line and there was also some sporadic shelling of news further back M36a, M35c and S36. 2 killed. 2 men had not walk fallen. At 4pm but not walk fallen. Enemy artillery normal. We again attacked TAIL TRENCH as I stated previous 4 p.m. (3/11th Royal Scots) 2 German Aeroplanes later driven down in our lines by our own crowd. Bombardments flare apr continued against the German trenches including a tr burst at intense nr. fire from M17 61 A to M17 a 47 German artillery quiet.	
	21			
	22		Much activity in the air today. We FIRST LINE (our	

WAR DIARY
or
INTELLIGENCE SUMMARY.

Army Form C. 2118.

Place	Date	Hour	Summary of Events and Information	Remarks and references to Appendices
	23		Hostile Artillery was troublesome all day also new trenches in front of the BUTTE. Enemy still quiet. A very misty morning and observation was much impeded. The GIRD LINE and BUTTE tac Rpts under continued fire with observation when the latter was possible.	
	24		Misty again. Yesterdays performance repeated. The enemy was rather active today on FLERS LINE. Observers today and much aerial activity. The GIRD LINE	
	25		bombarded as before. A/52 and D/52 came under the Bosche tactically and were replied today on the BUTTE. Every now and again today - intermittent shelling of HIGH WOOD FAUCOURT, MESA and FLERS LINE kept on most of the day	
	26		to Continued our bombardment of the GIRD LINE	
	27		GIRD LINE Rpt under fire as usual. A Battery very heavily shelled from 11am to 5pm one gun damaged and one casualty.	

WAR DIARY
or
INTELLIGENCE SUMMARY.
(Erase heading not required.)

Army Form C. 2118.

Place	Date	Hour	Summary of Events and Information	Remarks and references to Appendices
	28		Bombardment as usual and between artillery duels	
	29		Fairly hot. GIRDLINE fired on as much as possible	
	30		Enemy continues inactive. He fired as usual, and between 3.5 and 3.30 p.m. Corporal to the bombarded Whites LINE by heavy artillery. Also began to put heavy position	
	31		but continued no bombardment and also fired on a working party in the LEBARQUE Switch. At 2 pm and 4.30 pm the Corporal to the leaving in bombarded an ammunition dump reported to be at M11a 3.7. 9/50 battery was again shelled today with 5.9 but no damage was done.	

T2134. Wt. W708-776. 500000. 4/15. Sir J.C. & S.

WAR DIARY
or
INTELLIGENCE SUMMARY

Ammunition Expended during October

18 pdr   42,947
4.5" How   7,765
            ―――――
            50,712

Casualties Officers Killed 2Lt C.A. KINNEAR C/50   16/10/16
                          Wounded 2/Lt S.H. LEWIS B/50   15/10/16
                                     Capt J.W HOGGART C/50   21/10/16

Other Ranks Killed 4
             Wounded 8 (1 Died of wounds)

A.F.Brooke
Lt Colonel RFA
Commn'd 50th Brigade RFA

9th Divisional Artillery

50th Bde. R. F. A.

NOVEMBER, 1916.

Confidential

War Diary Vol 14

50th Brigade RFA
9th (Scottish) Division

November 1916.

Army Form C. 2118.

WAR DIARY
INTELLIGENCE SUMMARY.
(Erase heading not required.)

Place	Date	Hour	Summary of Events and Information	Remarks and references to Appendices
NEAR HIGH WOOD	November 1916.			
HR. S10.c.4.7. Reference to 57°S.W. 1/20,000	1		The enemy's artillery was normal today and continued our bombardment of the GIRD LINE.	
	2		Bombardment continued A/52 and D/52 reported. The enemy was quiet.	
	3		The enemy was not specially heavy – HIGH WOOD, M34b, M35a, M39b all coming in for attention chiefly with 5.9. Aeroplanes active.	
	4		Our barrage for the attack on the GIRD LINE (to take place tomorrow) was put today at 9am Y/15Thu and the enemy heavily bombarded our Centre at the Sunken road. Reply to our barrage was feeble but he put a fair amount of firing during the day. Several 5.9 in the vicinity of C. Battery.	
	5		We attacked the GIRD LINE at 9.10 am. Lt. JACOBSON of D Battery went forward as F.O.O. after the Infantry assault and succeeded in Establishing his Signalling Lamp on to BUTTE de WARLENCOURT at 9.25am. He subsequently had to look after his Battalion	

WAR DIARY
or
INTELLIGENCE SUMMARY.
(Erase heading not required.)

Army Form C. 2118.

Place	Date	Hour	Summary of Events and Information	Remarks and references to Appendices
			Commanders the fixed information he had received as to the position of the Infantry and in going back to Infantry Brigade HQ took the information as to the repeat of the Battalion Commander, he was wounded.	
			In support in support of the attack. The Rifle/Divisional Group at this time consisted of the 25th & 39th Brigades RFA (2nd Division) and the 50th, 58th & 64th Bdes (9th Div) &c attack which, on our front was carried out by the Infantry of the 50th Division (the Australians were on their right) was not successful. Our Rifle Battalion failed to reach their objective & were back in our front line in a few hours having suffered fairly heavily. The Left Battalion had past the BUTTE and were repulsed considerably to the NW put up to the BAPAUME road. They were forced to retire losses during the retreat & by the following morning our line was back again to SMAG & MAXWELL trenches.	

Place	Date	Hour	Summary of Events and Information	Remarks and references to Appendices
	6		To-day has been quiet. No fire occurred. Saluros on the GIRD LINE same as yesterday.	
	7			
	8		Bombardment of GIRD LINE continued. It reported to junction of HOOK SAP and the GIRD LINE (M.17.b.8.5) by aeroplane with platelets to (M.21.a.9.50) who are two lots (M.21.a.6) including A/50 and D/52. Enemy artillery & aeroplane fairly active to-day. M.28.5, M.28.d. the slope E of HIGH WOOD and the FLERS LINE was all shelled. German aeroplanes extremely active to-day & interfered considerably with shooting. An enemy on a "Chinese" attack at 3.15 p.m. turned on the GIRD LINE in M.17.b. The Enemy put up a heavy barrage in front of EAUCOURT	
	9		L'ABBAYE in response. 9 of 9th Divisional Artillery HQ were to-day shelled by that of the 15th Division. To-day this and back to ST GRATIEN Château. Be moved on yesterday, for 3 minutes at 9.10 a.m.	
	10			

WAR DIARY
or
INTELLIGENCE SUMMARY.
(Erase heading not required.)

Army Form C. 2118.

Place	Date	Hour	Summary of Events and Information	Remarks and references to Appendices
	11		The enemy was fairly active today on his usual targets. Another "Chinese" attack was made today at 12.15pm. Otherwise little activity on Either Side. Very misty all day. Observation was impossible throughout the two days owing to mist. Salvos were fired into the GIRDLINE at intervals the	
	12/13		usual programme of night firing was carried out	
	14		At 6.45 am the 149th Infantry Bde (50th Divn) attacked from GIRD LINE and BUTTE TRENCH when the area M18.a.3.1 – M18.a.0.3 – M17.b.3.5 – M17.a.7.0. The Australians attacked on their immediate right, & supported the operation, bombing in conjunction with 1st Bde Artillery. Owing to the difficulty of communications the situation was very obscure but the Australians succeeded in establishing themselves in the GIRD LINE from a point about 170 yards to the right of HOOK TRENCH and the 149th Bde obtained a temporary footing in the latter trench but were bombed out. The GIRD	

WAR DIARY or INTELLIGENCE SUMMARY

Army Form C. 2118.

Place	Date	Hour	Summary of Events and Information	Remarks and references to Appendices
	15		LINE opposite the 149th Bde is still in the Enemy's hands. Today there was much Enemy Shore machine gun FIRE	
	16		LINE and LE BARQUE SWITCH. The Enemy is very front to LA P. We city shell in the vicinity of Brigade H.Q. At 9pm Enemy artillery became more active - their usual objective was for a while shelled during the day and heavy barrage fire on our trenches during the evening. We have succeeded the H.Q.A again at 9pm but the operation was gradually cancelled & ordinary night find was carried out. Great Enemy activity in the air today.	
	17		4 two free balloons were seen. 1st Battn relieved by the 52nd Battalion and battalions and Brigade H.Q. moved down to forward lines into Reserve.	
	18/21		In Reserve	
	22		The Brigade (less C/50) marched at 9am for BAIZIEUX (C.11.a. Sheet 63D 1/40,000) C/50 remained to pull out	

WAR DIARY
or
INTELLIGENCE SUMMARY.
(Erase heading not required.)

Army Form C. 2118.

Place	Date	Hour	Summary of Events and Information	Remarks and references to Appendices
	23/4		Entrained 4 guns from the line. The Brigade was billeted near BAIZIEUX in "A" Camp.	
	25		In rest at BAIZIEUX	
			Marched to PIERREGOT. "C" Battery rejoined the Brigade here marching right through from their wagon lines near hourly hood	
	27		Marched to TALMAS	
	28		Marched to MEZEROLLES	
	29		Marched to Divisional Artillery Rest Area near FREVENT. Billets in PETIT BOURET & GRAND BOURET.	

Army Form C. 2118.

WAR DIARY
or
INTELLIGENCE SUMMARY.
(Erase heading not required.)

Place	Date	Hour	Summary of Events and Information	Remarks and references to Appendices
			Casualties. Officers. Wounded Lt. L.H. JACOBSON 5/11/16	
			Other ranks. Killed 3	
			Wounded 6	
			Died of accidental wound 1	
			Honours. Lieut L.H. JACOBSON. Military Cross.	
			2nd Lieut G. CUTTLE "	
			Ammunition. 18 pr. 40,452 rounds	
			4.5 How. 6,801 "	
			47,253	
			Whitesmith Lt Col RFA	
			Comm'd 50th Brigade RFA	

9th Divisional Artillery

50th Bde. R. F. A.

DECEMBER, 1916.

SECRET.

WAR DIARY.

50th BRIGADE R.F.A.
9th (SCOTTISH) DIVISION.

JUNE 1916.

EK 158.

H.Q. 9th D.A.

Herewith War Diary of the
50th Brigade R.F.A
for December 1916.

[signature]
for LT. COLONEL R.F.A.
COMMANDING 50th BRIGADE R.F.A

1.1.17.

CONFIDENTIAL WAR DIARY.

50th. BRIGADE R.F.A.

9th. (Scottish) Division.

DECEMBER 1916.

Army Form C. 2118.

WAR DIARY
or
INTELLIGENCE SUMMARY
(Erase heading not required.)

Place	Date	Hour	Summary of Events and Information	Remarks and references to Appendices
	DECEMBER 1916			
BOURET Sur CANCHE				
near FRENENT	1/25		In rest billets at BOURET-Sur-CANCHE. Nothing to report. On the 20th Bde received orders to relieve the 35th Divisional Artillery in the line on the nights of the 26/27th and 27/28th.	
	26		Marched to forward lines at WANQUETIN near ARRAS. Brigade and Battery Commanders, Adjutant and Orderly officers into billeting parties went on ahead by motor lorry.	
ARRAS	27		Battery brought head from into action after march into position to be occupied temporarily to prepare for new operation to take place on 31st January.	
51c51B NW3 1/10,000			A Battery at G20 a 3.4	
			B " G26 a 9.0	
			C " G26 b 3.1 (1 section with C/157 at G28 c 3.5)	
			D " G28 c 3.1½	
			Brigade H.Q. G21 c 5.4 (16 Rue des Ecoles, ARRAS)	

WAR DIARY or INTELLIGENCE SUMMARY

Army Form C. 2118.

Place	Date	Hour	Summary of Events and Information	Remarks and references to Appendices
	28		Reconnoitring OPs repairing wires laid. Two 4.5" Howitzer Batteries from VII Corps, D/746 & B/747, came into action after dark & were attached to the Brigade. D/746 at G.28.d.1.7. B/747 G.27.c.9.8.	
	29		Registering.	
	30		Registering. Orders received for operation on 1st prox.	
	31		D/50 in conjunction with 99th Siege Battery & medium T.M's cut wire in front of the hit to be raided tomorrow viz G.36.c.58.95 to G.36.c.30.80. D/50 firing on the latter point.	

J.W.Fisacke
LT. COLONEL R.F.A
COMMANDING 52nd BRIGADE R.F.A

CONFIDENTIAL.

WAR DIARY.

50th Brigade R.F.A.

9th (Scottish) Division.

JANUARY. 1917.

WAR DIARY
INTELLIGENCE SUMMARY

Army Form C. 2118.

Place	Date	Hour	Summary of Events and Information	Remarks and references to Appendices
January 1917	1st		The operation arranged for today was postponed. Gunners registration of targets was done between 7.30 am 8.30 am. before the Cancellation order was received.	
ARRAS Sheet 51B NW3 1/10,000	2nd		Registration & Calibration.	
	4	6.10.30 pm	The enemy shelled the town with gas shells. Our counter battery opened fire very quickly reducing his enemy fire. Approximately 500 shells were fired.	
	5		The enemy again shelled the town with gas shells.	
	6		The operation postponed from hit[?] was postponed by tomorrow. The 4 Siege expended by tomorrow fire and 2,680 18pdr shells were fired and 3050 4.5" How's, killing in addition 90 Smoke Shell. (BHow Batteries D/50, D/246, B/247) The Twenty	

WAR DIARY or INTELLIGENCE SUMMARY

Army Form C. 2118.

Place	Date	Hour	Summary of Events and Information	Remarks and references to Appendices
	7		Retaliation was not commenced for much. The raid was carried out by the 9th & 10th Bn S. Highlanders. Our casualties were slight but we took one prisoner and inflicted considerable loss on the Enemy.	
			Afterwards the leading sections of A, B & C batteries each sent them opposite number of the 157th Bde (35th Divn) in position:-	
			A G.20.d.6.0	
			B G.34.a.2.8	
			C G.28.c.3.6	
			The two VII Corps howitzer batteries B/247 and D/246 both took this evening with orders to rejoin their Divisions tomorrow.	
	8		The rest of the remainder of the 18pdr batteries of the 157th Bde was completed this evening:- D/157 remained in their position and formed part of the Right Group. D/50 also	

WAR DIARY or INTELLIGENCE SUMMARY

Army Form C. 2118.

Place	Date	Hour	Summary of Events and Information	Remarks and references to Appendices
	9		Remained in their position in the shelled at G28c 3.15. Brigade HQ. 161 siege bc 157th bde Hd & others Command of the Rapid Group.	
			Registration & Calibration. After dark the right section of C/156 became part of D/157 and the right section of D/152 moved up into his position & became part of D/150 making it a 6 gun battery. A, B, & C batteries took out gun lines at MONTENESCOURT from opposite number of the 157th Bde.	
	10		Registration & retaliation for TMs. D/150 took over section line of D/157 at MONTENESCOURT. After dark the battery sections of A and B/150 were relieved by leading sections of B/159 and C/159. They moved into position at G15a24 and G16c15 respectively with their respective Brigade HQ	

Army Form C. 2118.

WAR DIARY
or
INTELLIGENCE SUMMARY.
(Erase heading not required.)

Place	Date	Hour	Summary of Events and Information	Remarks and references to Appendices
	11		the Left Group.	
	12		Registration. Enemy artillery rather active during the afternoon.	
			Remarks of A + B Batteries rest relieved by Br C/157 D/157 fired 30 gas shell the 99th Siege Battery fired 34 H.E. at a position of a heavy T.M. broken at about G.2 a 7.6. A/50 fired 40 H.E. in conjunction.	
	13		After dark D/50 moved 4 Guns into action at G.15.a.1.4. these [?] under the Lift Group - the remaining 2 Guns were left at G.2.c.3.1.	
	14		A section of C/50 was relieved by a section of C/157 from its position at G.15.a.7.3 coming under the Centre Group.	

WAR DIARY
or
INTELLIGENCE SUMMARY.

Army Form C. 2118.

Place	Date	Hour	Summary of Events and Information	Remarks and references to Appendices
	15		The remains of O/50 were relieved by C/154. The Command of the Right Group was in consequence of this relief to O.C. 154 & O.C. 4 H.Q. 50th Brigade moved into billets at C.27 d 9.7.	
	16/31.		A, B, D Batteries were grouped under the Left Group (52nd Brigade) during the time and C Battery remained out of action. Estimates and plans were prepared for the Construction of new positions but all work was at a standstill owing to frost snow which lasted continuously.	

[signature]
LT. COLONEL R.F.A.
COMMANDING 50th BRIGADE R.F.A.

Brigade Major, R.A.

    9th. Division.

Herewith War Diary for month of February 1917.

                                  Lieut. R.F.A.
                     for Lieut. Colonel R.F.A.
                     Commanding 50th. Brigade RFA.

1.3.17.

CONFIDENTIAL WAR DIARY.

50th BRIGADE R.F.A.

9th (Scottish) DIVISION.

FEBRUARY 1917.

Army Form C. 2118.

WAR DIARY

INTELLIGENCE SUMMARY

(Erase heading not required.)

Instructions regarding War Diaries and Intelligence Summaries are contained in F.S. Regs., Part II. and the Staff Manual respectively. Title pages will be prepared in manuscript.

Place	Date	Hour	Summary of Events and Information	Remarks and references to Appendices
ARRAS	February 1917		During the whole of this month the Battery remained Brigaded under 51st Bde + 52nd Army F.A. Bde.	
Sheet 51B NW3 1/10,000			The cold weather allowed rapid work which had put all work on new positions out of the question, but not break whilst about the night of this month had was then pushed on, the positions ultimately secured as being	
			Bde HQ. G10a 2.1	
			A Bty. G10c 4½.6	
			B " G10c 6½.8	
			C " G10c 9½.4½	
			D " G10c 2.4	
			These are all North of the Suburb of ST. NICHOLAS, north of ARRAS. "C" Battery, being still out of action, took charge of the construction of positions for a reinforcing Brigade. These were all in the lines on the East Side of the main street of ST NICHOLAS in G16c and G16a with Bde HQ. at G16c.5.6.	

T3134. Wt. W708-773. 50000. 4/15. Sir J. C. & S.

WAR DIARY or INTELLIGENCE SUMMARY

Place	Date	Hour	Summary of Events and Information	Remarks and references to Appendices
			An Infantry working party of 100 men to work on wire positions was attached to "C" Battery on the 15th. They came from the 51st Division, (the 5th foremen) and were relieved on the 26th by a party from the 71st Royal Scots. (9th Divn) Work on O.P.'s was also taken in hand, the following being allotted to Battalions:-	
			A. G.22.b.2.0. ("De Bethy.")	
			B. G.22.a.6.7. ("The Granary.")	
			C & D ("Eva.")	
			and also O.P.'s in the Trenches at about G.5a.5.3 and 7.5	
	14th		A very successful raid was carried out by the 9th Scottish Rifles from opposite "KING" Crater to opposite "KITE" Crater. 43 prisoners were taken, also a machine gun and many dugouts containing Germans were destroyed. Our own casualties were slight.	

WAR DIARY
or
INTELLIGENCE SUMMARY.
(Erase heading not required.)

Army Form C. 2118.

Place	Date	Hour	Summary of Events and Information	Remarks and references to Appendices
	20"		"D" Battery today moved up into action in their new position and "C" Battery also went into action with 4 guns at 6.15 a.m., both Batteries coming into action under the orders of the O.C. 51st Bde.	
			Casualties	
			Officers —	
			Other ranks — 2 Bombr. "B" Battery wounded by a 4.2" shell which fell in Lt Nicholas killing 6 wounding about 8 men of the 34th Division —	

J.M. Plaroske
LT. COLONEL R.F.A
COMMANDING 50TH BRIGADE R.F.A

CONFIDENTIAL WAR DIARY.

50th. BRIGADE R.F.A.

9th. (Scottish) DIVISION.

MARCH 1917.

WAR DIARY
INTELLIGENCE SUMMARY

Army Form C. 2118.

Place	Date	Hour	Summary of Events and Information	Remarks and references to Appendices
March 1917	2nd		The Enemy attempted a raid on the Division front at 5am but did not reach our trenches.	
Map reference to ARRAS 51.B.N.W.3 1/10,000	5		Conference of Battery Commanders at B's position. Snow fell during the night and early morning but ceased quickly. This raid was carried out - one by the 51st Division (XVII Corps) next Division on our right by the 3rd Division (VI Corps) next Division on our left) and two other by the 34th Division (but one on our left) and the former captured one Officer and 18 other ranks and the latter 30 other ranks and two machine guns.	
	8		Very windy. The screens next new position blown down.	
	9		One section of A Battery was relieved tonight by a battery of the 34th Division. The guns were moved to C Battery position where they remained until 4 pm when (G15 a.7.7) personnel moved up to the Quarry next new position. (G10 c)	
	10		A Battery completed the move during the night.	
	11		Began to dump ammunition for active operations at our new	

WAR DIARY or INTELLIGENCE SUMMARY

Place	Date	Hour	Summary of Events and Information	Remarks and references to Appendices
	14		positions. 2/Lt. H.St.G. Talbott, B Battery was wounded in the left arm by a splinter of 4.2 Shell.	
	15		Major G.R. Holland DFA (T.F.) arrived & took Brigade & Battery Commander reconnoitred forward positions in G.11.d. New positions for the Brigade being before in G.16.a and c are practically complete and the infantry working party have under Major Holland to make ammunition dumps for his forward positions.	
	19		Orders were received to-day for A, B & C all to move to their new positions in G.10.c on the 22nd.	
	20		Information was received to-day that the enemy was evacuating his line (the final South of ARRAS & to hit the XVII Corps might possibly be ordered to attack at 2 hours notice.	
	21		A raid carried out by the 11th Royal Scots to-day into his trenches line in G.12.a+b and G.6.c+d met with determined resistance & proved that the line in this sector was strongly	

Army Form C. 2118.

WAR DIARY
or
INTELLIGENCE SUMMARY.
(Erase heading not required.)

Place	Date	Hour	Summary of Events and Information	Remarks and references to Appendices
	22		held & that time has no indication of withdrawal at this front. A & B Batteries moved up into new positions after dark and C Battery's Firing Section was relieved by one of the H.Q. Divisional Artillery, and moved up into its new position.	
	23/24		Remainder of C Battery relieved & moved to new position. Brigade H.Q. in ARRAS received a direct hit today from a 5.9" shell & two badly damaged.	
	25			
	26		H.Q. moved into dugouts (Battle H.Q.) at G.10.c.1.5.	
	27		The Battery (The Divisional Artillery Comm. up - 93rd Army D.A. Artillery)	
	28/31		H.Q. in forward positions in G.11.d Continued, also dumping of ammunition. The gradual of ammunition to G.P. dumps preparatory to active operations is 1500 rounds per 18 Pr. at rear positions and 600 rounds per gun forward, 2000 rounds per 4.5 How. and 600 rounds per How. forward.	

WAR DIARY
or
INTELLIGENCE SUMMARY

Army Form C. 2118.

Place	Date	Hour	Summary of Events and Information	Remarks and references to Appendices
			Making a total for the Brigade of :- 18pdr. Gun positions 24,000 Gun'd " 10,800 34,800 rounds 4.5" How Gun " 12,000 Gun'd " 3,600 15,600 " TOTAL 53,400 rounds Of this amount has been dumped at gun positions 38,930 18pdr 9,684 4.5 How TOTAL 48,614 rounds Casualties Offr. Coro 1 Wounded (2o N.S.G. Talcoult - B. Bty) O.R. 2 Killed 2 Wounded	

W.H.F.Brooke
LT. COLONEL R.F.A.
COMMANDING 50th BRIGADE R.F.A.

CONFIDENTIAL

WAR

DIARY.

50TH: BRIGADE. R.F.A.

9TH: (SCOTTISH) DIVISION.

APRIL. 1917.

WAR DIARY or INTELLIGENCE SUMMARY.

Army Form C. 2118.

(Erase heading not required.)

Place	Date	Hour	Summary of Events and Information	Remarks and references to Appendices
ARRAS	April 1914.			
"	2nd		Operation Orders received today for attack.	
FAMPOUX	3		"Z" day will be the 8th.	
Sheet 51B NW 1/20,000	4		Preliminary bombardment begun today. The 18pdrs not required to bombard but 'D' Battery bombarded in our zone and during the night searched CTs and roads. 18pdrs registered in our zone. Enemy quiet - little retaliation.	
	5.		Bombardment continued. "A" and "B" wire cutting. A rehearsal of the procedure to be carried out at Zero hour took place at 8am. Mobile barrage was on front line and supports up to BOSKY & OBSERVATORY REDOUBTS, also 35 rounds 4.4 from GOCPSS 69.5. A + B Batteries fired during the night on the Divisional Zone in H8 & H14.	
	6.		Zero hour has been postponed for 24 hours. A machine gun barrage has been fired during the morning and a Chinese attack carried out at 1.30 pm. 18pdrs wire cutting.	

WAR DIARY
or
INTELLIGENCE SUMMARY
(Erase heading not required.)

Army Form C. 2118.

Place	Date	Hour	Summary of Events and Information	Remarks and references to Appendices
	7		No practice barrage today. "A" Battery was shelled & train men destroyed. In ROCLINCOURT VALLEY was shelled with gas shell from 9 hr. 15am. Some "Tanks" arrived & were parked in the valley during the night.	
	8		"Y" day. Practice barrages were arranged with batteries on our flanks (135th Bty on the Right and a 34th Division Bty on the left) and another rehearsal took place at 11.15am. Sig. no. of SD/50 wounded this afternoon by S9 gun. "Zero" hour will be 5.30am.	
	9		In accordance with operation orders 'B' Battery fires Shell on Trench Junctions & battery positions during the night 8/9th. The attack took place at 5.30am. We were the right Division of this XVII Corps. The 34th Division on our left and next to them the 51st. On our right was the 15th Division of VI Corps. This Brigade covered the 24th Infantry Brigade. Major Holland (att. 16th Infantry Brigade) was Liaison Officer with the	

WAR DIARY or INTELLIGENCE SUMMARY

24th Inf Brigade and 2Lt C.C.Cannor, "A" Bty, was F.O.O. with 2t Lt H.S.ELLISON at a relay post in our support line in G.11.d. The range from our batteries to the enemy front line was about 2,500 yards and Zero Hour was fixed at 8.10 hours. The barrage already in line started punctually on time and from the beginning the operation went with Clockwork precision and uniform success. Communication was very good and early information was received that Capture of the first objective had been. On receipt of this "C" Battery moved forward into action in prepared positions in G.11.d., the remaining batteries divided the barrage between them and after Lts 2nd objective was taken when "C" Battery had opened fire from its forward position, "A" Battery moved forward to its own valley position. Similarly "B" Bty in its turn. These moves were all carried out deliberately and all arrangements including Communication to the new positions worked smoothly. The Stokes Mortar Battery moved to a position just

WAR DIARY or INTELLIGENCE SUMMARY

Army Form C. 2118.

the OIL FACTORY in GIVENCHY after the capture of the 3rd Objective. The 4th Objective was captured that evening, units of the 4th Division passing through the 9th to attack it, altogether Battalion was cleared out of range. 2nd Lt CROUCH was relieved by Lt. H.S. ELLISON at dusk & established himself near the HYDERABAD REDOUBT & kept the Brigade informed during the night of the progress of events. 2nd Lt A.C. BELL was at a relay station in OBERMEYER TRENCH in G.H.Q. line & fired our two S.O.S. calls but our own twice during the night in response to S.O.S. calls but our own position remained unaltered in the morning.

Place	Date	Hour	Summary of Events and Information	Remarks and references to Appendices
	10		The situation during the day was rather obscure and by air practically no firing going on. Orders to move batteries forward to be in HY and H8 were reconnoitred and preceded Brigade HQ in close C12.6.8.4.	
	11		At 1am Orders received to move forward at dawn to positions behind FAMPOUX and to ready to open fire by 10am. Arrived at 5am and took up positions in H22a + H15a hi.k. Brigade HQ in the farm on left bank his Ogulim at H22.c.5.6. Batteries all ropenra reported by 10.30am and at 11am a "Chinese Attack" took place followed at noon by an attack on ROEUX in support of which we barraged. Attack failed. Heavy Snow fell in the evening. Major Osborne (D/50) Slightly wounded - Remained at Duty.	
	12		The 27th I.B and the S.A. Brigade attacked the GAVRELLE - ROEUX road at 5pm and the 26th Brigade, when this objective was reached the 26th I.B. were to advance southward an attack ROEUX.	

WAR DIARY or INTELLIGENCE SUMMARY

Army Form C. 2118.

Place	Date	Hour	Summary of Events and Information	Remarks and references to Appendices
	14		This knowner has not carried out. Loss for 27th F.A. hd M.G. were heavy. Communication was bad and he considered our programme of barrage for the attack on ROEUX before it could be stopped. The situation was very obscure. Night was quiet. Batts. & v Brigade H.Q. (H15d & H22a) was shelled from 11.30 pm till (13th) 1.30 am with 5.9" shells and again from 10 am till 12 noon with 4.2". 6.5 & 7.30 pm 2nd S.R. ATWILL, Orderly Officer, was wounded by a shrapnel bullet in the left wrist. Communication was kept to an old German O.P. on GRANGE HILL (H35a) to be used as a Brigade O.P. Between 6 and 8 pm "D" Battery shelled the small spinney in H18d which was subsequently taken by us, together with a small trench in front of it. Rifle firing on Enemy Communications.	
	15		2nd Lt F.A A. BEAKE. A/50, and one gunner wounded by 4.2". He found Liaison Officer with 5th Canadians (51st Div.) today.	
	16		The 51st Divisional Artillery took over from ours today.	
	17		Enemy has active today until the evening when he started heavy	

Army Form C. 2118.

WAR DIARY
or
INTELLIGENCE SUMMARY.
(Erase heading not required.)

Place	Date	Hour	Summary of Events and Information	Remarks and references to Appendices
	18		In the vicinity of Battery, 2nd Lt A.J.B. MACNICOL and 3 men of D Battery were wounded. Lt MACNICOL subsequently died. Intermittent hostile shelling today. Batteries firing but harassing fire whenever possible. D Bty in trouble in I/a a.m.c.	
	19		Enemy shelled the neighbourhood at intervals again today. 2nd Lt A.C. BELL and 2 men of B Bty wounded. Quiet in evening on S.O.S. call.	
	20		Enemy quieter. Operation Orders received for fresh attack on 23rd. Preliminary Bombardment to begin tomorrow.	
	21		"X" day. Bombardment in Bigger Zone at the rate of 600 rounds per Battery for 24 hours began at dawn.	
	22		Batteries very heavily shelled in the early hours of this morning with K gas shells for about 1 hour, and again during the forenoon with S.O.9 and 2. Batteries had many casualties, wounded and gassed.	
	23		The 51st Division attacked at 4:45 a.m. the 17th Division were on our right (crossing the river SCARPE) and the 37th on our left.	

T.2134. Wt. W708-776. 500000. 4/16. Sir J. C. & S.

WAR DIARY
or
INTELLIGENCE SUMMARY

Army Form C. 2118.

Place	Date	Hour	Summary of Events and Information	Remarks and references to Appendices
	24 25		Besides ourselves the attack was supported by the 14th Brigade R.H.A, 23rd Army F.A. Brigade, 51st Brigade and the 255th + 256th Brigades of the 51st Divl. Artillery. 'A' Battery had a Lewis gun at H.23.b.6.4. to fire shrapnel along the Railway Cutting from T.13.d.9.2. to T.9.c.6.5.3. The 23rd 255th 256th + ourselves was ordered to be prepared to move forward. The attack was not a success. It was badly held up by machine gun fire & the CHEMICAL WORKS and ROEUX were from Safe obstacles. Lt. H.S. ELLISON wounded whilst at the O.P. 34th Divl. Artillery H.Q. Came in.	
	27 28		A quiet day. One Officer and 16 men per battery went into ARRAS for a bath and 24 hours rest. Orders received for a fresh attack tomorrow by the 34th Division. The 34th Division, 101st Brigade on his Right and the 103rd on the left, attacked at 4.25 a.m. The 12th Division were on his right divided by the SCARPE and the 37th on the left divided by a line Eastwards from I.7.c.7.7. to I.9.c.7.4. Left of line 1860m. Bround for fun	

WAR DIARY
or
INTELLIGENCE SUMMARY

Place	Date	Hour	Summary of Events and Information	Remarks and references to Appendices
	29		few minutes except for 6 minutes before the Infantry were to assault any objection when it was raised to 4 - found perform per minute on the protection - 2 rounds per Howitzer. This attack again failed and so was left in practically the same line as before. Batteries were heavily shelled during the moving. D Batteries was very heavily shelled again this morning and A, C & D batteries had casualties. Especially D who had 10. The enemy has become quicker and positions to cover that he for B and D towers to come under our C.P.R. again & his Brigade has to come under his return C.P.R. again & his Colonel sent his commentator in his neighbourhood. The P.O. NT on sour delivery started whilst very heavily with 8" again during the afternoon and D Battery had 3 officers killed by the shell, Major A.J. USBORNE, Lt. L.H. JACOBSON and Lt. T.A. TURNER. The Brigade never brought to before lines after dark.	
	30		Brigade & Battery Commanders reconnoitre new positions in the vicinity	

WAR DIARY
or
INTELLIGENCE SUMMARY.

Army Form C. 2118.

of the POINT on jour R. The moves up might however positions were
Cancelled. Lt R.G.Joice + Sergt Jackson (R.R.) Killed while marking out new
positions.

Casualties during the month :—

Officers.

Killed.
Major A.J. Osborne "D"
Lt. L.H. Jackson "
T.R. Turner "
A.J.B. Macneice "
R.G. Joice C

Wounded
2/Lt. A. Mackey B
S.R. Ahmed M.R. (Orderly Officer)
I.A.A. Blake A
A.C. Bell B
Lt. N.G. Stevens C

Other ranks.
Killed   14
Wounded   70
            ——
            84

R.A.H.Brooke Lt. Colonel
Cmdg 50th Brigade R.F.A.

CONFIDENTIAL

WAR

DIARY.

----- 50th: BRIGADE. R.F.A. -----

9TH: (SCOTTISH) DIVISION.

MAY, 1917.

Army Form C. 2118.

WAR DIARY
or
INTELLIGENCE SUMMARY.
(Erase heading not required.)

Place	Date	Hour	Summary of Events and Information	Remarks and references to Appendices
ARRAS	May 1917.			Casualties
FAMPOUX	1st		The Brigade Commander and Battery Commanders reconnoitred new positions for Batteries at H.9 central. Batteries went into action this after dark with the exception of 'A' Battery who went further forward to H.10.C, and were tactically under the 52nd Brigade. Brigade Headquarters moved from the waggon lines to H.7.a.7.8 in the evening.	
Sheet 51.B.N.W. 1/20,000	2nd		Orders were received for an attack and Batteries registered. The O.C. 50th Bde. proceeded to reconnoitre positions in H.18.a. and 6.§.2 men killed and to prepare to move forward on receipt of orders from the 9th Divisional Artillery when the final objective had been captured.	'C' B⁻⁶/₂ 2 men killed 2 " wounded
	3rd		The 9th Division attacked with the 4th West Divisional front, the 26th¾. Inf. Bde. on the right and the 27th Inf. Bde. on the left with the Inf. Bde. of the 17th Division in reserve. The South African Bde. were later in the line. The attack extended on a front of about 15 miles, the 1st and 5th Armies also taking part. We were between the 4th Div. on the right and the 3rd Div. on the left.	

WAR DIARY or INTELLIGENCE SUMMARY.

Army Form C. 2118.

Place	Date	Hour	Summary of Events and Information	Remarks and references to Appendices
	3rd cont'd		Zero hour was at 3.45 am and batteries opened fire at a range of about 4450 yards, the Howitzer B'y's barraging 200 yards further East. The width of the barrage for the 18 pr batteries was about 350 yards, and the rate of fire 3 rounds a gun a minute. The barrage crept East 100 yards every 2 minutes from Zero + 4 to Zero + 24, then 100 yards every 3 minutes till the final barrage was reached. The rate of fire for the 4.5 How was 2 rounds a gun a minute. Besides our own the following Field Artillery Brigades were supporting the attack: 32nd, 52nd, 152nd, 160th and 293 A.F.A.Bde. Our own front the attack was not a success, the Battalion approaching to the direction in the dark and then to hold up by machine gun fire from shell holes in rear of the Enemy's Trenches. Shortly after the final barrage was reached our Brigade was ordered to maintain a slow rate of fire over an S.O.S. lines. Owing to the mud being impassable the Howitzers were not able to carry out the bombardment with lethal shell, which had	

Place	Date	Hour	Summary of Events and Information	Remarks and references to Appendices
	3rd cont.		Orders from 3.0 am till 3.15 am on the railway. At 1.45pm orders were received for a local operation by the 27th Inf. Bde. against WIT TRENCH with a view of getting into touch with two companies of the K.O.S.B.'s who had not been heard of since the morning operation. Our Brigade was ordered to reinforce the 27th Inf. while Brigade 2nd with H.E. orshrapnel on an area North and South line thro' I 8 b. 5.0 from 2.0 till 2.50 + A.5. The attack took place at 8.0 pm and thereafter by various units objectives. But finding no trace of the missing companies returned to their trenches in accordance with the plan. Battalion carried out thurst fire on any enemy targets, and searching fire in Brigade zone by night. "A" Bttn remained in forward position but came under the orders of the New Brigdr.	Gallipoli
	4th 5th			
	6.		"B" "C" & "D" Battalion shelled in morning from 11.0 – 11.30 am with 7k. 5.9's and 4.2's and again from 6.15 pm 16 6.30 pm and 6.45 pm to 7.0 pm the 18 pdr carried out a practice barrage at 4.0 pm starting on the enemy front trenches	"B" 13/6 1 Killed. "C" 13/6 2 wounded "D" 13/6 21 wounded

Army Form C. 2118.

WAR DIARY
or
INTELLIGENCE SUMMARY.
(Erase heading not required.)

Instructions regarding War Diaries and Intelligence Summaries are contained in F.S. Regs., Part II. and the Staff Manual respectively. Title pages will be prepared in manuscript.

Place	Date	Hour	Summary of Events and Information	Remarks and references to Appendices
	7		'A' and 'C' B'rys have shelled during the day and 'C' B'15 had 1 gun damaged.	Casualties
	8		There was a conference of Brigade Commanders at R.A. H.Q. in the morning, and a conference of Battery Commanders at Bde H.Q. in the afternoon.	'C' B'15 { 1 wounded
	9		Quiet day.	'C' 1 wounded 'D' 1 killed
	10			
	11		The 9th Divn RA went out and the 50th B'de came under the orders of the G.O.C. RA 4th Divn. There was a conference of Brigade Commanders, and orders were received with reference to an attack. This took place at 7.30pm and was carried out by the 47th Divn and 2 companies of the 17th Divn against 'TRENCH at I.13.6.05 — I.13.6.½.8½ — CHEMICAL WORKS — Southwards to ROEUX Cemetery. In addition Trenches I.15.32½.25⁶¹⁵ 29⁷ᵗʰ 10⁷ᵗʰ 51ˢᵗ 25⁵ᴿ 23ᴿᴰ 48½ and 162 B'dies Supports the attack with the 4th Div R.A. and 7th 29³ʳᵈ 52ⁿᵈ 16.0⁷⁵ and 152 under the 17th Div. R.A. 'B' and 'C' B'16 of...... at a range of about 4,200 yards, 'A' B'de about 3200 and 'D' 4400 yards	

WAR DIARY
or
INTELLIGENCE SUMMARY
(Erase heading not required.)

Army Form C. 2118.

Place	Date	Hour	Summary of Events and Information	Remarks and references to Appendices
	11th Cont'd		The rate of fire for 18 pdrs was as follows :—	
			Zero — Zero +16 4 rounds a gun a minute	
			2+16 — 2+24 3 " " " "	
			2+24 — 2+40 2 " " " "	
			2+40 — 2+70 1 " " " "	

The barrage crept East at Zero + 2 by lifts of 50 yards at the rate of 100 yards in 4 minutes, then 100 yards East of objective found a protective barrage, batteries also searching forward by short lifts 400 yards E and back their line in each hour. The ammunition used was HE delay up till 4300. Thereon delay till 4 minutes after zero, protective barrage, after which shrapnel was used.

The rate of fire for the How. Btys. was 3 rounds a gun a minute from Zero to 2+16, 2 rounds a gun a minute from 2+16 to 2+24. Thereafter more than ½ round a gun a minute unless situation demanded it. At Zero + 3 hours or cease

WAR DIARY
or
INTELLIGENCE SUMMARY.
(Erase heading not required.)

Army Form C. 2118.

Place	Date	Hour	Summary of Events and Information	Remarks and references to Appendices
	11th Cont:d			Consolidation
			The G.O.C. R.A. 17th Div. was in command of the G.O.C. R.A. 4th Div. and Cavalry & the G.O.C. R.A. 17th Div. The barrage was exceptionally thick and good, our brigade having 3 18 pdr Bties + the Hvt 18's 2 00 [?] barrage. 200 yds higher 3 18 pdr Bties on a front of about 1200 yds. The attack was successful and the night fairly quiet.	
	12		At 6.30 am the attack was continued. The 32nd, 160th, 152nd, & 293rd Bgds also being under orders of the 17th Div R.A. A/ [?] Our creeping barrage started 150 yards in front of starting line, and moved from Zero + 3 minutes by lifts of 50 yards arriving "B" & "C" Bties Eastern most half the zone. "A" & "B" remain the whole. When the final Pufkelin barrage was reached "A" & "B" Bties the ground 500 yards East. The How Bties fired on C O D TRENCH till Zero + 4 and then railway from I.14.b.07 - I.9.c.63. From 75 pdrs the rate of fire was :—	{ A / 1 rounds D / 1 "
			Zero - Zero + 10 4 rounds a gun a minute.	
			Zero + 10 - Zero + 20 3 " " " " "	
			Zero + 20 - Zero + 90 1 " " " " "	
			Shrapnel being used till Pufkelin Barrage was reached, and then H.E.	

Army Form C. 2118.

WAR DIARY
or
INTELLIGENCE SUMMARY.
(Erase heading not required.)

Place	Date	Hour	Summary of Events and Information	Remarks and references to Appendices
	12th (n.7º)		The Rate of fire for the 4.5 How. was - Zero - Zero + 3 rounds a gun a min. b. and subsequently at half this rate of the 18 pdrs. The attack was unsuccessful, the 4th Div. front and north front of the village & that of the 17th Div. The left battalion found their objective but were bombed out, and others 16 their original line. The centre battalion was also unsuccessful. During the day also our battn'n fired on German lines with their new GREENLAND HILL with great effect. D.18.G. fires lethal shells from midnight at 1.30 am in bursts of 5 minute intervals followed by lachrymatory shells. During the night their parties worked apart at I.8.C.0.1 and N.31. a Quiet day. From 10.3 pm - 10.13 pm the Brigade gas covering fire for a rush by the infantry on CURLY TRENCH. This attempt failed, the enemy apparently having heavy Art.	Casualties
Aug 12/13.	13			"A" 21 amm-

Army Form C. 2118.

WAR DIARY
or
INTELLIGENCE SUMMARY.
(Erase heading not required.)

Instructions regarding War Diaries and Intelligence Summaries are contained in F.S. Regs, Part II. and the Staff Manual respectively. Title pages will be prepared in manuscript.

Place	Date	Hour	Summary of Events and Information	Remarks and references to Appendices
	14th 15th		Batteries Engaged in harassing fire. (Stopped for the day)	Casualties
	15th		" " "	'A' 2 wounded
	16th		" " intense	'C' 1 "
			Enemy harbour and fortified trenches. At 3.30 am an Infantry after a short bombardment attacked and succeeded in Capturing the CHEMICAL WORKS, CURLY CUPID and saw the trench. Our batteries fired on the S.O.S. lines. Our infantry counter attacked at 7.30 am, one Brigade being slated on CURLY TRENCH, and CUPID in another not to our S.O.S. lines. In attempting CURLY and CUPID but were not again. Fighting kept on all day near the river in the reception, the CHEMICAL WORKS and all the original trenches with the exception of CURLY and CUPID.	'A' 2 wounded
Nipur	17/18th		The 18th D.L.I. hlupin 15th the 31st Div. run hill attacked GAVRELLE TRENCH from C 25 b 1½ 2 to C 25 a 9½ 9½. The attack took place at 12.30 am and surrounded by the 5th Div. artillery and Heavy Artillery. 13th Corps carried out a feint attack on OPPY Our How Bttys supported the main attack searching the area	

WAR DIARY or INTELLIGENCE SUMMARY

Army Form C. 2118.

Place	Date	Hour	Summary of Events and Information	Remarks and references to Appendices
	17th / 18th cont?		C25d 4-3½ - I.1.b.5½.8 and I.2.a.4½.7½ - C26c.2½.4 from Zero to Zero+60. The range was about 5500 yds and the rate of fire as follows:- Zero - Zero + 30 2 rounds a minute Zero + 30 - Zero + 50 1 " " " at Zero + 50 talk died down. After Zero + 60 our guns had kept nothing and firing occasional until hostile running, the remaining guns firing on their S.O.S. lines. The infantry reached their objectives but were driven again by bombs. The presence of the Brigade with[drew] to their wagon lines during the afternoon leaving parties of about 12 men to guard the guns and teams near the gun dug outs. The strength of the zone was taken over by the 51st. 13th R.F.A. Rations at wagon lines, the weather being very good.	Casualties 2/Lt G.S. COOPER 'A' Bty
	18			
	18/25		The Brigade returned with a few taking and the 160th R.F.A. with the 152nd B.M. mm left and 57th on an sight. The zone was I.1.d.3½.6½ - I.3.c.2.9 + I.7.b.05 - I.9.a.08. All the batteries had registered the new zone by 6 Pm. Except 2 guns of 'A' B.G. which had amongst by shell fire, 3 shells falling in unit	2/Lt G.S. COOPER 'A' Bty wounded also Sgt ROBINSON —

Army Form C. 2118.

WAR DIARY
or
INTELLIGENCE SUMMARY.
(Erase heading not required.)

Place	Date	Hour	Summary of Events and Information	Remarks and references to Appendices
	26.) 27.)		Batteries engaged in Harassing Fire. Enemy's artillery have not active on Back Areas without the vicinity of Brigade H.Q. Chiefly with 4.2 guns and 77m guns, the Battn firing Whitshell at night.	
	28.		Batteries engaged in Harassing Fire and anything Targets.	
	29/30		"D" B/15 shelled HtQ in SQUARE WOOD with their Howitzer Batteries from 3.0 am – 5.0 am firing 10 rounds every 10 minutes. The 18 pdrs fired with same target with HE from 3.30 am – 5.0 am in reliefs.	
	30.		The Colonel reconnoitres for positions in I.13.a North of Road, previous orders having been received in view of the possibility of an enemy withdrawal. Hostile artillery very quiet.	
	31.		The 17th Divl RA were not and were relieved by the 34th Divl. A quiet day, with a certain amount of hostile shelling on roads and Tracks in back areas.	

Army Form C. 2118.

WAR DIARY
or
INTELLIGENCE SUMMARY.
(Erase heading not required.)

Instructions regarding War Diaries and Intelligence Summaries are contained in F. S. Regs., Part II. and the Staff Manual respectively. Title pages will be prepared in manuscript.

Place	Date	Hour	Summary of Events and Information	Remarks and references to Appendices
			Total Casualties for the month of May :—	
			2/Lieut G.S. COOPER wounded	
			O.R. 4 killed	
			19 wounded	
			Total 23	
			Ammunition Expenditure during May :—	
			18 pdr. Shrapnel 14359 rounds	
			(3 Batteries) H.E. 15003 "	
			Smoke 6 "	
			4.5 How. H.E. 7820	
			(1 Battery) Whd 250	
			Lachrymatory 32	

R.W.B.Brooke
Lt. Colonel R.F.A.
Commanding ... ... R.F.A.

CONFIDENTIAL WAR DIARY

FOR

JUNE, 1917.

50th BRIGADE, R.F.A.

9th (SCOTTISH) DIVISION.

WAR DIARY
or
INTELLIGENCE SUMMARY.
(Erase heading not required.)

Army Form C. 2118.

Place	Date	Hour	Summary of Events and Information	Remarks and references to Appendices
Shruli 51.B.N.W & 51.B.S.W.	June 1917 1		A quiet day.	
	2		The 160th Brigade R.F.A returns into action, so batteries 50th Bde registered new S.O.S. lines covering responsible for zones at 10.a.m. The zones are :- North lines I.7.a.9½.9½ to I.3.d.o.o. " South " I.7.d.½.9½ - I.9.b.o.o	
	3		Between the 51st Bde on the right and 160th Bde on the left. Batteries took part in a Chinese attack at 8.0.p.m. The 18 pdrs fired on the enemy front line for 2 minutes and then lifted 50 yards & remained to 4 minutes, then came back on front line again for another 2 minutes, after which they stopped firing. H.E was used on front line and shrapnel during the lift. Rate of fire was 4 rounds per gun a minute. D/50 shells also to finish in Brigade zone for the same burst at the rate of 2 rounds per howitzer per minute.	
	4		Another Chinese attack took place at 7.30.a.m. Batteries carried out the same programme.	

Place	Date	Hour	Summary of Events and Information	Remarks and references to Appendices
	5.		Orders were received for an attack by the 34th Div on left and 9th Div on right. The objective of the 34th Div was CURLY and CHARLIE and to establish posts in CUTHBERT & COD, while the 9th Div were to take COPID and a line 60 yards E of this and South of the railway. Besides ourselves the following brigades supported the 34th Div:- 51st, 160th, 152nd, 293rd, 223rd, 317th. Zero hour was at 8.05 pm. B/150 and C/150 opened on CHARLIE with H.E. A/150 just short of CHARLIE with shrapnel, but at zero + 2 lifted to same line as 'B' and 'C' B/150 with H.E. At zero + 4 its 3 batteries lifted 100 yards and fired shrapnel. At zero + 6 L/150 again a barrage of 50 yards ammunition on its final objective in which H.E. was used. At zero + 10 the barrage again lifted at 50 yards animals to protect the barrage line, where 'B' and 'C' B/150 fired a standing barrage with H.E. and 'A' B/150. Searched WEAK WEED WINDMILL COPSE in brigade zone with shrapnel. 'D' B/150 bombarded COD & CUTHBERT and at zero + 5 L/150 200 yards	

Army Form C. 2118.

WAR DIARY
or
INTELLIGENCE SUMMARY.
(Erase heading not required.)

Place	Date	Hour	Summary of Events and Information	Remarks and references to Appendices
Shuts 51.B.N.W & 51.B.S.W.	June 1917	1	A quiet day.	
		2	The 160th Brigade R.F.A. returned into action, so Batteries 50th Bde registered their S.O.S. lines (evening) responsible for zone at 10 a.m. The Zones are:- North line $I.7.a.9\tfrac{1}{2}.9\tfrac{1}{2}$ to $I.3.d.0.0$ South " $I.7.d.\tfrac{1}{2}.9\tfrac{1}{2}$ - $I.9.b.0.0$ between the 51st Bde on the right and 160th Bde on the left.	
		3	Batteries took part in a Chinese attack at 8.0 p.m. The 18 pdrs fired on the enemy front line for 2 minutes and then lifted 50 yards behind it to 6 minutes, then came back on front line again for another 2 minutes, after which they stopped firing. H.E. was used on front line and Shrapnel during its lifts. Rate of fire was 4 rounds per gun a minute. D/50 Shells also to points in Brigade zone for the same burst at the rate of 2 rounds per gun per minute.	
		4	Another Chinese attack took place at 7.30 a.m. Batteries carried out the same programme.	

Place	Date	Hour	Summary of Events and Information	Remarks and references to Appendices
	5.		Orders were received for an attack by the 34th Div on left and 9th Div on right. The objective of the 34th Div was CURLY and CHARLIE and to establish posts in CUTHBERT road, while the 9th Div had to take CUPID and a line 60 yards E of this and South of the railway. Besides ourselves the following b'gades. supported the 34th Div:- 51st, 160th, 152nd, 293rd, 223rd, 317th. Zero hour was at 8.0 p.m. B/150 our C/50 opened on CHARLIE with H.E. A/150 just short of CHARLIE with Shrapnel, but at zero + 2 b/[?] to saturate as 'B' and 'C' B/15gr with H.E. At zero + 4 for 3 b[?] in hills 100 yards and two shapnel. At zero + 6 b/150 again attacked at 50 yards annul on 15 final objective on which H.E. was used. At zero + 10 the barrage again b/150 at 50 yards annuals to protect the Barrage line, where 'B' and 'C' B/15gr formed a standing barrage with H.E. and 'A' B/15. Started WEAK. WEED. WINDMILL COPSE in brigade zone w/K Shrapnel. 'D' B/15 barbaned CO9 r CUTHBERT, and at zero + 5 b/[?] 200 yards.	

Army Form C. 2118.

WAR DIARY
or
INTELLIGENCE SUMMARY.
(Erase heading not required.)

Place	Date	Hour	Summary of Events and Information	Remarks and references to Appendices
	5. Cont?		The rate of fire was as follows:—	
			18 Pdr. Zero to Zero +10 4 rounds per gun per minute	
			Z+10 to Z+14 3 " " " "	
			Z+14 – Z+30 2 " " " "	
			Z+30 1 " " " "	
			4.5 Howr. Zero to Zero+14 2 " " " "	
			Z+14 – Z+30 1 " " " "	
			The barrage proved very well and appeared to be very effective. The attack was successful and position gradually consolidated. Throughout the manoeuvre Support the attack on this occasion. Apparently the Germans were taken by surprise believing it 16th another Chinese attack another has been a good number recently. "A" B"? was engaged in heavy fire from 10 pm till 3 AM in Brigade Zone, while "D" B"? to engage line with D/S1 shells SQUARE WOOD with gas shells at 11 am firing 50 rounds of BCBR in 3 minutes	

WAR DIARY or INTELLIGENCE SUMMARY

Army Form C. 2118.

Place	Date	Hour	Summary of Events and Information	Remarks and references to Appendices
	5 cont'd		followed by 75 rounds B.S.K. in 5 minutes. There was some firing in answer to S.O.S. calls during the night, but all attempts at enemy concentrations were broken up.	Casualties
	6.		A quiet day. A few S.O.S. calls.	"C" 1 wounded
	7.		Battries fired in answer to S.O.S. and some shells with gas shells during the night.	"C" 3 wounded.
	8.		Battries were again shelling with gas shells from 2.30pm - 3.0pm and also a little later. In the evening the whole Corps artillery opened barrage to support the Canadian Corps and 3rd Corps Australian to the left. Three similar barrages were put down at 8.30pm, 11.45pm and 12.55am. The 18pdrs started an S.O.S. burst for 2 minutes at 4 rounds per gun per minute. At zero +2 they advanced by lifts of 100 yards for 2 minutes at the rate of 3 rounds per gun per minute. At Z +10 guns burst out 16 S.O.S. burst at 2 rounds per gun per minute for 2 minutes, and then ceased fire. Half shrapnel and half H.E. was used	

WAR DIARY
or
INTELLIGENCE SUMMARY.
(Erase heading not required.)

Army Form C. 2118.

Place	Date	Hour	Summary of Events and Information	Remarks and references to Appendices
	8 Cont'd		"D" Bty. bombarded WIBBLE TRENCH during the burst firing 2 minutes broken by himself. The enemy replies very lightly over trenches. During the firing barrage at 11.45pm on infantry established 3 posts in C.O.D. which had been withdrawn.	Casualties.
	9.		A fairly quiet day.	D/1 wounded
	10.		The firing fired a few salvoes of 4.2's with "D", "B", "C", but did no damage. The Brigade commander reconnoitred possible positions with the C.R.A. 9th Div. in case of a change of some to move forward.	
	11		A quiet day. Orders received for the remainder more.	
	12.		Battery fired an organised shoot at 12 noon for 12 minutes. Brigade Commander with 105cm C.R.A. 9th Div.	
	13		further of Battery Commanders. Orders received for artillery operations on 14th 15th and 16th.	
	14.		Quiet on the whole.	D/2 wounded

Army Form C. 2118.

WAR DIARY
or
INTELLIGENCE SUMMARY.
(Erase heading not required.)

Place	Date	Hour	Summary of Events and Information	Remarks and references to Appendices
	15/		In accordance with operation order batteries carried out harassing fire from 12 noon till 6.0 p.m, special attention being paid to SQUARE WOOD, WEIRD TRENCH, tracks from BRICKWORKS in I 9 b, through junction of WASTE and WINE, through I 9 c also to WEED, and also the railway. This harassing fire was taking place along the whole divisional front. The Brigade continuing till 12 noon on the 16th. After dark the 50th Brigade came under the command of the right divisional Artillery (47th Div), and with the exception of 'A' Battery moved to new positions as follows:- Headquarters to Eventhurkervai H 13 d 9 9. B/50 to position B/50 at A 15 b 99, C/50 to position C/50 at H 9 d 9 2. D/50 to wagon lines. The 78th Bde R.F.A. took over the vacated positions.	Carvallin
	16/		Batteries registering their new zones. The North Boundary of the Brigade zone was I 8 c 3½ ½ to I 10 c 0 1 and the South Boundary I 14 c 77 to I 16 c 06. The G.O.C. 47th Div. and C.R.A. visit	D/ 2 killed (2 wounded)

Place	Date	Hour	Summary of Events and Information	Remarks and references to Appendices
	16 cont'd		round 'A', 'B' and 'C' batteries' positions. The 18 pdr batteries of the Brigade moved from the zone from 5.0 p.m. 'D' Battery came into action after dark occupying position vacated by D/256 at H.12.c.8.6. just South of the R. SCARPE. The 29th Bde R.F.A. with the 50th Bde came under the Command of O.C. 56 Bde.	Casualties
	17 18		Quiet	'B' 2 wounded
	19		Batteries carried out harassing fire from 12 noon till 12 mid- night on 20th firing 2/3rds of the allowance of ammunition at night.	
	20		'D' Battery fired killed shell during the night. At 5.0 p.m. the 18 pdr of the Left Group had an organised shoot searching shell holes. The 29th Bde. put a barrage from I.15.c. 10.50 to I.20.b. 95.75. and the 50th Bde. from I.20.a. 75.75. At 5.2 p.m. the 18 pdr began creeping 16 yards by 1/2 minute of 50 yards permanent toward East the until the 29th Brigade	'C' 1 wounded

WAR DIARY
or
INTELLIGENCE SUMMARY.
(Erase heading not required.)

Army Form C. 2118.

Place	Date	Hour	Summary of Events and Information	Remarks and references to Appendices
	20 Cont.		had reached the starting point of the 50th Bde and his reserve. 5.14 pm Wurfer Raid. The ammunition used was as follows. 29th Bde 5.0 pm – 5.6 pm H.E. 5.6 " – 5.14 " 50% H.E. and 50% Shrapnel. 50th Bde Shrapnel throughout. The rate of fire was 4 rounds per gun per minute. 'D' Bttn in conjunction with the 128th Bde barraged 100 yards East of the 29th Bde Zone, D/128 on right, D/150 on left moving thereonwards as the 78 Bde barrage continuing 3 rounds per how a minute. A/79 Battery covered the command of the O.C. 50th Bde. Remainder on lyst of 50th Bde.	
	21		Batteries carried out harassing fire from horn till horn with 235.	
	22.			
	23.		Batteries registered for forthcoming raid.	
	24.		A raid took place at 10.15 pm by the 1st Battalion Royal Irish Fusiliers. The artillery arrangements were in hands of the O.C. 50th Bde who, in addition to his own Brigade, had the artillery	

WAR DIARY
or
INTELLIGENCE SUMMARY
(Erase heading not required.)

Army Form C. 2118.

Place	Date	Hour	Summary of Events and Information	Remarks and references to Appendices
	24 Inst?		of 2.18 pr batteries of the 4th and 14.5 How Battery of the 29th Bde. 12 - 18 pdr guns of the 51st Bde, 32nd Bde and 2 section of 4.5 How. 1-18 pdr battery of the 31st Bde, and 1-15 pdr battery A179 & 9th Left Divisional Artillery. The Heavy Artillery also assisted containing HAUSH & DEZBAR woods and a hostile Gun battery was also engaged. The preparation bombardment and expert counter attacks. The barrage was extraordinarily good, and accurate, the infantry getting such close to bursting shrapnel with impunity. The enemy's reply was very feeble though at times 1.30 am he put up a barrage & hanging extensively on front, support lines and the railway bridge.	
	25.		Australian and 2 Divisions from Mesopotamia and took Gallery line – 15 306th Bde R.F.A. 65th Division, in advance on the 38th Bde had received orders to relieve the 308th Bde. After dark 1 section from each battery pulled out, and went to	

Army Form C. 2118.

WAR DIARY
or
INTELLIGENCE SUMMARY.
(Erase heading not required.)

Place	Date	Hour	Summary of Events and Information	Remarks and references to Appendices
	25 and 26.		The waggon lines for the night Batteries were shelled with 8" in morning, his German aeroplane apparently ranging on the lot. 2/Lieut QUINN 'A'Bty. was temporarily buried and got concussion. Otherwise no damage was done. The 2 remaining sections withdrew to wagon lines after dark, and the advance section hung up informing in new positions. HQ to wagon lines.	Casualties 'A' 2/Lieut QUINN wounded.
	27.		Brigade H.Q. moved up to new position behind WANCOURT at N22c88. Remaining section of batteries came in after dark to HENINEL. "A"/50 at N29a.74. B/50 N29a.I.I. C/50. 4 guns at N28B.98 2 guns at N29c.6.0. D/50 at N29a.96. Through for S.O.S. line was about 3600 yards. Wasunder the 56th Div. 6th Corps.	
	28) 29) 30.		Quiet. Batteries registering their new zones. At 3.0 pm "D"Bty. fired on NUT TRENCH and neighbourhood on hostile Trench hurler's and snipers. The 18 pdr batteries searched skill both in the neighbourhood. C.R.A. 9th Div. 10th (temporary command) of the 56th Div. Artillery.	

WAR DIARY
or
INTELLIGENCE SUMMARY.
(Erase heading not required.)

Army Form C.

Place	Date	Hour	Summary of Events and Information	Remarks and references to Appendices
			Honours & Awards. *for services since September 1916.*	
			Bar to D.S.O. Maj. C.W. McLEAN. C/50. Military medal. Sergt BROWNING. C/50.	
			2nd Bar " " " " (Continued) " KINDER T. "
			D.S.O. Maj. D.R.D. FISHER. A/50. " Bdr. HARRIS A.H "
			Military Cross Lieut C.W. ANDREW " " Gnr. FORBES P. "
			" " H.S. ELLISON C/50 " " MORTON P "
			" 2/Lt C.C. CROUCH A/50 " " CEDARGREEN R. "
			" " G.M. BONNIN C/50 " " Bdr. MEELING B. "
			" " Capt. A.V. CRAIG R.A.M.C. att. 50 TiBde. Meritorious Service medal.	
				R.S.M. E. DAWSON. H.Q.
			Military medal. Sergt CLAYTON A.W. A/50. Fitter S.Sergt J.B. HILTON. D/50.	
			" " Dvr. HENERY J " Mentioned in despatches.	
			" " Sergt. BEWSEY F.V. " Lieut G.B. TRAILL H.Q.	
			" " Gnr. GORMALLY. M. " " C.W. ANDREW A/50	
			" " Bdr. JEYNES A " " H.S. ELLISON C/50.	
			" " R.M.R RICHARDS E " B.S.M. DYER. late C/50.	
			" " Gnr. APPLEYARD A " Sergt BAKER A.V.C. att A/50	
				a/Sergt PETERS. N. H.Q.

R.J.M.C? Brooke Lt Col, RFA

Army Form C. 2118.

WAR DIARY
or
INTELLIGENCE SUMMARY.
(Erase heading not required.)

Place	Date	Hour	Summary of Events and Information	Remarks and references to Appendices
			Total Casualties for the month of June.	
			2/Lieut F.J. QUINN wounded.	
			O.R. 2 killed.	
			12 wounded.	
			Total. 14	
			Ammunition Expended during June.	
			18 Pdr. Shrapnel 9645.	
			(3 batteries) H.E. 9810.	
			Smoke 4.	
			4.5 How. H.E. 3975.	
			(1 Battery) Lethal 366.	
			Lachrymatory 33.	

SECRET.   50th. Bde. No. E.K. 216

LEFT GROUP ORDERS FOR MINOR OPERATION.

Reference attached Map PLOUVAIN 1/10,000 - Air Photo 13
AA 732 - 12/6/17.

1. A raid will be carried out at Zero Hour on Z. day by the 10th. Infantry Brigade with the object of securing an identification and obtaining information regarding the enemy's line.

2. Infantry form up in CROW Trench between I.14.c.5.2. and I.14.c.55.55.

   Objective:- The front I.14.c.75.10. to I.14.c.9.5. and to a depth of 75 yards, i.e. the German system of organised shell holes apparently in two systems.

3. The operation will be supported by the following 18 pdrs:-

   29th. Bde. R.F.A. .. .. .. 11 guns.
   32nd. Bde. R.F.A. .. .. .. 16 guns.
   50th. Bde. R.F.A. .. .. .. 18 guns.
   51st. Bde. R.F.A. .. .. .. 6 guns.
   Left Div. Arty. (A/79) .. .. 6 guns.

   and by the following 4.5" Hows:-

   128th. Bty. R.F.A. .. .. .. 29th. Bde. RFA
   "D" Bty. R.F.A. .. .. .. 50th. Bde. RFA
   1 Section .. .. 32nd. Bde. RFA

4. Barrages and Rates of Fire as per attached Tables Y and Z.

5. Ammunition.

   For all 18 pdrs.   Shrapnel throughout the operations, except Barrage B which will be H.E.
   4.5" Howitzers   H.E.

6. Arrangements will be made for Counter-Battery work and for Heavy Artillery on HAUSA WOOD and DILBAR WOOD.

7. The 50th. Brig. will find Liaison Officer at Battalion Hd.Qrs.

8. Action of Infantry.

   Zero   Infantry leave assembly trench and advance.
   Z plus 3   Troops reach and clean up 1st. system.
   Z plus 5   2nd. wave of troops advance on second line of shell holes.
   Z plus 6   Troops clean up 2nd. line.
   Z plus 11   Advanced troops start to return and pass through 1st. system.
   Z plus 12   Troops holding 1st. system follow.

9. If it is required to stop the fire of Artillery before zero plus 30 the message "O.K." will be sent to Batteries. On receipt of this all guns will stop firing and be ready to repeat their Barrage if required.

10. If it should be found necessary to repeat any barrage the rate of fire will be 2 rounds per gun per minute and only the barrage letter, followed by a figure indicating the number of minutes for which the barrage is required, will be sent to batteries, e.g. "H.5" will mean "Repeat Barrage H. for 5 minutes at 2 r p g p m".

11. Z. day and Zero hour will be notified later.

12. Watches will be synchronised from this Office.

13. Acknowledge by wire.

Lieut. R.F.A.

23/June/1917.   Adjutant, 50th. Brigade, R.F.A.

Copy No. 1   to 4th. Div. Arty.
"   2-5   to 29th. Bde. R.F.A.
"   6-10   to 32nd. Bde. R.F.A.
"   11-15 to 50th. Bde. R.F.A.
"   16-17 to 51st. Bde. R.F.A.
"   18   to A/79 Battery.
"   19   to 10th. Inf. Brig.
"   20-21 to 1st. Bn. Royal Irish Fusiliers.
"   22-24 Spare.

18 pounder Barrage Table Y.

Btys.	Hour	Barrage Letter.	Task	Rate of Fire.
2 Btys. 29th. Bde. 11 guns. & B/50 6 guns. 10.16½	Zero to 3 plus 1½	A	I.14.c.70.00. to I.14.c.95.60.	4 r p g p m.
	3 plus 1½		Lift 50 yards towards line I.20.b. 10.85. to I.14.d. 35.50.	-do-
	10.17½ 3 plus 2½		-do-	-do-
2+3½ 10.18½	3 plus 3½		-do-	-do-
2+4½ 10.19½ 10.45	3 plus 4½ to 3 plus 30	B	Form standing barrage on line I.20.b.10.85. to I.14.d.35.50.	4 r p g p m to 3 plus 15 then 2 r p g p m till 3 plus 30 then cease firing.
32nd. Bde. 16 guns.	Zero to 3 plus 30 10.15-10.45	B	Form standing barrage on line I.20.b.10.85. to I.14.d.35.50.	4 r p g p m till 3 plus 15 then 2 r p g p m till 3 plus 30 then cease firing.
A/50 Bde. 4 guns.	Zero to Zero plus 30. 10.15 to 10.45	C	Form flank barrage from I.14.c.70.00. to I.20.b.10.85.	4 r p g p m till 3 plus 15 then 2 r p g p m till 3 plus 30 then cease firing.
C/50 Bde. 4 guns.	3 plus 30 10.15 to 10.45	D	Form flank barrage from I.14.c.95.60. to I.14.d.35.50.	4 r p g p m till 3 plus 15 then 2 r p g p m till 3 plus 30 then cease firing.
A/50 Bde. 2 guns.	Zero to 3 plus 20. 10.15 to 10.35	F	Sweep from I.20.a. 70.50. to I.20.a. 70.80. and search 200 yards East.	3 r p g p m till 3 plus 15 then 1 r p g p m till 3 plus 20 then cease firing.
C/50 Bde. 2 guns	Zero to 3 plus 20 10.15 to 10.35	E	Sweep from I.14.c. 90.80. to I.14.a. 90.20. and lengthen searching for 300 yards.	3 r p g p m till 3 plus 15 then 1 r p g p m till 3 plus 20 then cease firing.
I Bty. 51st. Bde. 6 guns.	Zero to 3 plus 15 10.15 to 10.30	J	1 Section enfilade sunken road in I.20.b. & I.14.d.	2 r p g p m till 3 plus 15 then cease firing.
		L	2 Sections between road & HAUSA WOOD	
A/79 6 guns.	Zero to 3 plus 15. 10.15 to 10.30	G	Search Railway Cutting and track South of it in I.14.b. 1 gun on Windmill.	2 r p g p m till 3 plus 15 then cease firing.

4.5" Howitzer Barrage Table A.

Bty.	Hour	Barrage Letter.	Task	Rate of fire.
32nd. Bde. 2 guns.	Zero to Zero plus 15.	K	CHALK PIT I.20.b.	3 r p g p m.
29th. Bde. 6 guns.	-do- 10.15 to 10.30	I L	2 Sections CYPRUS. 1 Section searching between road and HAUSA WOOD from CHALK PIT for 300 yards.	3 -do-
D/50 Bde. 6 guns.	-do-	H	I.15.c.00.65. to I.14.b.30.40.	3 -do-

E.K. 216/2.

1. Z Day is today and Zero hour will be between 10 and 11 p.m. The exact time will be notified by wire in the evening - one word only will be sent indicating the number of minutes after 10 p.m.

   e.g. "Fifteen" , 10.15 p.m.

2. In the event of the wind being favourable gas shell will be fired for the first minute at the Rate of 4 r p g p m by D/60 on Barrage H and by Howitzers of 29th Bde. on the <u>further</u> end of Barrages I and L.

   If gas shell are to be fired the code word "REVENGE" will be sent.

3. The following amendments in E.K.216 are to be noted -
   Table Y, Column 2,
   for Z + 4½ read Z + 3½ and
   " Z + 5½ " Z + 4½
   In the same Column, the time for Barrage D should read "Zero to Z + 3g."

4. Please acknowledge by wire.

   G.B.Grant
   Lieut: R.F.A.
   Adjutant 50th Bde. R.F.A.

Copies to :-

29th Brigade R.F.A.
32nd " "
A,B,C & D/60. Btys.
51st Brigade R.F.A.
A/79 Battery.

4th Div. Artillery   )
10th Inf. Brigade.   ) For information.
1st Battn. Royal Irish Fusrs.)

24/6/17   E.K. 219/4/   SECRET.

The following alterations are made in the rates of fire :-

1. Barrage A will be 4 r p g p m.

2. Barrages B, C and D will be 4 r p g p m till Z + 15 then 2 r p g p m. till Z + 30.

3. Howitzers will all fire 3 r p g p m.

[signature]
Lieut: R.F.A
Adjutant 50th Bde. R.F.A

Copies to :-

29th Brigade R.F.A
32nd   "   "
A, B, C & D/50 Btys.
51st Brigade R.F.A.
A/79 Battery.
4th. Div. Artillery   )
10th Inf. Brigade   ) For information
1st Battn. Royal Irish Fusilrs)

-SECRET-

10th Brigade No.B/ 398

O.C.50th Bde R.F.A.

    Herewith copy of Scheme for a minor operation to be undertaken by the 10th Inf. Brigade on the night 24/25th not 25/26th as previously arranged.

    The scheme will of course conform to the revised Artillery programme which we have not yet received.

Please acknowledge

[signature]

Captain B.M.
10th Infantry Brigade.

22/6/17.

SECRET

4th Division "G".

Reference Trench Map PLOUVAIN 1/10,000.
Aeroplane Photos (13 L.A.752, 51B, I.14, 12/6/17.
                  (13 L.A.764, 51B, I.13,14,19,20. 12/6/17.

In accordance with G.S.78 dated 18th, I forward the following scheme.

1. **OBJECT.-** To ascertain system of defence of organised shell holes- inflict loss on the enemy, and obtain identification.

2. **OBJECTIVE.-** German system of organised shell holes, apparently in two systems.
   Front - I.14.c.75.10 to I.14.c.90.50 and to a depth of 75 yards.
   This is shown on Map A.

3. **ZERO HOUR & DATE.** The raid to take place on night 25/26th June - ZERO hour will be notified later (probably at 11p.m.)

4. **TIME TABLE.**

Time.	Action of Troops.	Remarks.
ZERO.	Barrage comes down on Front Line Shell Holes. Troops leave Assembly Trench and advance.	Barrage between I.14.b.3.0 and I.20.a.7.5.
Z + 1 minute.	Creeping Barrage lifts 50 yards.	Creeping barrage is between I.14.c.9.7 and I.20.a.7.9. which leaves 100 yards gap on each flank.
Z + 2 minutes.	Creeping barrage lifts 50 yards. Troops reach and clean up 1st system.	
Z + 4 minutes.	Creeping barrage lifts 50 yards. 2nd wave advances on 2nd system.	
Z + 5 minutes.	Creeping barrage lifts 50 yards and stands. Troops clean up 2nd system.	
Z + 10 minutes.	Advanced troops return and pass through 1st system.	
Z + 11 minutes.	Troops holding 1st system follow.	
Z + 15 minutes.	Barrage slackens off.	

5. **STRENGTH.** 4 Officers, 90 O.R.

6. **ASSEMBLY.** Troops taking part in the raid will assemble in CROFT TRENCH, I.14.c.60.20 to I.14.c.85.55. Opportunity will be given all ranks to study the ground over which they will pass.

-2-

7. ACTION.   All men engaged will be arranged in Sections of 1 N.C.O and 8 men, definite groups of shell holes being allotted to each section.

The sections detailed for 1st system of shell holes move forward followed at 25 yards distance by those detailed for the 2nd system of shell holes.

Flanking sections will be provided with Lewis Guns.

No hand grenades will be carried.

Return.   At Z + 10, or on completion of mission, Very Lights will be sent up at intervals from the flanks of the assembly position.

8. M.G.CO-OPERATION.
M.Guns. (Map B).

1 M.G. in CROFT Trench at I.14.a.52 to fire on a bearing 100° True.

1 M.G. of 11th M.G.Company by arrangement with 11th Brigade to fire from COLOMBO about I.20.a.55 on a bearing of 50° True.

1 M.G. on railway embankment about I.13.c.15 to employ long range fire and search railway from about I.14.b.07 to I.8.d.80.

4 M.G's in CORDITE trench to employ long range fire and barrage CYPRUS trench from I.14.d.63 southwards, and CARROT trench from I.20.b.74 Northwards, and front edge of HAUSA WOOD.

All guns fire sustained rate of fire from Zero to Zero plus 15, then slow rate until Zero + 25.

9.   Artillery programme is attached.
all shrapnel   The Barrage on front raided being of H.E. with shrapnel on the immediate flanks as a guide to raiding troops.

Lieut.Colonel,
19/6/17.   Commanding 10th Infantry Brigade.

REPORT ON RAID BY ROYAL IRISH FUSILIERS - 24th June 17.

Result.
S Prisoners were taken (Hanoverians). Shell holes inspected. A few were organised for defence. Not a great deal of work had been done. A shallow trench had been begun between 2 or 3 holes, about 1 foot deep 1½ ft. broad.

Our casualties were 5 wounded and 2 Officers and 19 men missing.

Barrage.
Heavies opened at least 30 seconds too soon. 18-pdr. barrage opened splendidly, and was very good. Bursts were low and only 3 or 4 rounds were short. Owing to the Heavies starting early, the Infantry got out of the trench and were starting to advance before the 18-pdr. barrage came down. The Infantry, after crossing the crest got very close to the barrage indeed many shells bursting over or just in front. The accuracy of the barrage made this all right.

Intelligence.
Our right advanced without any opposition. Some Germans appear to have been seen, but a Lewis Gun fired from the hip of a man advancing on the flank dealt with these.

The left met opposition early, but after capturing 5 prisoners went on to second objective. It was on this flank that the missing men were.

One Officer was seen to trip over a wire, get up and bayonet a Hun, but was not seen again. The other missing Officer was seen shooting Germans with his revolver. Our patrols went out immediately after but found no trace. German patrols were also out, and it is possible had taken the missing men in, as they had removed all their own dead.

Before Zero 4 German machine guns were firing, but none fired during the raid except one from the German line of Defence at about Zero + 7 minutes.

(Sd) A A TYER
LT. RFA

25/6/17.

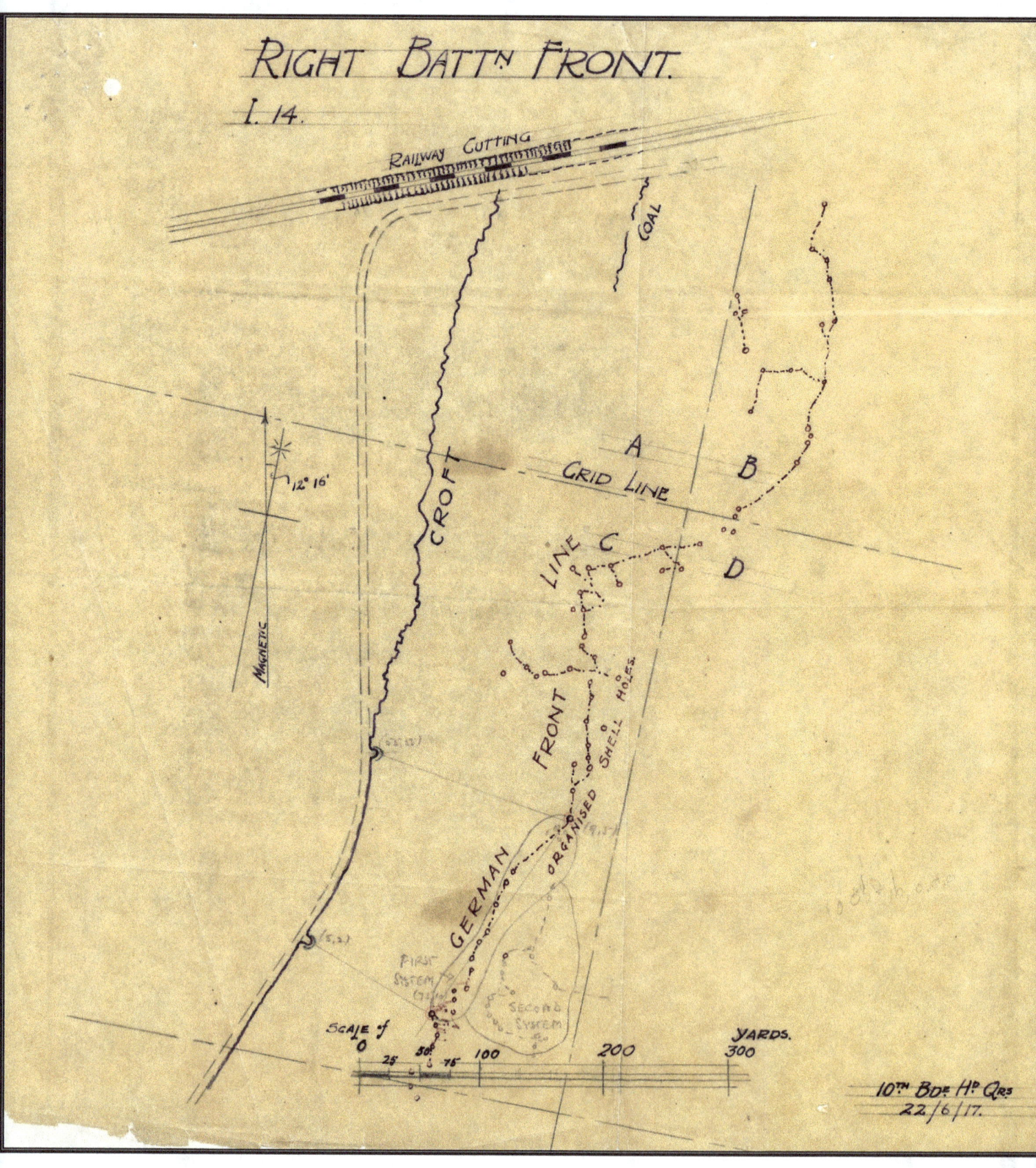

CONFIDENTIAL

WAR

DIARY.

-:-:-:-:-:-

JULY. 1917.

-:-:-:-:-:-

50TH. BRIGADE R.F.A.

9TH. (SCOTTISH) DIVISION.

Army Form C. 2118.

WAR DIARY
or
INTELLIGENCE SUMMARY.
(Erase heading not required.)

Place	Date	Hour	Summary of Events and Information	Remarks and references to Appendices
Ref sheet 51B.S.W.	July 1917 1) 2) 3)		Quiet days. Special shoots arranged to take place on receipt of code word from infantry, also mutual support schemes with Divisions on flanks.	
	4.		The 50th Brigade R.F.A. came under the command of CRA 50th Division. The Zone remained the same.	
	5.		The 251st Bde R.F.A. having gone out of the line the 251st Bde R.F.A. switched their line aim from the zone of the 50th Bde. In our therefore between the 251st Bde on the left and the 250th Bde on the right. D/162 came under the tactical command of OC 50th 13th R.F.A.	
	6.		Liaison under the O.C. 251.13th R.F.A. for liaison purposes.	
	7.		Special work programme arranged to harass short batteries carrying out short or wiring a certain number on him from the Brigade.	
	8) 9) 10)		Quiet. Slight alteration in S.O.S. lines.	

WAR DIARY
or
INTELLIGENCE SUMMARY.

Army Form C. 2118.

Place	Date	Hour	Summary of Events and Information	Remarks and references to Appendices
	July '17			
Right	11/12		D/50 fired chemical shell at 11.15 pm and 2.15 am. The 162nd Bde R.F.A. went out. A/50 came under the tactical command of O.C. 250½ Bde R.F.A. covering right infantry Brigade. The 50th 13th Bde A/50 covering via Left infantry Brigade with the 257th 13th R.F.A. Duties of A/50 were to SOS lines were amended and became from 9.0 pm 11th
			B/50 O 20 d 68½ to O 20 b 61	
			C/50 O 20 b 61 " O 20 b 63	
			D/50 O 20 d 81 " O 20 d 93	
			After dark 1 Sec A/50 moved to N 28 b 32.	
	August 12/13		Another section A/50 moved to N 28 b 32. The 9th D.L.I. made a small raid on L. TRENCH at 10 pm after a bombardment earlier by the 50th, 13th R.F.A. At 3.30 pm the infantry withdrew from Pots 1 and 2. The Brigade fires as follows:-
	13.			

Army Form C. 2118.

WAR DIARY
or
INTELLIGENCE SUMMARY.
(Erase heading not required.)

Instructions regarding War Diaries and Intelligence Summaries are contained in F.S. Regs., Part II. and the Staff Manual respectively. Title pages will be prepared in manuscript.

Place	Date	Hour	Summary of Events and Information	Remarks and references to Appendices
	13 Aug		15 bdr.	
			B/50 3 guns O 26 c 3 5½ to O 26 c 3 6½	
			C/50 3 guns O 26 c 3 6½ to O 26 c 3 7½	
			Trier 4.0 to 4.5 pm 2 rounds per gun per minute	
			4.5 " 4.10 " 1 " " " " "	
			4.15 " 4.25 " 1 " " " " "	
			4.45 " 5.0 " ½ " " " " "	
			7.0 pm H - 3-gun salvos from B/50 and C/50	
			10.0 – 10.2 pm 2 rounds per gun per minute on Tarralone	
			10.2 – 10.15 " 1 " " " " " on	
			O 26 c 65 to O 26 c 33 B/50 right half, C/50 left half.	
			4.5 How. D/50 3 guns O 26 c 35½ to O 26 c 37½	
			4.0 to 4.5 pm 2 rounds per gun per minute	
			4.30 ; 4.40 " 1 " " " " "	
			4.55 " 5.0 " 1 " " " " "	
			Ammunition 50% H.E. for 18 pdrs.	

WAR DIARY
or
INTELLIGENCE SUMMARY.

Army Form C. 2118.

Date	Hour	Summary of Events and Information	Remarks and references to Appendices
13 cont		Amnis the bombardment from 4.0 pm to 5.0 pm the enemy guns of batteries fires in dug outs in TRIANGLE WOOD 1/2 round per gun per minute. The 257th Brigade R.F.A. carried out a shoot at the same time on enemy trench O.21.a.0.5 1/2 to O.14.d.9 1/2. 1/2 to ascertain the enemy. The infantry outran and found his trench badly damaged but no Germans there.	
14.		A quiet day.	
15		D/50 shelled O.27.c.28 to O.27.a.20 with chemical shell during the night.	
16		In conjunction with the Harris and Trench Mortars D/50 bombarded OBENA at 3.0pm O.32.a.23 to O.32.a.25, B/50 put up a smoke barrage from O.27.c.28 to O.21.central to O.21.d.3. During the night D/50 bombarded from O.27.c.28 to O.27.a.20 with chemical and lachrymatory shell.	
17.		A few shells near HENINEL. Hostile aeroplane active in balloon	

WAR DIARY
or
INTELLIGENCE SUMMARY
(Erase heading not required.)

Army Form C. 2118.

Place	Date	Hour	Summary of Events and Information	Remarks and references to Appendices
	18		Maj. General LEWRY. M.G.R.A. 3rd Army went round battery positions with the Brigade Commander. A quiet day	
	19		An attempt raid was made by Enemy on LONE SAP, but completely failed.	
	20		Quiet day. Considerable hostile aeroplane activity.	
	21			
	22			
	23		Attempted hostile raid on No. 3 Post failed.	
	24		D/SD fired chemical shell.	
	25		Hostile bombardment on CHERISY	
	26		Quiet	
	27		B/SD shelled in afternoon and evening with 77 m/m & 5.9's. No. 1.	2/Lieut ALDER slightly wounded
	28		Guns hit and carriage & sights damaged	B/SD wounded
	29		Quiet	
	30		B/SD shelled with 4.2's	
	31		Orders came in for forthcoming move. Quiet.	

Army Form C. 2118.

WAR DIARY
or
INTELLIGENCE SUMMARY.
(Erase heading not required.)

Place	Date	Hour	Summary of Events and Information	Remarks and references to Appendices
			Casualties during July.	
			2/Lieut. F.H. ALDER wounded.	
			O.R. 1 "	
			Ammunition expenditure during July :—	
			18 Pdr. Shrapnel 4325	
			(3 Batteries) H.E. 3573	
			Smoke 225	
			4.5 How. H.E. 2508	
			(1 battery) Lethal 711	
			Lachrymatory 429	
			J.R. Hutton	
			Major R.F.A.	
			Lt-Colonel R.F.A.	
			Commanding 50th Brigade, R.F.A.	

CONFIDENTIAL

WAR

DIARY.

AUGUST 1917.

50TH. BRIGADE R.F.A.

9TH (SCOTTISH) DIVISION.

Army Form C. 2118.

WAR DIARY
or
INTELLIGENCE SUMMARY.
(Erase heading not required.)

Instructions regarding War Diaries and Intelligence Summaries are contained in F. S. Regs., Part II. and the Staff Manual respectively. Title pages will be prepared in manuscript.

Place	Date	Hour	Summary of Events and Information	Remarks and references to Appendices
Sheet 57C NE, 57C SE.	Aug. 1.		A quiet day. Preparation for move continued.	
	2.		1st Stage of exchange with 290th Brigade R.F.A. carried out. Brigade Commander and Adjutant with half gun line personnel and one officer from each battery proceeded at 9.0 am from MERCATEL X roads by motor bus to BUS. "B" and "D" Btys. went on into action behind HARRINCOURT WOOD and came under the Tactical command of 51st Brigade R.F.A. The remainder went to wagon lines at P33a. Half the wagon line of each battery proceeded by road at 7.0am to P33a. A similar number of the 290th Brigade R.F.A. arrived at the HENINEL position. They did not take on our wagon lines.	
	3.		Operation order was issued for Brigade to assist infantry returning from a raid in HENINEL sector. Infantry did not reach German Sap so Artillery was not required.	
	4.		A quiet day.	
	5.		Remainder of 50th Bde wagon lines left by road at 7.0 am.	

WAR DIARY
or
INTELLIGENCE SUMMARY.

Date	Hour	Summary of Events and Information	Remarks and references to Appendices
5 cont^d		Remainder of personnel in lorries at 9.0 a.m. Guns and stores were handed over, and the Command passed to O.C. 290th Brigade. The wagon lines at P33a are moved slightly to higher ground. The Brigade with 9th Div under C.R.A. 9th Div.	
6-18		Resting at wagon lines. Ten 'B' and 'D' batteries who were in action. 'A' and 'C' batteries training.	
19		O.C. 50th Bde R.F.A. took Command of the left group covering 27½ Inf. Bde in the HERMIES sector, relieving the 210th Bde R.F.A. The Group consisted of B/50, who came from 50?? Bde R.F.A. on the right, at Q7a14. A/293 at J33b85, and a coy pn. How. Bty. consisting of 1 Section 130th Bty and 1 Section D/51 at J35a52. The front to be covered was nearly 4000 yards.	
20		Batteries registered. C/50 relieved B/50. Also personnel went up to man D/50 Howitzer, the latter's personnel relieving 16 wagon line. During to the width of front covered in addition to the normal S.O.S. lines the defence	

Army Form C. 2118.

WAR DIARY
or
INTELLIGENCE SUMMARY.
(Erase heading not required.)

Instructions regarding War Diaries and Intelligence Summaries are contained in F. S. Regs., Part II. and the Staff Manual respectively. Title pages will be prepared in manuscript.

Place	Date	Hour	Summary of Events and Information	Remarks and references to Appendices
	20 (cont[d])		of the Zone was obtained by various concentrations and mutual support schemes.	
	21-27		Very quiet. 'B' and 'D' batteries training at wagon lines. Higher firing normally 10.0 rounds per 18 pdr battery and 30 rounds per How. Bty. Thereon a Corps Concentration East night on schedule points lasting a 1 minute. All batteries firing that could bear on the target. Amm allotment reduced to 10 rounds per gun, 5 " " How.	
	28.		The 13th Div Engaged in wire cutting. During the night 28/29 one section of C/50 moved to J.35.b.95.15.	
	29/30		Detached section C/50 Engaged in wire cutting for raid. At 8 p.m. on the 30th the 10th A.& S. Highlanders, 26th Inf. Bde. & 16 carried out a raid to clean YORKSHIRE BANK K.32.a and b, 16 raid quarries at K.32.b.49 and to ascertain the Enemy wire having. The left group Artillery arrived as follows:- A/62.93. 1 Section Enfilade road K.33.a.25.80 to K.32.b.98 Shrapnel.	

WAR DIARY
or
INTELLIGENCE SUMMARY

Army Form C. 2118.

Place	Date	Hour	Summary of Events and Information	Remarks and references to Appendices
	30 (cont.)		1 Sector : ETNA CRATER. Amm. H.E.	
			" Barrage K33a.00.95 to K26d.95.05 Amm Shrapnel.	
			Rate of fire.	
			Zero to Zero +5 4 rounds per gun per minute	
			Zero +5 " Zero + 15 3 " " " "	
			Zero +15 " Zero + 35 2 " " " "	
			C/S20 : Smoke barrage K27c.30.25 to K26d.15.55. from	
			Zero to Zero + 35. First half minute 4 rounds per gun per minute	
			Then 3 R.P.G.P.M.	
			4.5 How 13¹⁶⁄₂ Trench K27c.25.70 to K26d.20.95. Zero to Zero + 35	
			2 rounds per gun per minute. Howitzer firin west of K26d.78	
			all H.E. Howitzer from East of K26d.78 1 round per minute	
			H.E. 1 round per minute gas shell. The T.M's barrelain also	
			on target. The infantry met with no opposition time, found no	
			Germans and no signs of mining. After destroying a few shelters	
			they returned. After the action A/z.93 pulled out and returned to their trench lines	

WAR DIARY
or
INTELLIGENCE SUMMARY.
(Erase heading not required.)

Army Form C. 2118.

Place	Date	Hour	Summary of Events and Information	Remarks and references to Appendices
	31		The relief of the 9th Div'l Arty by 36th Div'l Artillery began as follows:. Also with D/50's Amm pulled out after dark without being relieved and returned to wagon lines leaving on Hows and stores 16 D/50. Left group. C/50 section at J36a93 and 1 section from Q7a14 relieved by a battery of 173rd Bde. Right Group. sections going into action at Q7a14. 1 Section of 16th Cwzn How (B/51) relieved by 2 section D/173. Two sections of B/173 went into action in position marked by A/h93 at J336.85.	
			Casualties N.L.	
			Ammunition expenditure (Withdrawn Cwzn How & Mtgs).	
			18 pdr. Shrapnel. 2389 H.E. 1673 4.5 How. H.E. 1135 Lethal. 47 18. pdr. Smoke. 754	

W McKern —
LT. COLONEL R.F.A.
COMMANDING 50TH BRIGADE, R.F.A.

CONFIDENTIAL

WAR

DIARY.

SEPTEMBER 1917.

50TH. BRIGADE R.F.A.

9TH. (SCOTTISH) DIVISION.

Army Form C. 2118.

WAR DIARY
or
INTELLIGENCE SUMMARY.
(Erase heading not required.)

Place	Date	Hour	Summary of Events and Information	Remarks and references to Appendices
Ref. Sheet 28.N.W. 28.N.E.	Sept. 1.		The command of the Brigade Zone passed to O.C. 173rd Brigade R.F.A. on completion of relief after dark. Remainder of 50th Bde on relief returned to wagon lines. Advance parties from batteries went to rest area at SERPIGNY, N.W. of BAPAUME.	
	2.		Preparing to march.	
	3.		The Brigade moved by road at 7.0 a.m. to rest area and settled in.	
	4.		Resting. M.G. R.A. 3rd Army came round.	
	5.		Review of Brigade in line by General ? the C.R.A. 9th Division	
	6.		Resting.	
	7.		Brigade proceeded to WATOU AREA, W. of POPERINGHE by train from MIRAUMONT. Also left lines at 4.0 a.m. H.Q. 8.0 a.m. and B.C. & D/50 at 4-hour intervals. Train journey varied from 7½ to 10 hours. Each unit detrained at PROVEN.	
	8.		Batteries arrived and settled in	

WAR DIARY or INTELLIGENCE SUMMARY

Army Form C. 2118.

Place	Date	Hour	Summary of Events and Information	Remarks and references to Appendices
	Sept.			
	9.		Brigade Commander and Signal Officer with air Officer and 3 Signallers from each battery went by lorry to H.Q. 42nd Div. R.A. at BRANDHOEK. Then on to Ramparts YPRES to O.C. 210th Brigade R.F.A. who took parts round position. Brigade Commander returned after reconnaissance. The remainder stayed.	
	10.		Observation of each battery marched to new wagon lines at H15d. Pt 6. Two Section went on. Their guns up to new battery position East of POTIJE. A/50. I.15 a.15.09, B/50. I.4.b.78.44. C/50. I.4.b.25.90. D/50. I.4.b.21.44.	A/50 1.90.20 D/50 1.90.20
	11.		Remaining section of batteries came up to new wagon lines. The guns going into action after dark.	
	12.		The Brigade belongs to anti aircraft group with 57th 210th 211th under 42nd D.A. Brigade H.Q. was in the Ramparts. Batteries busy making positions. Enemy shelling throughout.	C/50 1 wounded D/50 4 gassed D/50 Henning w

T2134. Wt. W708-776. 500090. 4/15. Sir J.C. & S.

WAR DIARY or INTELLIGENCE SUMMARY

Army Form C. 2118.

Place	Date	Hour	Summary of Events and Information	Remarks and references to Appendices
	Sept.			
	13		Brigade heavy bont of hostile/Enemy with 50th and 64th A.F.A. Bdes.	H.Q. 1 wounded A/50 1 wounded B/50 1 killed 1 wounded
	14		Brigade was part of No 3 Group with 50th Bde.	Also 1 wounded B/50 1 "
	15 } 16 }		Battering his Task barrages. D/50 100th park in gas bombardment during nights.	9/50 1 wounded Lr. ANDREW wounded
	17 } 18 }		Came under C.R.A. 9th Division.	A/50 2 wounded A/50 1 dis.w wounded
	19		Bombardment began at 3.0 am for forthcoming operations. This bombardment was divided into seven periods.	B/50 1 wounded D/50 3 wounds w.
	20		Zero hour was at 5.40 am. The attack 17th, 15th, 9th Division, 29qst, 296th, 210th, 211th, 50th, 57th 64th and D/86 battery. The 18pdr barrage was divided into (a) creeping (b) searching, the latter composed of 2 sections per brigade searching 100 to 500 yards in advance of the creeping barrage. Enemy attitude gun with Corps tunes fires on round of smoke annuals while infantry was advancing.	

WAR DIARY or INTELLIGENCE SUMMARY

Army Form C. 2118.

Place	Date	Hour	Summary of Events and Information	Remarks and references to Appendices
	21		After the attack at certain times during the day the Brigade reached certain areas.	
	22		Battery fired in answer to S.O.S. calls and swept see shell holes in Brigade Zone.	D/50 1 wounded 9/50 1 killed 1 wounded
	23		The Brigade came under CRA 3rd Div.	9/50 2 gunners 1 and gunner
	24		Fairly quiet.	B/50 2 gunners 1 wounded
	25		D/50 came under CRA 39th Div. tactically. Barrages took place in the morning and afternoon.	D/50 1 wounded
	26		Two hours bar at S.50 am. Intermittent fire kept up all night. The barrage was of the same type as previous attacks. After the final protective barrage was reached guns ceased forward track 3 hours in 1 1/2 hours. Then kept up intermittent fire in protective barrage line till end of the day.	
	27 28 29		Battery strafing forward positions. Sweeping barrage at intervals. 16 HUSSAR FARM.	9/50 1 killed 1 wounded

WAR DIARY
or
INTELLIGENCE SUMMARY.

Army Form C. 2118.

Place	Date	Hour	Summary of Events and Information	Remarks and references to Appendices
	Sept 30.		A/50 and 1 Section D/50 now to new position at I 6 d 88 and I 10.11½ each with morning.	
			Casualties	
			Lieut. Cw. ANDREW wounded.	
			O.R. 3 killed	
			2 died of wounds.	
			20 wounded	
			9 gassed	
			Total 34	
			Ammunition Expenditure	
			18 pdr. Shrapnel. 23,160	
			H.E. 22,840	
			Smoke. 1,100.	
			4.5 How. H.E. 8000	
			Gas }	
			WMcKeown.	
			Lt. Col. i/c	
			Cmdt 50th Bde R.F.A.	

CONFIDENTIAL

WAR

DIARY.

OCTOBER 1917.

50TH BRIGADE R.F.A.

9TH. (SCOTTISH) DIVISION.

Army Form C. 2118.

WAR DIARY
or
INTELLIGENCE SUMMARY.
(Erase heading not required.)

Instructions regarding War Diaries and Intelligence Summaries are contained in F.S. Regs., Part II. and the Staff Manual respectively. Title pages will be prepared in manuscript.

Place	Date	Hour	Summary of Events and Information	Remarks and references to Appendices
	Oct. 1st		Renewing two sections of each battery moved to new position behind FREZENBURG RIDGE just south of the railway. Batteries registered and fired practice barrages.	2/Lt LUCKHAM. D/50. wounded.
	2} 3}			2/Lt WARD. D/50. killed.
	4.		The attack was resumed at 6.0 a.m. 50th Bde R.F.A. supported the 10th Australian infantry Brigade, 3rd Australian Division. All objectives were gained.	2/Lt HICKMAN. C/50. killed. Lt YOUNG. D/50 missing. Lt WHITE. D/50. wounded.
	5.		Teaching barrages were fired. Batteries started to build forward positions behind Northern end of WINDMILL HILL.	
	6.		The 50th Bde was relieved by 240th Bde R.F.A. 48th Division, and moved to new wagon lines near POPERINGHE on the ELVERDINGHE road.	
	7.} 8.}		At wagon lines	
	9.		Batteries were in to action at ST. JOLIEN, under B.G. 63rd Bde R.F.A. Rtd KM. during the afternoon. An attack took place at 6.30 a.m. only partially successful on 48th Div. front.	

WAR DIARY
or
INTELLIGENCE SUMMARY.
(Erase heading not required.)

Army Form C. 2118.

Instructions regarding War Diaries and Intelligence Summaries are contained in F. S. Regs., Part II. and the Staff Manual respectively. Title pages will be prepared in manuscript.

Place	Date	Hour	Summary of Events and Information.	Remarks and references to Appendices
	Oct.			
	10. } 11. }		Battery registered and fired test barrages. 2000 rds of 18pdr ammunition and 650 rounds for 4.5" how were received to bring us up to the guns. The work of bringing the ammunition up was most difficult owing to mud and hostile shell fire.	
	12.		The attack was resumed. We covered the 9th Div, forming the Centre Group with 160 & 161 Bde. The right group (D/V AFA Bde and 200 Bde RFA) also supported the and left Group (51st AFA Bde, 126th AFA Bde, 291 Bde RFA) also supported the division. The weather conditions and state of the ground hampered the attack which was only partially successful.	2/LT. COOPER also wounded
			Battery looking after positions and getting up ammunition.	
	13.)14.)15.)16.)17.		D/50 moved down the POELCAPPELLE road to ARTILLERY HOUSE. B/50 moved to D/50's old position. During this period there was very considerable counter battery work on the part of the enemy. Brigade and Battery Commander of the 2nd Divisional Artillery	2/LT. DAVIS 15/10 " CAYE 5/10 gassed. MAJOR HOLLWAY
	18.		arrived to see positions	
	19.		50th Brigade relieved by 38th Bde 2nd Div. Battery returned to wagon lines.	2/LT. CROUCH also wounded (since died of wounds)

T2134. Wt. W708-776. 500030. 4/16. Sir J. C. & S.

WAR DIARY or INTELLIGENCE SUMMARY

Army Form C. 2118.

Place	Date	Hour	Summary of Events and Information	Remarks and references to Appendices
	Oct.			
	20.		The Brigade marched to wagon lines 1½ miles N.W. of POPERINGHE on the PROVEN road.	
	21.		March continued to WORMHOUDT.	
	22.		March continued to Staging area at GHYVELDT. Came under 42nd Div. Arty, 15th Corps, 4th Army.	
	23.) 24.)		Resting.	
	25.		Bde and Battery Commanders went up to reconnoitre positions behind NIEUPORT on right Division front under 42nd D.A.	
	26.) 27.)		Resting.	
	28.		1 section each battery went to new wagon lines at LA PANNE and later Bdes to relieve a 187 Bde. R.F.A. 41st Div. Arty. on left front.	
	29.		Remainder of Brigade moved to new wagon lines. Remaining section relieving rest of 187 Bde. with him under 9th Div.	
	30.		Batteries registered.	
	31.		Quiet. D/50 Engaged a hostile Trench mortar during his altercation.	

WAR DIARY
or
INTELLIGENCE SUMMARY.
(Erase heading not required.)

Army Form C. 2118.

Place	Date	Hour	Summary of Events and Information	Remarks and references to Appendices
			Casualties for October	
			Officers Killed 2	
			Missing 1	
			Wounded 3	
			Gassed 5	
			Total 11	
			O.R. Killed 30	
			Missing 4	
			Wounded 59	
			Gassed 64	
			157	
			L. McKean	
			LT. COLONEL, R.F.A.	
			COMMANDING 60TH BRIGADE, R.F.A.	

CONFIDENTIAL

WAR

DIARY.

NOVEMBER 1917.

50TH BRIGADE R.F.A.

9TH. (SCOTTISH) DIVISION.

WAR DIARY
or
INTELLIGENCE SUMMARY.

Place	Date	Hour	Summary of Events and Information	Remarks and references to Appendices
	Nov. 1.		Except for reginhlin of zero line and S.O.S. lines days were my quiet	
	12.		There was a certain amount of hostile shelling in our of dinner.	
	13.		French Officers came round to reconnoitre our	
	14.		Enemy artillery more active than usual.	
	15.		'A' Battery shelled all day	
	16. 17. 18.		Quiet days.	
	19.		Half of each battery was relieved by 55th Div French Artillery Regt but took to wagon lines	
	20.		Half of each battery marched during early hours of morning to new wagon lines at GHYVELDE. Remaining half R Each battery and Brigade H.Q. relieved by the French	
	21.		Remainder of Brigade marched to GHYVELDE in early hours of morning	
	22		The Brigade marched to WORMHOUT	

Army Form C. 2118.

WAR DIARY
or
INTELLIGENCE SUMMARY.
(Erase heading not required.)

Place	Date	Hour	Summary of Events and Information	Remarks and references to Appendices
	Nov.			
	23.		The Brigade continued march to WEMAERS CAPPELL.	
	24.		The Brigade continued march to WARDRECQUES.	
	25.		The Brigade marched to THIENBRONNE.	
	26.		The Brigade continued march to retaure. H.Q. at BEAURAINVILLE. 'A' B'ty at HESMOND 'B' B'ty at BEAURAINVILLE. 'C' B'ty at LOISON. 'D' B'ty at OFFIN.	
	27.		The Brigade was resting.	
	28.		Training began. A Programme was made out for the weeks training. The first week Section training, the second week Battery training; the next week Brigade training. Training Area about 3 miles x 2 miles S.E. of the BEAURAINVILLE - ROYON road.	
	29/30		Training continued.	

Army Form C. 2118.

WAR DIARY
or
INTELLIGENCE SUMMARY.
(Erase heading not required.)

Instructions regarding War Diaries and Intelligence Summaries are contained in F. S. Regs., Part II. and the Staff Manual respectively. Title pages will be prepared in manuscript.

Place	Date	Hour	Summary of Events and Information	Remarks and references to Appendices
			Casualties April 1916	
			Killed	
			Wounded	
			Officers — 3 (1 since (wounds), 1 remains at duty)	
			Other ranks 10 11 (1 since (wounds).	
			W. Milton	
			LT. COLONEL R.F.A.	
			COMMANDING 50TH BRIGADE, R.F.A.	

WAR DIARY or INTELLIGENCE SUMMARY

50th Bde

Date	Hour	Summary of Events and Information	Remarks
December 1		Orders were received in the early hours of the morning for the Brigade to be prepared to entrain at our from HESDIN. H.Q. Entrained at 4.15pm. A/50 6.8pm, B/50 9pm, C/50 midnight D/50 3am (2nd Dec).	
2		H.Q. arrived at PERONNE at 4.30am; A/50 at 9.30am, B/50 at 2pm, C/50 at 4pm, D/50 at 9pm. The Brigade on arrival proceeded to POIGNY.	
3		The Brigade went up into action in centre 53rd Divisional Artillery. Bde HQ near ST. EMILIE. Guns were registered before dark and Communication lines established to all batteries and O.P. was run to ROISEL.	West of RONSSOY
4		Fired on S.O.S. lines for 10 minutes at 5.45am. Otherwise batteries were registering.	
5		Short on S.O.S. lines at 7am and 8am.	
6, 7.		Quiet day.	

WAR DIARY or INTELLIGENCE SUMMARY

Army Form C. 2118.

Place	Date	Hour	Summary of Events and Information	Remarks and references to Appendices
Peronne	8		Orders are received for the Brigade to be transferred to the 9th Divisional Artillery. The Brigade was relieved by the 65th Army F.A. Bde. Half the personnel went on to the new position in cars, went with him laid out on own roads Gouzeaucourt in case of a withdrawal.	
	9		Remainder of personnel and Horses relieved by the 65th A.Bde. Brigade Commanders and Battery Commanders went on to reconnoitre position of the 235th Brigade just north of Gouzeaucourt Wood. Wagon lines moved to HURLU.	
	10		The Brigade went in to their new position relieving the 235th Bde. and found the establishments with the 70th Brigade, and were carried out and having pits and six Regulation war carts out and ------ of ----- 10pdr.	
	11			
	12	3. a.s.	night. 20 German guns and several quantities of other material. from close to front line trenches.	
	13	15. Afternoon	Abandoned and seized by the Brigade and a quantity	
	14			
	15			

WAR DIARY
or
INTELLIGENCE SUMMARY.
(Erase heading not required.)

Army Form C. 2118.

Place	Date	Hour	Summary of Events and Information	Remarks and references to Appendices
	December			
	16.		At 7.30pm The Brigade fired a concentration shoot in conjunction with the division on our right and with the Heavy Artillery. The barrage was for 17 minutes and ran to the right.	
	17.		M-our 20nd were salvage was anti-aft dark. Harassing fire on movement.	
	18.		During the night 18th/19th the 70th Brigade was out and the 50th Bde. Coming into position.	
	19.		During the night 19th/20th 3 18-pdr Batteries came into position relieved by the 70th Bde. They were under the O.C. 50th Bde tactically.	
	21.		The Brigade fired for 5 min at 6.30am and 6.45am on roads and tracks with Brigade zone. The Heavy Artillery cooperated.	
	22.			
	23.		Harassing fire on enemy movement.	
	24.		Fired a barrage on S.O.S. lines at 6.15am reaching 300 yards, information having been received that the Germans were 'standing to' expecting an attack.	
	25.			
	26.			
	27.		Quiet days.	

WAR DIARY
or
INTELLIGENCE SUMMARY.

(Erase heading not required.)

Army Form C. 2118.

Place	Date	Hour	Summary of Events and Information	Remarks and references to Appendices
	December			
	28		2 Guns of A/310 and 1 Howitzer of D/310 shot at 100 forward positions and fired at a rate of an edge of wood in front of BONNELIEU about 450 rounds.	
	29		A quiet day.	
	30		At 6.20 am the Germans started a heavy barrage on our front line and carried on at 2 points about 6.40 am. We fired S.O.S. at 6.45am and again at 7.5am. The German infantry is getting in at our front line along our own front. They also attacked the 63rd (Naval) Division on our left and at our front held our front trench. During the morning we fired in support of the left division and again at 2.15pm and 2.30pm. Firing fire at 3.12pm. At 4.40pm our fire again in support to counter attack which attained its objective reaching at 5.12pm. Another heavy German barrage on divisional left at 4.30 am. At 10.25 am Brigade fired for 3 minutes in conjunction with our left Brigade on the German front line S.E. of BONNELIEU on about 200 Germans. At 10.45 am fired on our front N. of BONNELIEU for 3 minutes.	

Army Form C. 2118.

WAR DIARY
or
INTELLIGENCE SUMMARY.
(Erase heading not required.)

Instructions regarding War Diaries and Intelligence Summaries are contained in F. S. Regs., Part II. and the Staff Manual respectively. Title pages will be prepared in manuscript.

Place	Date	Hour	Summary of Events and Information	Remarks and references to Appendices
	December		Casualties for the month of December.	
			1 O.R. wounded.	

W M°heen —

LT. COLONEL R.F.A.
COMMANDING 50TH BRIGADE, R.F.A.

50 Bde Army Form C. 2118.
Vol 28

WAR DIARY
INTELLIGENCE SUMMARY.
(Erase heading not required.)

Instructions regarding War Diaries and Intelligence Summaries are contained in F.S. Regs., Part II. and the Staff Manual respectively. Title pages will be prepared in manuscript.

Place	Date	Hour	Summary of Events and Information	Remarks and references to Appendices
Shutsyc.	January 1918.			
	1, 2		Quiet days.	
	3		Also went out to rest at wagon lines.	
			Fired a barrage at 6.15 am on the German lines having in view trenches. 65th Brigade withdrew to wagon lines. at NURLU	
	4-10.		Quiet days. Ordinary harassing fire carried out.	
	11.	6.17 am	Barrage on enemy Trenches in anticipation of a strike.	
			Enemy action Quiet. Also came back into action.	
	12.			
	13.		The Brigade changed wagon-lines with the 150th Brigade near FINS.	
	14-23		Ordinary harassing fire at enemy movement and tracks.	
	24-27.		Some Guns & wagons were sent from the vicinity of BOUZEAUCOURT including German 4.25 & 7.7cm and French Howr.	
	28		Over to more at Feb 2 and 3rd record.	
	29-31		Quiet. With the exception of the 2 barrage mentioned above the month passed in ordinary trench warfare, with generally harassing fire on transport and tracks.	

WAR DIARY
or
INTELLIGENCE SUMMARY.

(Erase heading not required.)

Army Form C. 2118.

Place	Date	Hour	Summary of Events and Information	Remarks and references to Appendices
			Casualties during January.	
			2 O.R.'s wounded	
			Honours and awards.	
			Capt E. B. Train military cross (adjutant)	
			Sergt Ison. B/50. Bar to military medal	
			Dr Sharpe A/50 military medal	
			" Wilson B/50 " "	
			" Mackay C/50 " "	
	1-2-18.			

E. R. Bovill Major
COMMANDING 50TH BRIGADE, R.F.A.

Army Form C. 2118.

5 D Bde L.T.M.

WAR DIARY
or
INTELLIGENCE SUMMARY.
(Erase heading not required.)

Instructions regarding War Diaries and Intelligence Summaries are contained in F. S. Regs., Part II. and the Staff Manual respectively. Title pages will be prepared in manuscript.

Place	Date	Hour	Summary of Events and Information	Remarks and references to Appendices
	February.			
	1		Quiet	
	2		Battery withdrew to trench lines after dark. Took over the defence of the line. The 65th A.F.A. Bde	
	3		Guards took over the 39th Division. Took over the Brigade position from rear parties. Battery marched to LA NEUVILLE SUR SOMME near BRAY.	
	4–17		Training.	
	18		Inspection by G.O.C. VII Corps.	
	19–28		Training.	
			Honours.	
			B.S.M. ROSE } Medaille militaire Belgian	
			Cpl. WILKINSON }	
			W. McEwan	
			Lt. Colonel, R.F.A. Commanding 5 Div. H. Brigade, R.F.A.	

9th Div.

Headquarters,

50th BRIGADE, R.F.A.

M A R C H

1 9 1 8

50th Bty

WAR DIARY
or
INTELLIGENCE SUMMARY.
(Erase heading not required.)

Army Form C. 2118.

Place	Date	Hour	Summary of Events and Information	Remarks and references to Appendices
	13th March		Orders received at 3 a.m. for the Brigade to march to HAUTE ALLAINES. Battery moved off at 10 a.m.	
	27-3.3		Remained at HAUTE ALLAINES. Battery moved off the village itself to get some shelter owing to the severe weather.	
	4		The Brigade moved to HALLE. Continued training.	
	5-10			
	10		Leading section to battery proceeded to wagon-line at NURLU and up into action in old position after dark relieving 174th Bde RPA 39th Div.	
	11		Remained in action relieving remaining section of 174th-Bde in the line, forming left group with the 65th Bde RPA.	
	12-20		Harassing fire was kept up, hostile by special counter-battery taking place from time to time owing to hostile battery attack. Battery was shelled with gas shell during this period.	
	21		At 4:30 a.m. the hostile went began. Enemy using gas shell to a large extent against battery positions. No S.O.S. Signal was sent up, but battery-low-barded. Team was bringing out of battery after dark. Battery withdrew during hostile to vicinity of battery to position south of DESSART WOOD to cover yellow line.	

Army Form C. 2118.

WAR DIARY
or
INTELLIGENCE SUMMARY.
(Erase heading not required.)

Instructions regarding War Diaries and Intelligence Summaries are contained in F. S. Regs., Part II. and the Staff Manual respectively. Title pages will be prepared in manuscript.

Place	Date	Hour	Summary of Events and Information	Remarks and references to Appendices
	22nd		Battery chiefly engaged in shelling roads between GOUZEAUCOURT and GONNELIEU. About 7 a.m. owing to the right flank running exposed a withdrawal took-place to position by RIVERSIDE WOOD to cover NURLU–FINS road. During the retirement the last gun of B/50 Brigade their limber on open sights assisted advancing enemy. H.Q. moved to MOISLAINS.	
	23rd		Orders for a further retirement were received at 6 a.m. Battery withdrew section at half hour intervals to SAILLY-SAILLISEL, but after shewing a few hours then withdrew again to position just behind MORVAL to cover the BAPAUME–PERONNE road. The 26th Inf. Bde. established their H.Q. close to Battery with the O.C. 50th Bde. who sent out mounted officer patrols. Considerable losses were inflicted on the enemy owing to the efforts received from this patrols. About 10 a.m. Battery began retiring to ridge in rear but was unable to communicate with infantry on covering the ridge by LEUZE WOOD.	
	24th		British were found here for German infantry was driven back by fire on open sights by Battery of the Brigade, and a hostile gun which advanced itself to within 400 yards was silenced by B/50	

WAR DIARY or INTELLIGENCE SUMMARY

Army Form C. 2118.

Place	Date	Hour	Summary of Events and Information	Remarks and references to Appendices
	24th Cont'd		The Brigade had to retire again and finally came into action S.W. of MARICOURT covering the line from HARDICOURT to TRONES WOOD. Hostile artillery of harassing began to come into action.	
	25.		Batteries fired on TRONES WOOD and BERNAFAY WOOD. When enemy came in mass from TRONES to their. During the afternoon batteries took up a position 500 yards in rear of a Dep. Ravine which made position difficult making a ford withdrawal from their former position difficult. During the night continued harassing fire was kept up by each battery in turn to cover the withdrawal of the Infantry. Each battery that withdrew in an completion of its task of firing, the last battery leaving at 3 a.m.	
	26		Batteries in the early morning at BUIRE and took up position on slopes ground north of the BUIRE - DURNANCOURT road. In the afternoon owing to the enemy occupying the high ground South of the ANCRE batteries changed their position to behind the crest. H.Q. moved from BUIRE to MILLENCOURT and amalgamated with the 57th Bde H.Q.	
	27.		Hostile artillery action up to 10 a.m. in Buire, an Battery covert in Enfilade by a 7 mm and forced to retire, all Batteries in new position LAVIEVILLE - MILLENCOURT - HENENCOURT. Targets principally VIVIER MILL and DURNANCOURT. Bde H.Q. HENENCOURT.	

Army Form C. 2118.

WAR DIARY
or
INTELLIGENCE SUMMARY.
(Erase heading not required.)

Instructions regarding War Diaries and Intelligence Summaries are contained in F. S. Regs., Part II. and the Staff Manual respectively. Title pages will be prepared in manuscript.

Place	Date	Hour	Summary of Events and Information	Remarks and references to Appendices
	28.		Situation quieter. 4th Australian Division in action on 50th Bde. area under their orders.	
	29.		No further developments. Batteries withdrew 16 Kilo wagon lines at TOUTENCOURT at 7 p.m.	
	30.			
	31.		Brigade marched to BEVELINCOURT. Resting at BEVELINCOURT.	
			Casualties — missing 2/Lieut HARKER	
			wounded Lt. Col. McLEAN. Capt. VENNING. 2/Lieut MORLEY. Lieut BECHER (at duty).	
			O.R.'s killed 12	
			wounded 131	
			missing 6	
				31.3.18

[signature]
LT. COLONEL R.F.A.
COMMANDING 50TH BRIGADE, R.F.A.

9K 21st Divisional Artillery.

50th BRIGADE R.F.A.

APRIL 1918.

Headquarters,
9th D.A.

[50TH BRIGADE R.F.A. stamp]

Herewith War Diary for the month of April 1918.
Kindly acknowledge receipt.

R. Tyrell
for
Mason
~~Lt. Colonel~~ R.F.A.
COMMANDING 50th BRIGADE R.F.A.

30/4/18.

50th Bde
R.F.A.

9/A/31

WAR DIARY
INTELLIGENCE SUMMARY.

Army Form C. 2118.

Place	Date	Hour	Summary of Events and Information	Remarks and references to Appendices
	1st April		50th Bde resting and refitting at Bevelincourt.	
	2nd		During afternoon Bde marched from Bevelincourt to St Roch Station Amiens to entrain for the Ypres salient.	
	3rd		Detrained at Hopoutre and marched to the La Clytte area, wagon lines remaining here, one section per battery going straight up into action, the last two batteries marched after dark on the night 3rd, 4th.	
	4th		Remainder of batteries went into action on the night of 4th, 5th. Taking over from the 2nd Australian F.A. Brigade at 6pm & came under the command of the 1st Anzac Corps. Battery positions in the Vanbrandmolen area.	
	5th	10 am	1X D.A. took over from 1st Anzac Corps.	
	6 – 9		Quiet.	
	10		'B' & 'D' batteries withdrew about 1000' in a N.W. direction.	
	12th		B/246 (39th Div Arty) came under the command of the 50th Bde	
	13th	12 noon	C/50 was attached to 51st Bde	
	16th		All batteries moved to positions just South of the Dickebusch Lake. B/246 left command of 50th Bde.	

Army Form C. 2118.

WAR DIARY
or
INTELLIGENCE SUMMARY.
(Erase heading not required.)

Place	Date	Hour	Summary of Events and Information	Remarks and references to Appendices
	16th		In evening fired barrage for our infantry to take northern edge of Whytshaete. Attack only partially successful.	
	25th		Enemy attacked on a six mile front, batteries withdrew to position north of St Hubertushoek, as enemy advanced to Vierstraat. Bombardment was very heavy with a hour gas.	
	28th		HQrs. moved to just north of Rinnenhilst. Grouped with 51st Bde 50th Bde grouped with 122 Bde R.F.A.	
	29th	3am	Enemy put down very heavy barrage on our front. During morning enemy attacked five different times, each time repulsed with heavy losses. have casualties.	

Casualties.
Killed
2Lt Shannon (died of wounds) ORs
Lt Harder   Killed. 12
                                  Wounded. 94
                                  Died of wounds. 2

Wounded.
Capt Abraham.
2Lt Quinn.
Lt Wallis
Lt McDougall.
2Lt Cooper (at duty)
Lt Andrew (at duty)
L.Col J de B Owen (gassed)

30.4.18

50th Bde RFA

Army Form C. 2118.

WAR DIARY
or
INTELLIGENCE SUMMARY.
(Erase heading not required.)

Instructions regarding War Diaries and Intelligence Summaries are contained in F. S. Regs., Part II. and the Staff Manual respectively. Title pages will be prepared in manuscript.

Place	Date	Hour	Summary of Events and Information	Remarks and references to Appendices
	MAY 1st		A quiet day.	
	2nd		French gunner officer came round battery position, as it was intended that their guns should come alongside, which they did after dark.	
	3rd		French Brigade staff shared H.Q. with 50th Bde. At 8pm S.O.S. went up on our hundredth right and on the French front, but there was no development.	
	4th		An enemy attack was expected and the S.O.S. went up at 6 a.m., but there was no infantry action. There was considerable artillery fire on both sides during the evening. French officer manned the H.Q.'s and guns to their position. Batteries fired a large amount of harassing fire and counter preparation. Hostile fire was chiefly of a harassing nature chiefly on battery areas.	
	5th 6th 7th		Enemy barrage began at 3 a.m. Gas firing used as usual at 8 a.m. his infantry attacked and gained ground in the MEERSTRAAT info opposite the 30th Corps. Brigade met again/the French on the right.	
	8th		No S.O.S. signals were seen owing to enemy smoke barrage. A counter attack in the evening restored our line except on the right when the French failed.	

Army Form C. 2118.

WAR DIARY
or
INTELLIGENCE SUMMARY.
(Erase heading not required.)

Instructions regarding War Diaries and Intelligence
Summaries are contained in F. S. Regs., Part II.
and the Staff Manual respectively. Title pages
will be prepared in manuscript.

Place	Date	Hour	Summary of Events and Information	Remarks and references to Appendices
May	9th		Quiet day. Usual harassing fire and enemies preparation	
	10th		Quiet day. S.O.S. went up in enemies line but no development.	
	11th		The French infantry took over our front.	
			Enemy artillery again active chiefly on battery area and line	
			of DICKEBUSCH - LA CLYTTE road	
	12th		Batteries withdrew to their wagon lines at 8 am.	
	13th		The Brigade marched to the WINNEZEELE area to rest and train.	
	14th			
	15th			
	16th		Training and resting.	
	17th			
	18th			
	19th			
	20th		The Brigade marched to CAMPAGNE area to continue resting and training enjoying the division	
	21st			
	22nd			
	23rd		Resting and training. 18 pdr Calibration	
	24th			
	25th			

Place	Date	Hour	Summary of Events and Information	Remarks
	May 26th		The Brigade move up into action in support of the South African Brigade in the METEREN sector. Brigade relieve the 148th Brigade. Battery positions are behind FLETRE, this are also Silent positions to move to in the event of main positions being heavily shelled.	
	27th 28th 29th 30th		very quiet.	
	31st		Batteries registered and carried out harassing fire. The enemy carried out a shoot on A/50 at 6.15am, short, also at 6.15am.	
			Casualties 2/Lt. L.G. BROOKS killed 2/Lt. P.A. WARD died of wounds. 6.d. GIBSON gassed OR's killed 6 wounded 35.	

E.R. Groom
LT. COLONEL R.F.A.
COMMANDING 50TH BRIGADE, R.F.A.

50. BDE. RFA WAR DIARY or **INTELLIGENCE SUMMARY**

Army Form C. 2118.

VA 33

Place	Date	Hour	Summary of Events and Information	Remarks and references to Appendices
June	1st		Harassing fire was carried out during the month on roads tracks & farms in the Bde Zone. 40 rds per gun for 24 hours.	
	2nd		A/50. B/50 & forward section of C/50 fired barrage to assist Australians in a minor operation near Morris. Remainder of C/50 & D/50 fired on their own zones.	
	3rd–14th		Batteries carried out observed shoots on Metaren firing at likely enemy O.Ps.	
	15th	1 a.m.	Batteries fired for raid by S.A.(28) 13ae	
	15th	11.55am	Fired for raid by 26th Bde.	
	20th	1.30am & 5.30am	Fired demonstration shoot with smoke as left Bde were making a raid.	
	23rd	12.30am	Fired creeping barrage for S.A. Bde to advance line in conjunction with Australia.	
	24th–25th		During night no: of rds for harassing for was doubled.	
	23rd		D/50 carried out experimental shoot with various gas shell. To test its hanging.	
	26th	3.30pm	Fired a smoke barrage to cover discharge from gas projectors on Metaren.	
	27th–30th		Usual harassing fire.	
			Casualties. ORs 1 Killed. 5 wounded. 5 gased (remaining at duty).	

W M Thom Lt Col
Comd" 50 B Bde

50 Bde RFA

Vol 34

WAR DIARY
INTELLIGENCE SUMMARY

Place	Date	Hour	Summary of Events and Information	Remarks and references to Appendices
	July 1st to 6th		All batteries of 50th Brigade carried out harassing fire in the Bde lanes on houses trenches tracks etc at various times.	
	6th		All batteries fired a barrage of Smoke T.H.E. for gas bombs to be fired on METEREN.	
	12th	1 am	Fired a box barrage for a raid by the S.A. Inf. Bde. One prisoner was captured.	
	night of 17th/18th		17th Bde 29th Div. moved into positions just north of METEREN. also batteries of 50th Bde moved to their operation positions.	
	19th	7.54 am	Batteries fired creeping barrage for infantry to take METEREN. lasting 57 mins. Batteries withdrew to their former positions	
	night of 19th/20th			
	22nd		Batteries began to prepare more forward positions.	
	night of 23rd/24th		No. of rds for harassing fire was doubled.	
	25th	2 am	Enemy attack our outpost line with 4 platoons, between GAZA CROSS Road and ALWYN FARM. S.O.S. rocket was put up, batteries replied.	

WAR DIARY
or
INTELLIGENCE SUMMARY.

Army Form C. 2118.

Place	Date	Hour	Summary of Events and Information	Remarks and references to Appendices
	night 25th/26th cont		attack was entirely unsuccessful. Counter preparation was fired by batteries at 2 a.m. which caused heavy casualties to the enemy in addition to the S.O.S. All battery lines were swept out as the infantry reported the enemy came up to occupy his night posts at this time.	
	27th	7pm	Battery Commanders of the 307th Bde 61st D.W. were shewn battery positions in case they were sent up to reinforce the 60th Bde. Working parties also arrived to improve the positions.	
	29th		61st Dvl. Arty. went out of the line to continue their rest & training.	
			Casualties. { 2 O.Rs wounded { 1. O.R. killed.	

Army Form C. 2118.

WAR DIARY
or
INTELLIGENCE SUMMARY.

(Erase heading not required.)

Instructions regarding War Diaries and Intelligence Summaries are contained in F. S. Regs., Part II. and the Staff Manual respectively. Title pages will be prepared in manuscript.

Place	Date	Hour	Summary of Events and Information	Remarks and references to Appendices
During METEREN operation.			The Battalion Commander of the South African Composite Battn. highly complimented a forward section of A/50 for the excellent work they did in harassing the roads & tracks in METEREN, until all their ammunition was expended. The following letter was received from G.O.C. S.A. Inf. Bde. " May I offer our sincere appreciation of the splendid work of the artillery, which enabled the infantry to accomplish their part of the task successfully & with comparatively small loss" W McKeen Major Comd.g 50th Bde R.F.A. 4.5.18	

50th BDE

WAR DIARY
or
INTELLIGENCE SUMMARY.
(Erase heading not required.)

Army Form C. 2118.

Place	Date	Hour	Summary of Events and Information	Remarks and references to Appendices
Aug.	1st		Harassing fire was carried out during the month on roads, tracks & occupied areas in the brigade zone.	
	2/3rd 15th		Harassing fire was doubled during the night. 186 Bde moved up to reinforce 50th Bde after the attack. All guns were put into silent positions.	
	15/16th			
	16th		Brigade registered on Hoegenacken Mill.	
	18th	11 a.m.	Fired a barrage for our infantry to extend their front southwards along the Hoegenacken Ridge. All objectives were taken.	
	19th	10.35am	Fired in reply to S.O.S. rocket put up by our infantry. No attack was made.	
	19th	5 p.m.	Howitzer Battery fired a gas concentration to create a diversion while the 29th DW on our right improved their position along the Bailleul-Hazebrouck railway.	
	21st	4 p.m.	186 Bde R.F.A. (39th Division) withdrew from action.	
	23rd/24th		93rd Inf Bde relieved the 27th Bde in the right divisional sub-sector.	
	27th/28th		50th Bde covered the 31st DW.	
	26th	10 a.m.	Bde Zone moved north to just in front of Meteren.	
	29th	10 p.m.	A/50 pulled out of action. Going to train W.Ls to train for 10 days.	
	30th		A/50 came back into action	

Army Form C. 2118.

WAR DIARY
or
INTELLIGENCE SUMMARY.
(Erase heading not required.)

Place	Date	Hour	Summary of Events and Information	Remarks and references to Appendices
August cont.	30th		Enemy were reported to have withdrawn on our front.	
	30th/31st		Batteries moved up to positions near Epsom Cross Roads.	

L.M^cL──
LT. COLONEL R.F.A.
COMMANDING 147th BRIGADE, R.F.A.

WAR DIARY
or
INTELLIGENCE SUMMARY

Army Form C.2118.

50 Bn ~~~~

Vol 36

Place	Date	Hour	Summary of Events and Information	Remarks and references to Appendices
September	1.		at rest in wagon lines at FLETRE	
	2.			
	3.		moved up in afternoon to position west of NEUVE EGLISE	
	4.		Supported 29th Div. with Lewis gunfire barrage for attack on Hill 63 at 9 a.m. Barrage from wagon lines. During day find execution from position till 6 pm. Withdrew at night to wagon lines billets BAILLEUL	
	5.		Battalion moved back to wagon lines just off the FLETRE – METEREN road.	
	6. 7. 8. 9. 10. 11. 12.		Resting and training In Reserve	
night 12/13			Brigade marched to HAANDEKOT area	

Army Form C. 2118.

WAR DIARY
or
INTELLIGENCE SUMMARY.
(Erase heading not required.)

Instructions regarding War Diaries and Intelligence Summaries are contained in F. S. Regs., Part II. and the Staff Manual respectively. Title pages will be prepared in manuscript.

Place	Date	Hour	Summary of Events and Information	Remarks and references to Appendices
	Sept. 13th		Resting and training. Battrin had forward parties working on position behind POTIGE also filling their with ammunition. Position also prepared for 153rd Brigade, RFA.	
	26th		Guns went up into action. Wagon lines moved to HAM HOEK and North of POPERINGHE.	
Anjou	26th/27th		No movement from guns. Detachments came up after dark. Batt'd in Rampark YPRES.	
	27th		Belgian and 2nd Army attack began. Supported 28th Bde in carrying barrage at 5.25 am. D/So moved forward about 7.30 am to position west of FREZENBERG ridge. Remainder of Brigade moved to same area about 9 am. Arriving thru they joined in a creeping barrage up to ridge South of ZONNEBEKE. At 1.30 p.m. whole Brigade advanced to third BROODSEINDE ridge. Considerable difficulty in getting into action owing to mud and tracks being blown in. Guns in action by dark. Also had a forward section in close support of the infantry after the advance from FREZENBERG. Battries engaged positions of enemy round KEIBERG with thaws fire. Also slur in close support. Brigade advanced to KEIBERG ridge	
	29th			

Army Form C. 2118.

WAR DIARY
or
INTELLIGENCE SUMMARY.

(Erase heading not required.)

Place	Date	Hour	Summary of Events and Information	Remarks and references to Appendices
Sept.	29th	contd	Also had a return attack to this line reading Battalion.	
	30th		The Brigade advanced at 7.0 am to position west of WATERDAMHOEK - DADIZEELE road. Batt H.Q. at WATERDAMHOEK. Battalion had a counter battalion on HILL 41 to support 35th Div. on our right at the afternoon, also later on LEDEGHEM and also Ammunition supply and rations very difficult owing to this state of roads in rear.	

W McKeown
Lt. Col.
Cmdg. 50th Bde R.F.A.

50 Bde R114ay
Nov 37

WAR DIARY
INTELLIGENCE SUMMARY

Place	Date	Hour	Summary of Events and Information	Remarks and references to Appendices
	Oct. 1st 1918.		Supported an attack at 6.15am with a barrage lasting 30 minutes owing to the Belgians on the left and the 36th Division on the right not advancing our troops had to retire from west of the ground gained, but remained in possession of LEDEGHEM Station. Also's forward guns did magnificent work in open sights firing on Hill 41 on our right and 3 times caused SOS action in front of our own infantry. Also withdrew 16 gun position to 1 gun field S.O.S. in afternoon on Counterattack on our right battalion and on the 36th Division front. This short quick barrage on Hill 41 enabling 36th Division to recover lost ground. B. E and D Batteries hand back further behind crest. C Battery hand back slightly. Bde H.Q. moved back from WATTERDAMHOEK to about 1500 yards behind battalion.	
	2nd			
	3rd		Harassing fire during day and night. Also's forward gun fired on open sights on the church steeple LEDEGHEM with good result, also on DADIZEELEHOEK and road to KESELBERG.	
	4th		Harassing fire night and day. Battery getting up ammunition to forward position and for Tomorrow. Brigade.	
567				

WAR DIARY
or
INTELLIGENCE SUMMARY.
(Erase heading not required.)

Army Form C. 2118.

Place	Date	Hour	Summary of Events and Information	Remarks and references to Appendices
October	8th		The Remnant of A/50 and also went back to rest at HAMHOEK leaving a guard behind and then first line. 'A' and 'B' Batteries 51st Bde came under the Tactical Command of O.C. 50th Bde.	
	9) 10)		Battries did light harassing fire on roads and tracks. Also continued to get up ammunition to forward positions.	
	11.		Heavy hostile barrage on Battery positions at 5.30 p.m. Field Amb. Preparation.	
	12.		A.T.O. Battries returned to their own Bde from HAMHOEK. A. & B. Batteries 51st Bde were tied to Command of O.C. 51st Bde. 4 guns per Battery moved up after dark to forward positions. Rest remaining gun continued normal harassing fire. 28th A.F.A. Bde came up to Harassing fire by Stars section. Remaining guns moved up to forward position after dark.	
	13.		Rainfall.	
	14.		The Mission was resumed by the Belgian, French and British 2nd Army. Attack started at 5.35 a.m. with a creeping barrage. Bde H.Q. moved up to a farm just behind railway north of LEDEGHEM at 2 a.m. & 70 B/50 moved to a Gunnery Repairs Station in a cow Corn high ground near WINKEL-ST-ELOI. At first the situation	

WAR DIARY or INTELLIGENCE SUMMARY

Army Form C. 2118.

Place	Date	Hour	Summary of Events and Information	Remarks and references to Appendices
Out in the open	14th/Oct/18		was very distant. In addition to the smoke and to barrage there was a thick ground mist. The enemy was holding his forward zone in strength. Our first line broken thro' with very little opposition. C/50 went forward at 7 am. with 2 guns working in close support of the infantry. Remainder of the Brigade advanced shortly after. 8 am. and first came into action when a the ridge running South from BONKEL-ST-ELOI. About 1 am the Brigade again advanced to close behind the crest to run the advance to the high ground round STEENBEEK. During the afternoon C/50 and D/50 went forward. O.C. C/50 (Major F.W. HOBART MC) came to action in a most gallant manner under heavy H.F. and shell fire and engaged the fires North of STEENBEEK. Casualties H.E.'s on open sight. They eventually withdrew slightly, but continued to fire at short range. Also advanced into action East of the BONKEL-ST-ELOI – GULLEGHEM road, but at dusk the whole Brigade withdrew to their former positions behind the crest.	
	15th		The attack was resumed with one the barrage at 9 am. with out of the enemy barrage the 50th Bde. Rpt. the Bois d'HEULE.	

WAR DIARY or INTELLIGENCE SUMMARY

Army Form C. 2118.

Place	Date	Hour	Summary of Events and Information	Remarks and references to Appendices
	Oct 15th 1918		under fire using smoke shell. Considerable opposition was met with from M.G. fire but this was overcome and the advance continued. The Brigade were forward to N.E. of STEENBEEK and at about 10.30 am and fired on the vicinity of LE CHAT. During the afternoon batteries were forward to another position South of ST. CATHARINE CAPPELLÉ and finally commenced action from the night just West of LE CHAT.	
	16th		Batteries bombarded road on East side of river running S.W. from HARLEBEKE at 14.00, 15.30 and 17.00. Harassing fire at 19.50 fired on Ships of church containing M.G. at 20.00 the same bombardment was put down for 3 min. B/50 had a forward gun firing on open sights from QUERNE. A/50 formed took on M.G.'s and a hostile Observation T. in a farm house bridge at HARLEBEKE the infantry succeeded in crossing the river opposite QUERNE and taking the road opposite HARLEBEKE the sappers suffered heavy casualties from M.G. fire and were unable to establish bridges at 6 am. Batteries fired on S.O.S. lines and there was no catastrophe. D/50 had 2 forward guns	
	17th		The Enemy attacked	

Army Form C. 2118.

WAR DIARY
or
INTELLIGENCE SUMMARY.
(Erase heading not required.)

Instructions regarding War Diaries and Intelligence Summaries are contained in F. S. Regs., Part II. and the Staff Manual respectively. Title pages will be prepared in manuscript.

Place	Date	Hour	Summary of Events and Information	Remarks and references to Appendices
Oct. 17 (cont)			In QUERNE. At 16.45 p.m. batteries again reported S.O.S. call, and fire concentration at 17.30 and 18.15. QUERNE was set on fire by hostile artillery. The 29th Div'n took over 9th Divisional front and 50th Bde RFA and 28th RFA until 10 am on the 18th. The 57th Bde and 28th HFA Bde. being grouped under O.C. 50th Bde R.F.A.	
	18.		The Brigade still supported 16 corn. The 9th Divisional Inf on his Right, going into action near HULSTE. The 57th Bde and 28th RFA were still grouped under O.C. 50th Bde.	
	19.		The infantry carried the line after dark and advanced 1000 yds under cover of a barrage. Barrage fire at 21.15.	
	20.		At 0.6.00 a barrage was put down and the infantry advanced. At 8.0 am. the 57th Bde built a raft in order to support our march to give an artillery Bridge on Itoarne river was down then by 8.30 and batteries crossed on C/50 guns in close support of the infantry. The Remaining batteries TORKAP arrived by position between HARLEBEKE and DEERYVCK and at start retire First his concentration at 12.35 and 13.45 as our Reverend south from further position has been running his bn. and batteries in their position for the night.	

WIGHT

Army Form C. 2118.

WAR DIARY
or
INTELLIGENCE SUMMARY.
(Erase heading not required.)

Instructions regarding War Diaries and Intelligence Summaries are contained in F. S. Regs., Part II. and the Staff Manual respectively. Title pages will be prepared in manuscript.

Place	Date	Hour	Summary of Events and Information	Remarks and references to Appendices
BULFER	21st		Battalion moved up to behind BELBEK during morning to form a further advance, but owing to division on left not advancing it was not considered advisable for the 9th D.L.I. to go forward. Hostile artillery continued to be active and at dusk battalion pursued km. 20.0. detachment under an Officer withdrew to advanced army line following.	
	22nd		The attack was resumed at 6.30 am the 10th D.L.I. forming up at 0.9.0 m. 13/50 had formed at the end of the honour and did my good luck notice them on open sight on the will and high ground East of NEHTE and reaching to attack hadown just before dark the evening batten moved up to position SE of BELBEK and 13/50 to the same area.	
	23rd		A comparatively quiet day. O.C. Bde and Battery Commander reconnoitre position East of NEHTE.	
	24th		Battalion moved up to position reconnoitred the previous day afternoon Bde HQ going to NEHTE CHATEAU. Thus position was very close up to front line, but small patterns to fire both honours repurred rather following day without moving further.	

Army Form C. 2118.

WAR DIARY
or
INTELLIGENCE SUMMARY.
(Erase heading not required.)

Instructions regarding War Diaries and Intelligence Summaries are contained in F. S. Regs., Part II. and the Staff Manual respectively. Title pages will be prepared in manuscript.

Place	Date	Hour	Summary of Events and Information	Remarks and references to Appendices
October	25		Attack was resumed under cover of a creeping barrage at 09.00. The second barrage due to begin at 12.30 was brought back on the SOS Bde RFA front at that moment, but this order was sent to batteries who had started on this line. The infantry however did not advance further.	
	26.		A quiet day. Hostile patrols pushed down to the L'ESCAUT as the enemy had withdrawn on our immediate front. The infantry line relieved after dark by the 30th Div. the 92nd Bde covering their left Brigade, the 93rd Bde.	
	27.		The Brigade was relieved by the 165th Bde 31st Div Arty after dark and withdrew to rest billets on the west bank of the YRS [Yser] approx HARLEBEKE.	
	28.		Relieving O.C. 92nd Bde RFA attended a conference at HQ. 31st Div Arty at STEENTJE at 12 noon with a view to reconnaissance of Bde sector being young for support in attack.	
	29.		Battery commanders went up to survey for positions behind INGOYGHEM [Ingoyghem]. Reinforcement to units being taken up after dark, the No 1 Section of the D.A.C. being at the disposal of the 92nd Bde.	

WAR DIARY or INTELLIGENCE SUMMARY

Army Form C. 2118.

Place	Date	Hour	Summary of Events and Information	Remarks and references to Appendices
Ocleke	30th		Battalion went up into position after dark. Brigade HQ. were at the WHITE HOUSE on the Eastern outskirts of the VIJFWEGE. The Brigade was under the Command of the CRA 33rd Div. The remainder of the ammunition required for the operation was brought up during the night.	
"	31st		The attack began at 05.25. The artillery covering the Divisional front being the 165th, 170th Bdes (31st Div Arty) 28th AFA Bde and the 3rd Bde RFA. As the cos of the first barrage began the attack was for 2 hours after which the second barrage began. The attack was very successful, the 16th artillery fire was very slight. At 2 pm the Brigade moved forward and (accurate action behind) BERGHUT, but was not called upon to fire. At 18.0 orders were received for the Brigade to withdraw to their first billet.	

WAR DIARY or INTELLIGENCE SUMMARY

Army Form C. 2118.

Honours Award

Lieut R. MORLEY — Military Cross.
89950 Sgt CRAIK N — Bar to military medal.
736797 Dr DOUGLAS J — military medal.
93136 A/Bdr CAMERON C — "   "   "
181   Dr FOTHERINGHAM W — "   "   "
98391 Gnr FAIRBAIRN W — "   "   "
37028 Gnr OAKES E — "   "   "
3832   Sgt JONES G.E. — "   "   "
74935 "   PINK F.W. — "   "   "
99759 "   MARSH G — "   "   "
8922   Bdr BALDWIN WA — "   "   "
27740 Dr BILLINGH. J — "   "   "

Casualties   Killed   Wounded
Officer   —   —
Other   2   8
O.R.'s   16   105

W. M°Keuer —
Lt Col. Cmdg 7.5th Bde R.F.A.

WAR DIARY
or
INTELLIGENCE SUMMARY.

Army Form C. 2118.

50 Bde R.F.A. / V.B. 38

Place	Date	Hour	Summary of Events and Information	Remarks and references to Appendices
Noremken 1918	1/2/3		The Brigade was resting and refitting.	
	4.		There was a practice ceremonial parade and march past of the whole division at 11 a.m.	
	5.		The whole Division was inspected by the King of the Belgians accompanied by the Queen on a flying ground east of BAVICHOVE. The division subsequently marched past.	
	6.		Resting.	
	7.		Orders received for the Brigade to be ready to go into action on the night 10/11th under the orders of the C.R.A. 31st Div. Arty to fire a barrage in support of an attack over the SCHELDT by the 19th Divn.	
	8.		The Brigade Commander and Battery Commanders went up to reconnoitre positions just West of the Scheldt N.E.A. AVELGHEM about in the front line. Our Officers reconnoitring a working party were sent to prepare position and their ammunition After dark batteries both up 2 wagon loads of ammunition being taken to the gun. Also taking up 1 wagon load per gun. D.A.C.	

Army Form C. 2118.

WAR DIARY
or
INTELLIGENCE SUMMARY.
(Erase heading not required.)

Instructions regarding War Diaries and Intelligence Summaries are contained in F.S. Regs., Part II. and the Staff Manual respectively. Title pages will be prepared in manuscript.

Place	Date	Hour	Summary of Events and Information	Remarks and references to Appendices
Noruntu (cont.)	9.		The Divisional Commander came round telling him during the morning with the C.R.A. One wagon load per gun of ammunition taken up to position. In some cases began an ordered new teams that no more ammunition was to be taken up as it was unlikely that the Brigade would be required.	
	10.		The Brigade received at inst and did not go into action. News of the Armistice reaching from General Division in the Evening.	
	11 } 12 } 13.		Resting and preparing to march to Germany. Warning order received for move on 14th.	
	14.		Division moved to VICHTE - CASTER area, just east of INGOYGHEM. The Division was marching in rear of the 41st Division.	
	15.		March continued across the SCHELDT to RENAIX area. The Brigade being to billets East of RENAIX.	

Army Form C. 2118.

WAR DIARY
or
INTELLIGENCE SUMMARY.
(Erase heading not required.)

Instructions regarding War Diaries and Intelligence Summaries are contained in F. S. Regs., Part II. and the Staff Manual respectively. Title pages will be prepared in manuscript.

Place	Date	Hour	Summary of Events and Information	Remarks and references to Appendices
November (cont'd)	16.		The Brigade halted for the day. Batteries to be Li-gun batteries. One section per battery to be ready to move under orders of 19th Bde.	
	17.		The Brigade still remained at same place. The Station to be detached were inspected by the Brigade Commander during the morning. They went off in the afternoon to assemble in one area with the Second Section of the 51st Bde R.F.A, and came under the orders of the 19th Corps at 4 p.m.	
	18.		Continued march thro' NEDERBRAKEL. to hitch about 6 miles East of that place.	
	19.		Resting.	
	20.		Bde.H.Q. C/50 and D/50 moved to DETTINGE in order to get further South. A/50 & B/50 not required to move.	
	21.		The 9th Division became leading division having this H.Q.'s Division. The Brigade moved to GOYCK. B/50 came under the orders of 60'r 26th hy/Bde. During the march orders received for C/50 to go on to GANSHOREN near BRUSSELS. They got in at 7 p.m.	

Army Form C. 2118.

WAR DIARY
or
INTELLIGENCE SUMMARY.
(Erase heading not required.)

Instructions regarding War Diaries and Intelligence Summaries are contained in F. S. Regs., Part II. and the Staff Manual respectively. Title pages will be prepared in manuscript.

Place	Date	Hour	Summary of Events and Information	Remarks and references to Appendices
Norunta (cont'd)	22.		C/50 under the command of Major J. HOGGART D.S.O. N.C. took part in the entry of King Albert into BRUSSELS and are billeted in barracks there for the night. The remainder of the Brigade rendered at GOYCK.	
	23.		March resumed to RHODE ST GENESE. C/50 rejoined the Brigade. Resting. Personnel ran over to visit BRUSSELS and WATERLOO.	
	24.			
	25.		March continued thro' Forêt de SOIGNES to WAVRE.	
	26.		Resting.	
	27.		Brigade marched to HUPPAYE.	
	28.		March continued to AVESNES.	
	29.		March continued to AMAY in valley of the MEUSE.	
	30.		Orders received at 2 am cancelling march owing to supply train being late. Brigade therefore to be preparing to resume the march on Dec 1st.	

Army Form C. 2118.

WAR DIARY
or
INTELLIGENCE SUMMARY.
(Erase heading not required.)

Instructions regarding War Diaries and Intelligence Summaries are contained in F. S. Regs., Part II. and the Staff Manual respectively. Title pages will be prepared in manuscript.

Place	Date	Hour	Summary of Events and Information	Remarks and references to Appendices
			Honours & Awards. (Mounted)	
			Maj. J. HOLLART M.C. awarded D.S.O.	
			" C.W. ANDREW M.C. " Bar to Military Cross	
			Lieut / S/C BECHER " Military Cross	
			Sergt TENNY.H. } B&HQ Military Medal	
			Corpl SKIRROW R " "	
			Gnr. Oakes. E B/50 " "	
			Sergt Pink A.W. C/50 " "	
			" Jones G.E. B/50 " "	
			" March G. C/50 " "	
			Bdr. Baldwin W.A. " " "	
			Dvr. Gillings J. " " "	
			" Weedon V. B/50 " "	
			" Broad J.J. " " "	
			Gnr. McGuyer J " " "	
			Sigr Murray H C/50 " "	

WAR DIARY
INTELLIGENCE SUMMARY

Honours Award (Noncomm) Cont'd.

Dr. Poole R.	D/50	awarded Military Medal
Corpl Boardman A.	D/50	" " "
Gnr. Chapple B.	"	" " "
Dr. Robinson E.	"	" " "
" Bowler C.	C/50	" " "
Gnr. Bird G.	"	" " "
Dr. Goddard C.W.	C/50	" " "
Gnr. Brooke W.A.	"	" " "
Br. Harris E.H.	"	" " "
Tpr Worby C.H.	"	" " "
Bdr. Pelerin W.F.	D/50	" " "
Sergt Loan T.	B/50	Bar to Military Medal.

30.11.18.

J. Hoggas, Major.
for Lt. Colonel, R.F.A.
COMMANDING 50TH BRIGADE, R.F.A.

Army Form C. 2118.

50 Bde RFA
VSI 39

WAR DIARY
or
INTELLIGENCE SUMMARY.
(Erase heading not required.)

Instructions regarding War Diaries and Intelligence Summaries are contained in F. S. Regs., Part II. and the Staff Manual respectively. Title pages will be prepared in manuscript.

Place	Date	Hour	Summary of Events and Information	Remarks and references to Appendices
	December 1918			
	1.		March continued along valley of the Meuse into valley of the VESDRE passing just south of LIEGE and halting at CHAUDFONTAINE. Orders received at 6 a.m. cancelling march owing to hitch in supplies.	
	2.		The Brigade remained at CHAUDFONTAINE.	
	3.		March continued to VERVIERS. All the horses in the Brigade were under cover.	
	4.		Remained at VERVIERS.	
	5.		Remained at VERVIERS. General was able to get baths. The C.R.A. and D.A.D.V.S. inspected the horses of the Brigade in the morning. At 11.30 received sudden orders to move in afternoon. The Brigade crossed the frontier into GERMANY and stayed the night at EUPEN.	
	6.		Continued march at 6.30 a.m. to BRAND.	
	7.		March resumed to DEREICHSWEILER near DUREN.	
	8.		" " " KERPEN.	
	9.		" " " EHRENFELD a suburb of COLOGNE.	
	10.		B/50 rejoined from 26th Inf. Bde.	
	11. 12.		Remained at EHRENFELD cleaning up.	

Army Form C. 2118.

WAR DIARY
or
INTELLIGENCE SUMMARY.
(Erase heading not required.)

Instructions regarding War Diaries and Intelligence Summaries are contained in F. S. Regs., Part II. and the Staff Manual respectively. Title pages will be prepared in manuscript.

Place	Date	Hour	Summary of Events and Information	Remarks and references to Appendices
December	13th		The whole Division crossed the RHINE marching past Lt. Gen. FERGUSON in MULHEIM. The Brigade went to BURRIG.	
	14th		Remained at BURRIG.	
	15th		The Brigade had the final march to No 1 Sub Area. Also there SOLINGEN attached to 26th Inf. Bde. Balloon and Craterfaller in trainers. the 6th 3 bry Clow Kühlin in HOCHSCHEIDE.	
	16th–22nd		In S.E. side of SOLINGEN. Brigade and Balloon getting settled etc but up and improved with the help of civilian labour.	
	23.		Commenced meetings & funds sports to March Ch. G.O.C. 26th Inf. 13th came round talking kilts.	
	25th–29th		Football competition started.	
	30th		Training in morning begun	
	31st		G.O.C. R.A 2nd Corps came round Followin	

Army Form C. 2118.

WAR DIARY
or
INTELLIGENCE SUMMARY.
(Erase heading not required.)

Instructions regarding War Diaries and Intelligence Summaries are contained in F. S. Regs., Part II. and the Staff Manual respectively. Title pages will be prepared in manuscript.

Place	Date	Hour	Summary of Events and Information	Remarks and references to Appendices
Annex v Annexes				
French-Cross de Guerre	9th Slai.	Maj. J. Laidman M.C.	
	Silver Stai.	Capt. J. BALDERSTONE	
	Bronze Slai.	Capt. A. C. 13644 M.C.	
	" "	B.Q.M.S. LAW C/50	
	" "	Sergt H. JENNY HQ	

A. A. Tye Capt.
for L. .... COLONEL R.F.A.
COMMANDING 50TH BRIGADE, R.F.A.

50 Bde RFA

WAR DIARY
or
INTELLIGENCE SUMMARY

Army Form C. 2118.

Instructions regarding War Diaries and Intelligence Summaries are contained in F. S. Regs., Part II. and the Staff Manual respectively. Title pages will be prepared in manuscript.

1438

Place	Date	Hour	Summary of Events and Information	Remarks and references to Appendices
	January 1919 1st to 5th		Batteries did training in the mornings and had minor sports in the afternoon. Foot ball competition etc. There was also firing competition, events F. Education classes also continued.	
	January 6th to 11th		Batteries did training in mornings. Driving drill, laying signalling, musketry. Junior Officers noted were told, also miniature ranges. Sports in afternoon, Football, running, jumping etc. Educational classes continued.	
	January 12th to 31st		Battery training continued in mornings; gun drill, F.C.'s rides musketry F.S.S.s instruction. Junior Officers rides + miniature ranges. Physical training for all ranks. Football matches, paper chases etc in afternoons. Educational classes continued.	

G.B. Darby
LT. COLONEL R.F.A.
COMMANDING 50TH BRIGADE, R.F.A.

WAR DIARY
or
INTELLIGENCE SUMMARY.

Army Form C. 2118.

Place	Date	Hour	Summary of Events and Information	Remarks and references to Appendices
	Jan 1919		Honours & Awards. January 1919.	
			Belgian Croix de Guerre. Capt. A.A. Tyer, M.T.O. H/qrs 50thBde R.F.A.	
			" " Capt. H.H. Ashton c/50 R.F.A.	
			" " 29780 F.W./Sergt. T. Pride c/50 R.F.A.	
			" " 59472 B.Q.M.S. G.K. Smith D/50 R.F.A.	
			" " 23725 S/Sergt. T. Joyce, R.A.V.C. Att. D/50 R.F.A.	
			" " 32185 Sergt. H. Graham C/50 R.F.A.	

G.R. Davidson
Lt. Colonel, R.F.A.
Commanding 50th Brigade, R.F.A.

Army Form C. 2118.

WAR DIARY
or
INTELLIGENCE SUMMARY.
(Erase heading not required.)

Instructions regarding War Diaries and Intelligence Summaries are contained in F. S. Regs., Part II. and the Staff Manual respectively. Title pages will be prepared in manuscript.

Place	Date	Hour	Summary of Events and Information	Remarks and references to Appendices
SOLINGEN	Feb. 1st to 16th		Training continued consisting of driving drill, meeting drill, laying, NCO's reskilling, section drill order. Animation ranging for Junior Officers. Also gun and tank infantry instruction in musketry. Physical Training. Also a route march tank meet. Football, sports &c. and Education classes carried on.	
	17th		Artillery position and roads also the River WUPPER was reconnoitred to a C Battalion line. Maj GOC RA 2nd Army came round in motor with the CRA and went round C Battery line.	
	18th to 28th		Training &c. as before. Inspection mean by Paten chinen None Being accepted were held.	

E.B. Denham
LT. COLONEL, R.F.A.
COMMANDING 50TH BRIGADE, R.F.A.

50. BDE. R.F.A.

WAR DIARY
or
INTELLIGENCE SUMMARY.
(Erase heading not required.)

Army Form C. 2118.

WO 462

Place	Date	Hour	Summary of Events and Information	Remarks and references to Appendices
SOLINGEN	March 16th 1919		Training Continued. Driving Drill, Riding Drill, Laying, N.C.O's Redrilling, Section drill order, Lecture, physical training and Route march each week. Football Education carried on. Divisional Boxing Competition held on by Artillery Review on WUPPERHOF ground by G.O.C. 2nd Corps. The G.O.C. addressed the men and the Brigade marched past.	
	20th			
	21st to 31st		Training etc continued. On return to billets made up with Army of Occupation men in order to start programme Section training.	

A.G. Tyer Capt
for
LT. COLONEL R.F.A.
COMMANDING 50TH BRIGADE R.F.A.

WAR DIARY or INTELLIGENCE SUMMARY

50th Bde RFA

Army Form C. 2118.

Place	Date	Hour	Summary of Events and Information	Remarks and references to Appendices
Solingen	April 1st 1919		Section Training Gun Drill, Driving & Riding drill laying.	WW 43
	2nd		Section Gun Drill Section Drill riding, Physical Training.	
	20th to 30th		Battery Staff training, Brigade route march each week. Brigade Football League. Educational classes carried on. Holiday. Batteries with wounded sports & football matches. The Second Section per Battery made up with Army of Occupation men. Training commenced;— Riding drill, gun horse, riding, "skeleton driving drill and drill Physical Training, marching, "Stabling" Drill. Signalling Battery Staff training, Lectures. Gunnery (care of stores, Equipment, Harness, Horsemanship etc.	
	15th		Capt "G.S" L.A.P. Tozer M.C. left Bde for demobilization —	
	26th		Capt (A/Major) I.M. Fleyrose took over command of B/50 R.F.A. from Maj. C.H. Andrews M.C.	

M. Tozer Capt.
H. Ev. Colonel R.F.A.
Commanding 50th Brigade, R.F.A.

Army Form C. 2118.

WAR DIARY
or
INTELLIGENCE SUMMARY.
(Erase heading not required.)

Place	Date	Hour	Summary of Events and Information	Remarks and references to Appendices
SOLINGEN.	MARCH 24.		HONOURS & AWARDS.	
			BELGIAN DECORATION MILITAIRE (2nd Class)	
			& CROIX DE GUERRE awarded to	
			No 100544 Cpl. J. CAMPBELL. C/50 R.F.A.	
			No 249813 Sergt. R. SKIRROW M.M. HQ 50th Div. R.F.A.	
			(R.E. SIGNALS).	
	April 1st.		BELGIAN DECORATION MILITAIRE awarded to	
			No 3532 Sergt. S. JONES M.M. B/50 R.F.A.	

F. ERNEST ENK.
COMMANDING 50TH BRIGADE, R.F.A.

50th Bde. R.F.A

Army Form C. 2118.

WAR DIARY
or
INTELLIGENCE SUMMARY.

Place	Date	Hour	Summary of Events and Information	Remarks and references to Appendices
SOLINGEN.	MAY 1st to 12th		Section training continued. Driving & Riding drill, laying. Section gun drill. Section skill orders. Physical training. Signalling etc. Battery Staff training. Subsector football competition.	
	May 13th		Entry of teams to represent II Corps at French Horse Show, WIESBADEN. Field Coaching of Firing Batteries from C/50 R.F.A., D/51 R.F.A. & from 113th Brigade R.F.A. & Hampden R.H.A. completed. The teams were judged by Brig. Gen. J.G. Rotton C.B. C.m.G. C/50 R.F.A. were selected to represent the II Corps at above Show.	
	MAY 14th to 31st		Section training continued. Driving & Riding drill. Signalling gun drill. Laying. Fuze setting. Lectures to Officers etc. Battery drill orders with full detachments + battery staff.	

A.W.C. Mallock
LT. COLONEL R.F.A
COMMANDING 50th BRIGADE R.F.A.

50th BDE R.F.A

Army Form C. 2118.

WAR DIARY
or
INTELLIGENCE SUMMARY.
(Erase heading not required.)

Instructions regarding War Diaries and Intelligence Summaries are contained in F.S. Regs., Part II. and the Staff Manual respectively. Title pages will be prepared in manuscript.

Place	Date	Hour	Summary of Events and Information	Remarks and references to Appendices
SOLINGEN.	June 1st		Battery Training Commenced.	
	June 2nd		Inspection of 50th Bde R.F.A. by Maj Gen Sir W. R. Robertson G.C.B. G.C.M.G. K.C.V.O. D.S.O. A.D.C. at WUPPERHOF near SOLINGEN. Extract from letter from G.O.C. Lowland D.A. "The G.O.C. 1 British Army of the Rhine wishes to convey to all ranks of the 50th Bde R.F.A. his satisfaction at the turn out of the Batteries this morning & in particular his appreciation of the condition of the horses."	
	June 3rd to June 30th		Battery Training. Batteries held Drill Orders twice weekly, Artillery gun drill, signalling, Riding School, Trumpet, Staff & Forge setting, Battery Staff training etc. Blocks carried out.	
	June 19th		A/50 moved from Hohscheid to Grafsrath [Map Elberfeld 4720 2500] Reconnoitred to Bde to prepare to advance in the event of Germany refusing to sign Peace terms.	

Army Form C. 2118.

WAR DIARY
or
INTELLIGENCE SUMMARY.
(Erase heading not required.)

Place	Date	Hour	Summary of Events and Information	Remarks and references to Appendices
			The following Honours & Awards have been published in the Peace Gazette.	
			50th Bde R.F.A.	
			Major C/H.W. 6 H.W. Maclean D.S.O. awarded C.M.G.	
			74935 Sergt A/H.W. Fink M.M.	D.C.M. C/50.
			49479 Staff Sergt Farrier J. Arnell	M.S.M. D/50.
			16901 Cpl. R.J. Furlong	M.S.M. B/50.
			17121 Dr. G. Arrowsmith	M.S.M. B/50.

Army Form C. 2118.

WAR DIARY
or
INTELLIGENCE SUMMARY.

(Erase heading not required.)

Place	Date	Hour	Summary of Events and Information	Remarks and references to Appendices
SOLINGEN	June 28th		Pieces signed	
	June 30th		A/SD returned to Adacked from Griffith Arrumeenthal	

50th Bde. RFA

WARDIARY
or
INTELLIGENCE SUMMARY.

Army Form C. 2118.

Place	Date	Hour	Summary of Events and Information	Remarks and references to Appendices
SOLINGEN	July 1st 2nd		Battery Frames. Sports Practise.	
	July 2nd		50th Bde Sports. wounded Sports held at GLÜDER in very inclement day.	
	July 3rd		50th Bde Sports. Resumed. Sports held on the RITTERSTRASSE GROUND at SOLINGEN. The ANDREWS CHALLENGE CUP awarded for highest aggregate of points gained in Athletyo won by Hq @co R.F.A.	
	July 9th		Inspection of Divisional Artillery Sports at HAUS. HORST.	
	July 11th		50th Bde R.F.A. marched out of SOLINGEN in order to relieve the 245th Bde R.F.A. LIGHT DIVISION. 50th Bde was billeted at MÜLHEIM for night of 11/12.	
	July 12th		50th Bde marched to POLL HEIM	
	July 13th		50th Bde arrived in new Billeting area. Hqrs Also ↓D/50 at NIEDERKEMPT. B/50 at ESCH. A/50 at ANGERDORT.	

Army Form C. 2118.

WAR DIARY
or
INTELLIGENCE SUMMARY.
(Erase heading not required.)

Place	Date	Hour	Summary of Events and Information	Remarks and references to Appendices
NIEDERKRT.	July 1st to July 30th		Horses Exercised. Battery Staff & Trek & Riders duty morning. Battery Cricket match on Sunday & Wednesday. Saturday afternoon held Divisional Artillery Competition. Eliminating Competition held at KIRCHTROISDORF. 16 Meids Right Gun team should represent the Divisional Artillery at the Rhine Horse Show. Judges for the Competition were Major Gen'l. H.H. Tudor C.B. C.M.G. O.Subsection II/50 were selected.	

[Signature]
LT. COLONEL. R.F.A.
COMMANDING 50th BRIGADE R.F.A

Appendix No. CCXXXII
Army Form C.2118.

WAR DIARY
or
INTELLIGENCE SUMMARY

(Erase heading not required.)

50th Bde R.H.A.

Place	Date	Hour	Summary of Events and Information	Remarks and references to Appendices
NIEDEREMBT	Aug 1st 1919		Orders Ridden, Battery Staff Rides, Exercise etc. Cricket v Sports in afternoon. A Thursday in each week all Batteries hold Drill orders in Shuttle v Ten grounds in vicinity of NIEDEREMBT, ESCH, OBEREMBT v ELSDORF.	
	Aug 4		Cavalry Division Horse Shows. I/50 R.H.A. represented the 50th Brigade in competition for Best turned out Gun v Team with their Grey Team belonging to "J" Subsection. They were awarded 1st Prize.	
	Aug 8th		Southern Division Horse Show. I/50 were again successful with their Grey Team in competition for Field Artillery team.	
	Aug 16		Army of Rhine Horse Show. I/50 were again successful in competition for Best turned out Gun v Team with their Grey Team.	

J.M. McCall
LT. COLONEL R.F.A.
COMMANDING 50TH BRIGADE R.F.A.

APPENDIX No. CCLXXXII

Army Form C. 2118.

WAR DIARY
or
INTELLIGENCE SUMMARY.
(Erase heading not required.)

50 A Bde R.F.A.

Place	Date	Hour	Summary of Events and Information	Remarks and references to Appendices
NIEDERKEM BT.	SEPTEMBER		Drivers Ride, Battery Staff Rides exercise in the morning. Cricket v football in the afternoon. Standing Sunday afternoon. Football Competition for "inter battery" challenge cup commencement Sep 11/14.	
	Sept 7.		C/50 R.F.A. moved from ANSELSDORF to ELSDORF. During the month the Brigade was considerably depleted by demobilisation of De RB/. MEN	

M.M.Hurdcroft
R.F.A.
CAPTAIN 50 BRIGADE R.F.A.

www.ingramcontent.com/pod-product-compliance
Lightning Source LLC
Chambersburg PA
CBHW082356010526
44111CB00041B/2561